METHAMPHETAMINE

METHAMPHETAMINE

A LOVE STORY

Rashi K. Shukla

 UNIVERSITY OF CALIFORNIA PRESS

University of California Press, one of the most distinguished
university presses in the United States, enriches lives around
the world by advancing scholarship in the humanities, social
sciences, and natural sciences. Its activities are supported by
the UC Press Foundation and by philanthropic contributions
from individuals and institutions. For more information, visit
www.ucpress.edu.

University of California Press
Oakland, California

Library of Congress Cataloging-in-Publication Data

Names: Shukla, Rashi K., 1971- author.
Title: Methamphetamine : a love story / Rashi K. Shukla.
Description: Oakland, California : University of California
    Press, [2016] | Includes bibliographical references and index.
Identifiers: LCCN 2015050884 (print) | LCCN 2016000505
    (ebook) | ISBN 9780520291010 (cloth : alk. paper) | ISBN
    9780520291027 (pbk. : alk. paper) | ISBN 9780520964891
    (e-edition)
Subjects: LCSH: Methamphetamine abuse—Social aspects—
    United States. | Drug traffic—Social aspects—United
    States.
Classification: LCC HV5822.A5 S58 2016 (print) | LCC HV5822.
    A5 (ebook) | DDC 362.29/95092273—dc23
LC record available at http://lccn.loc.gov/2015050884

Manufactured in the United States of America

25   24   23   22   21   20   19   18   17   16
10   9   8   7   6   5   4   3   2   1

For Krishna Kumar and Jaya
Who loved ceaselessly, sacrificed selflessly,
and crossed oceans to offer us lives enriched with opportunities

"Words have no power to impress the mind with the exquisite horror of their reality."

—Edgar Allan Poe

CONTENTS

FOREWORD

Criminology has an urban bias. It is easy to forget that much crime occurs in small towns and other rural areas, and that city crime often depends on a rural hinterland for obtaining its illegal product. The days of bootleg liquor bring Al Capone to mind, evoking memories of Chicago organized crime and the equivalent in other cities. We forget that the urban bootleg whiskey came from the hills of Appalachia, where hill farmers speaking heavy dialects produced corn whiskey using fuel chopped down with an ax.

Rashi Shukla counters the urban bias by interviewing people in many-sized places, many of them rural or small in scale, to understand the production, transportation, and consumption of methamphetamine. She has a passion for interviewing, for asking good questions, for figuring out the offenders' viewpoints, how and why they act a certain way. She avoids the very general questions about why they are bad, or what they think is wrong with the world, preferring not to waste good interview time.

Her skilled interviewing brings forth a tale of offenders loving meth, dealing it, struggling to get away from it, but missing it afterward and struggling to keep away from it. Her skill shows even in her first phone encounters with users, when she dances around sensitive topics to assess what they might have to say about manufacturing illicit drugs. Not one of the thirty-three interviewees withdrew consent, demonstrating her success in developing and maintaining rapport. Her tenacity was maintained for the four years it took to obtain the final interviews.

Her rapport did not lead her to "go native." She recognized the harm to people while looking from the outside, without losing sight of their viewpoints on that harm. She also showed that choices seeming irrational to outsiders make sense to meth users, given the values they held during their drug-use period. In other words, Professor Shukla never forgot that the offenders' viewpoints are central for understanding the crimes they commit.

Thus she maintains empathy for the people she studied while also emphasizing the need to do something about the problem. She points out that meth use grew despite an era of prohibition, adapting to changing enforcement strategies. The result of her policy analysis is to recommend both comprehensive approaches and that no single antimeth technique works for all parts of the problem. Her independent thinking has led her to interesting suggestions, including the use of drug hotlines for users to talk about their own risky behaviors without threat of prosecution.

Not only is this a scientific contribution, it also informs policy, and is a very useful book to assign to a class. Most of all it is a good read.

Marcus Felson
Texas State University

ACKNOWLEDGMENTS

I am honored to have shared this life with my loving parents, Krishna Kumar and Jaya Shukla. Thank you for sacrificing everything to give your children a better life, and for setting the example of what it means to live purposefully with character, integrity, and intention. Your unconditional love and support made all the difference. Everything I am is because of you. Thank you for believing that I could do anything before I ever did anything.

I will forever be indebted to the amazing men and women who participated in the interviews and shared their life experiences. Without them, this book would not exist. I am honored that they entrusted me with their life stories. Thank you for speaking for those without a voice.

Thank you to my muse CD for encouraging my first project, and for inspiring me do something original again. You always challenge me—reminding me that the road ahead is much longer than it appears, and that the work completed thus far is not enough. Without your ongoing love and support I may not have found my way back.

I am privileged to have family and friends who never tire of putting up with crazy, and am grateful for all of the dedicated supporters along the way. Named here or not, you know who you are. While some had no idea what methamphetamine was, or why I was doing this, there were always countless others who never doubted the worthiness of this endeavor and path. Thank you to Kanchana, Tulsi, and Dev Saha, to Neel, Patty, Emma, Sage, and Xavier Shukla, and to the rest of my family for your endless love. Thank you to Amrita Srinivas, Deepa Narayanan, Christen Moroz, RJ Woods, Michaela Smith,

Maryann and Sid Brown, Elsa Gonzalez, Jared Matheson, Christie McDonald-Hamm, Cindy Mueller, Anje Vela, Mrs. Grooms, Michael Ray, Rick, Michael Price, Mena Ganesan, Saba Hameed, Mouna Kaul, Misty Kint, Ranell Collins, Jeffrey Freshour, Austin Ralstin, Kody Young, Josh Massad, Victoria Tjahjo, Jermaine Peterson, Dee Dee Wise, and Bobby Cross for your constant encouragement.

This project would not have been possible without the financial support of the University of Central Oklahoma (UCO) Office of Research and Sponsored Programs, College of Liberal Arts, and School of Criminal Justice. Thank you to Greg Wilson, John Barthell, William Radke, Patricia LaGrow, Pamela Washington, Gary Steward, and especially to E. Elaine Bartgis, my early collaborator, for sharing in the excitement of this project. I am beholden to David Ford and DeWade Langley for providing words of strength and inspiration during my moments of doubt. I am appreciative of Elizabeth Maier, Patti Loughlin, Xiao Bing Li, Shawna Cleary, Jaime Burns, Don Mizell, Jere Roberson, Burle Steeleman, Mike Jenkins, Mark McCoy, John Mabry, Niki Morgan, Brad Watkins, Doug Reed, Darian DeBolt, James Lofton, Leeda Copley, Jerry Roberson, Keith Killian, Dallas New, Ramario Holland, Katie Richárd, Pam McDown, Janie Leftwich, Pam Lumen, Kelly Ross, members of the UCO Institutional Review Board, and the countless others who assisted in various capacities along the way.

I would like to express my gratitude to my network of mentors and colleagues who provided advice and input over the years, including Gisela Bichler, Miriam Boeri, Sharon Chamard, Aldo Civico, Ronald V. Clarke, Todd Clear, Randol Contreras, Derek Cornish, Paul Eckblom, Allen Futernick, Kevin Hayes, Scott Jacques, Leslie Kennedy, Jennifer Lanterman, Edith Laurencin, James LeBeau, Travis Linnemann, Estee Marchi, Eric McCord, Mangai Natarajan, Jerry Ratcliffe, George Rengert, Kim Rossmo, Judi Ryder, Susan Sharp, Marti Smith, Mercer Sullivan, Angela Taylor, Rebecca Tiger, Klaus von Lampe, Jeffrey Walker, Ralph Weisheit, and Bonita Veysey. I am especially indebted to Phyllis Schultz, the Countess of all things criminal justice, for encouraging me to be creative and for making me coffee every day as I struggled. Special thanks to the Rutgers University School of Criminal Justice for awarding me a visiting library fellowship during my sabbatical and for providing the space and resources to immerse myself in this project so I could complete the first draft of this manuscript. Thank you to Marcus Felson for providing the foreword to this book and to Mary Eckhart for your ongoing encouragement.

I will forever be grateful to those on the front lines of this battle who were willing to take time to help a curious researcher over the years. Their patience and the selfless giving of their time and expertise will always be appreciated. Thank you to John Duncan, the godfather of this project, for inspiring my research. Special thanks to Tanner Beckner, Kathy Bell, Robert Block, Mike Connelly, Jim Cox, Bill Coye, Tom Cunningham, David Hale, Robert Heidlage Jr., Don Hewett, Reginald Hines, Chuck Jordan, Justin Jones, Kody Kinder, Brian Serber, Jon Shepard, John Singer, Ronald Thrasher, Dub Turner, Bei Xu, Darrell Weaver, Lonnie Wright (deceased), Mark Woodward, the team who allowed me to accompany them on a pseudoephedrine sting operation, and the many others still fighting the good fight.

This project could not have been completed without the indispensable work of numerous research assistants who have been the backbone of this project, including Emelia Chrisco, Jordan Crump, Lacey Elmange, Amanda Gautier, Shannon Jackson, Kathryn Letourneau, Matt Magness, David Newton, and Danielle Stoneberg. I am especially grateful to Cora Bradley, who assisted with this project in the beginning and at the end, to David Cea for intellectually challenging me and reminding me of the importance of telling the truth of this tragedy, and to Kristina Kave for her invaluable assistance trimming the final manuscript and tightening the storyline. Each of you provided essential feedback at various critical junctures. Special thanks to Angela Myers for volunteering to help with the earliest stages of data analysis and to those who read the initial chapters as they were drafted, particularly Phyllis and Gordon Schultz, Sue and Steve Marom, CD, Melissa Smith, and to Robert Mather and Greg Scott for reviewing early drafts of the proposal. The book is stronger due to your input.

Thank you to the new friends who cheered me on during my sabbatical, including Zachary Kelliher, Marin Kurti, Jacqueline Rouse, Marjorie, everyone at Roberts Pizza in Newark, and Arthur Miller, the cab driver who reminded me that "every transaction may be your last." The sabbatical experience would not have been what it was without Alina Istrate, who made my journey to New Jersey and back pleasurable and stress free, and Anisha Kansal and Erik Satre, who provided feedback from the earliest stages and never failed to pull me back from the darkness as I struggled through the writing process. It was a pleasure to spend time with Carol Roehrenbeck and Elizabeth Hull, who made me feel at home during my time in New Jersey.

It was an honor to work with Maura Roessner, the insightful editor at the University of California Press, who recognized the power of this story from the very beginning. Thank you for gently prodding this project along during some of the most difficult days of my life. I am also appreciative of the UC Press Editorial Board for taking the chance to publish this work and to the anonymous reviewers for their ingenious comments and suggestions. I am grateful to the entire UC Press team for their assistance getting this manuscript to publication. I hope the final product demonstrates that your comments and concerns were taken to heart.

I will always be thankful to the incredible nurses who, while caring for my father during the final days of his life, reminded me of the importance of this work. It will always be ironic that the publication of this book coincided with the most difficult period of my life—the death of my father. Though it is heartbreaking that the man who was the inspiring force behind all that I have ever done did not live to see this project come to fruition, I am grateful for the lessons of life forced upon us by the universe.

Thank you to the numerous others who provided input and support over the years, including the anonymous key informants who informally "participated" in this project and tirelessly provided invaluable insight, and to the former manufacturer who first brought the issue of methamphetamine to my attention many years ago when he handed me his tried-and-true methamphetamine recipe on a worn-out, discolored, piece of paper upon his exit from the lifestyle. One can only hope that by the end of one's life, he or she has done something that actually mattered. Together, this is our contribution.

AUTHOR'S NOTE

This account is based on 1,238 years of life experiences shared during interviews conducted over a four-year period of time. Names and dates have been changed.

This book contains materials not appropriate for young children, the faint of heart, and those not interested in knowing.

CHAPTER I

An Introduction to Darkness

At twenty-two years old, Evan found himself addicted to methamphetamine and the lifestyle associated with manufacturing. Even as he sat across from me and talked about his journey into this dark world and back, he struggled to make sense of it and resist the elusive hold it seemed to have on him. As he spoke, I wondered if remembering his journey would lure him back. He didn't just talk about shooting up. He opened sugar packets in the restaurant and put them in a spoon. He didn't just describe preparing the right amount of meth. He poured sugar on the table, slicing the powder into thin, equally sized lines.

Evan: I was involved, but it was a lie, you know. I thought it was . . . I thought I was a big man when I was selling it and usin' it and stuff.

Q: Was it like an illusion?

Evan: Yeah. It was . . . What can I compare it to? I don't know. It's incomparable. Just like if someone handed you a stack of a bundle of hundred dollar bills or something, and you thought, "Wow, thanks, ten thousand dollars," and then you looked, and only the top one was real . . . All the money, all the, feeling important about having it, all the money that you get from it, it all goes right back into it, so you don't actually get anything out, all that power, is just people wantin' what you have and it's dangerous, you know. At first, I could only remember the good times I had on it, but I've started being able to see it all now and think, "No," I think, "Well, was that good times?" But that wasn't good times at all. That was probably the lowest part of my life. That wasn't the fun times. I don't want to live that again.

During the course of the interview, I asked Evan multiple times if this was too much. If remembering and recalling the life he had once lived was somehow too powerful and seductive, strong enough to entice him back to the life he had escaped—and to using meth. I never anticipated the issue prior to this moment. There seemed to be a danger in remembering, in reliving the experience, in talking about what he gave up. The methamphetamine. The manufacturing. The money. The sex. The addiction. The power.

Toward the end of the interview Evan pulled off his ball cap, and I saw the misshapen part of his left temple. I didn't quite understand until he said:

Evan: Yes, it was killing me. It was, it was killing me. I couldn't stop doing it. I got so addicted to it that it just took over everything else. I don't feel like I'm a liar, or a thief, or violent, or untrustworthy or dishonest, but I was then . . . it's really strong, it, it took my whole life over, and it took anything that mattered to me, [everything] took a back seat to it. That was it. It was anything I could do, whatever I had to do to get it, I would do it. I couldn't stop doing it. I could not stop doing it, and I got really depressed. I couldn't see the good anymore. I just couldn't see. I had a gun, a pistol, because I didn't want anybody tryin' to rob me or come in my home and hurt me or my family, and I started having thoughts of suicide. And, I mentioned to my wife, and she kinda just acted like I was just tryin' to get some attention or anything. "Oh shut up about that." I was serious. I didn't know what else to do. I didn't feel like I could talk to anybody about it and, I didn't feel like I had any friends anymore, only customers. And I . . .

Q: This was when you were heavy into meth?

Evan: Oh, yeah. I couldn't stop doing it. I was more addicted than anybody I knew. There were some friends of mine that would not come around me because I was too gone. And, on March the eleventh of 1997,[1] I took the nine millimeter and put it in my mouth and fired it. And I shot the top of my head off. [He points to the places where plates are.] And this is a metal plate, this is a metal plate, this is a metal plate, and so is this, and this is where they don't come together, and if you'll look at the roof of my mouth, there's a very small hole from the bullet. [He opens his mouth and shows me the hole.] And they had to remove a third, that's what happened to my teeth, the recoil when it went into my mouth. They had to remove a third of my brain from bone splinters. And I was in the hospital for almost six months, and I wasn't supposed to live. And I, I lived. And I stopped using methamphetamine.

He stopped for a period of time. However, shooting himself in the head wasn't enough to stop completely. It wasn't enough to escape the grip meth had on him. He got back into the lifestyle and started using again, only later finding his way back out once more. And here he sat before me—clean for five years, clean for now.

The illusion of methamphetamine is that it gives you everything you've ever wanted. The truth of the tragedy is that it takes everything you have. It destroys lives.

There is darkness in the deepest depths of the world of methamphetamine. There is no light in the pits of despair that overtake those who become seduced by meth and all it seems to offer. In these corners of reality, those who find themselves immersed beyond control come face to face with the darkness that permeates this world. It is blackness at its very core; something not comprehendible to those who have never known it. It is here, in the deepest levels of the world, that the tragic power of methamphetamine lies. It is the point at which all bets are off. Where there is no turning back—no resetting of the clock, no erasing of time. It is the point at which they cease to be who they always were and truly are. For some, it is a point of no return.

Those who become enthralled are forced to confront a hard-core reality: there is only one way to survive this murky and dangerous world—by meeting darkness with darkness. It is the reality lived by those who told me their stories; they were among those who survived—the few who escaped. They lived to tell about it. But it was not by chance.

They survived because they did what they had to do, no matter how damaging and destructive. They visited edges and corners of reality where few ever go. It is a place from which some never return and even fewer ever admit to. They shared what they had seen, experienced, and participated in, so that we would know. They shared it so that you would know. It is by every measure the essence of the truth of the tragedy that is methamphetamine.

In lieu of judgment, I challenge you to appreciate the opportunity provided to see what goes on in the deepest corners of the world of methamphetamine. I challenge you to respect their honesty and appreciate their willingness to share some of the most tragic and soul-crushing experiences of their lives. It is critical that we see things as they really are. The fact that they were willing to admit to some of the most ominous truths about their lives and the things they had done so that we could understand and learn is as inspiring as it is heartbreaking.

WHY IS THIS IMPORTANT?

Methamphetamine has been around in various licit and illicit forms for decades. It is a derivative of amphetamines. Methamphetamine[2] is ingested, smoked, injected, snorted, or inserted.[3] The drug is known by various street names including crank, ice, crystal, chalk, and speed.[4]

Its effects are long lasting; the high can last for hours. Users may stay awake for several days on drug-fueled binges. The powerful effects of this synthetic drug, combined with the lack of sleep that accompanies extended use, result in serious behavioral and mental consequences. Users may experience meth psychosis, which can cause extreme paranoia, hallucinations, and delusions,[5] leading them to sometimes be referred to as *tweakers*.[6]

The *Faces of Meth* campaign was one of the first means by which people came to learn about methamphetamine. Post-arrest images illustrated physical effects of methamphetamine over time. These were among the first images to provide undeniable, visual evidence of the extreme deterioration that can accompany addiction to the drug. The persons in the "after meth" versions of these pictures appear dangerous and scary. While such images provide visual validation of the external deterioration that can accompany methamphetamine abuse, self-neglect, and involvement in the lifestyle, the message conveyed is incomplete. The photos seemingly suggest that users can be identified on the basis of physical characteristics related to their consumption of the drug.[7] These depictions, however, fail to account for the reality that not everyone who uses meth ends up looking like the images portrayed. They add an additional layer of stigma.

News stories represent another important source of information. Local and national headlines include the following: *Police: Meth addiction led Utah mom to kill 6 newborns*,[8] *Boy riding on father's bicycle handlebars burned when "shake-and-bake" meth lab explodes*,[9] *Porta-potty meth lab found on golf course*,[10] *Meth lab found under toddler's mattress*,[11] *My home was a former meth lab*,[12] *Bloomfield man found with needle stuck in his arm*,[13] *13-Person meth case ends with sentencing*,[14] *Two charged for making meth in front of a child*,[15] *Mexico seizes record amount of methamphetamine*,[16] and *Australian police make record meth seizure*.[17] The headlines serve as reminders of the need for more effective responses and solutions.

The problem is composed of three distinct but highly interrelated facets: use, trafficking, and clandestine manufacturing. The drug is supplied to local communities via traditional sources of drug distribution as well as local production in clandestine laboratories. Changes or shifts in one method of supply influence the other. As local production increases, the demand for trafficked methamphetamine declines, and vice versa.[18] While manufacturing is a serious problem in specific regions, the problem is not limited to the United States.[19]

Three main types of laboratories exist. Super labs, originally found in California, produce the largest quantities of finished product (e.g., ten or more pounds).[20] Today, the largest super labs operate out of Mexico. Mom-and-pop laboratories, also known as small toxic laboratories (STLs), are medium sized and produce enough to supply small networks of users (e.g., one to four ounces). Shake-and-bake laboratories, also known as the one-pot method, represent the smallest and newest type of laboratory.[21] Shake-and-bake laboratories produce small quantities of the drug, generally only enough for individual consumption.[22] Different manufacturing processes can be utilized within a single type of laboratory.[23]

Many of the ingredients used to manufacture the drug are legally available, because they have legitimate household, commercial, and industrial uses. For example, red phosphorus can be used as a fertilizer, pesticide, and in the manufacturing of pyrotechnics.[24] Anhydrous ammonia, a common farm fertilizer, is stolen from tanks in farming communities or obtained from over-the-counter cold packs.[25] Other commonly used ingredients include drain cleaner, muriatic acid, and lithium batteries, all of which can be purchased at regular stores. Key precursor chemicals used to make meth include ephedrine, pseudoephedrine and phenylpropanolamine. While the former are found in cold and allergy products, phenylpropanolamine is only available by prescription for animal use. The chemicals can be extracted from products that contain them.[26]

In the United States, responding to the clandestine manufacturing component of the problem took priority due to the imminent dangers posed by lab-related fires, explosions, and contamination. Highly specialized skills, expertise, special equipment, and mechanisms for safe disposal[27] are required for proper response. The costs of cleaning up a contaminated laboratory site can be thousands of dollars depending on size and the extent of contamination that has occurred. In recent years, the burdens of remediation have shifted from the federal level to the local and state levels.[28,29]

Federally, legislation aimed at stopping clandestine manufacturing was enacted in each of the last three decades.[30] The most significant of these was the Combat Methamphetamine Epidemic Act (CMEA) of 2005,[31] which enhanced controls on access to products containing key precursor chemicals. Today, purchasable quantities of pseudoephedrine are limited to 3.6 grams per day and 7.5 grams in any thirty-day period without a prescription.[32] At the state levels, legislative initiatives vary widely[33] and include the reclassification of pseudoephedrine as a controlled substance available only by prescription.[34] Evaluations of effectiveness have documented short-term and limited victories at best.[35]

The costs of this problem are both direct and indirect. Direct costs include expenditures for law enforcement personnel time, equipment, and biohazard suits, and risks related to the disposal of contaminated chemicals and other leftover materials. Indirect costs include those related to environmental contamination, property damage, medical care, child social services, and the criminal justice system.[36]

The misconception is that methamphetamine "happens somewhere else" or is a concern only for those directly affected. The truth is that the two worlds—the one of methamphetamine and the one we live in—are inextricably interconnected. While the world of methamphetamine may seem far from the reality you and I live in, it has the potential to exist next door. Six main public health issues often overlooked in responses to the drug problem include: child endangerment, abuse, and neglect; toxic places; intravenous drug use; risky sex; risky drug use; and drug-related violence.

Child Endangerment, Abuse, and Neglect: To the extent that drug-related activities take place in the home, children may be forced to come into contact with those engaged in the drug lifestyle, placing them at risk for exposure to drugs and criminal activity. Preoccupied parents and caregivers may place children's well-being second to the drug. Children are at risk of physical, psychological, and emotional neglect and abuse. The perils for children are even greater when methamphetamine is manufactured in the home. In addition to harms from exposure to toxic fumes and chemicals, children may be harmed by injuries resulting from fires, explosions, and burns.

Toxic Places: Manufacturing is volatile, toxic, and dangerous. Production processes require the use of hazardous and poisonous chemicals. Noxious gases are released during the production process and contaminated waste materials remain following the completion of a cook (i.e., manufacturing session). The locations and sites where production occurs as well as disposal sites for residual chemicals and supplies result in environmental contamination. Because those engaged in manufacturing often go to great lengths to evade detection, manufacturing-related activities place themselves, those around them, and first responders at risk.

Intravenous Drug Use: People continue to use drugs intravenously in spite of few sources of legal access to needles. In the face of limited legitimate options, injecting drug users often obtain needles from illicit sources, share needles to inject drugs, and dispose of needles in an unsafe manner. Risky injection practices include the sharing of syringes, which increases the likelihood of the transmission of blood-borne diseases, such as hepatitis B and C[37] as well as HIV.

Risky Sex: In the underground world, sexual activities are often exchanged for drugs or the money to purchase them. Risky sex includes having multiple sex partners and engaging in sexual activities in particularly risky ways (e.g., without condoms, with prostitutes, or with known intravenous drug users).[38] In addition, the enhanced sexuality and loss of inhibition that accompanies use has the potential to contribute to drug-facilitated sexual assaults.[39] Heightened sexuality, one of the side-effects of methamphetamine, may be a contributory factor for the sexual abuse of children among those who use drugs. It is not uncommon for those on the front lines to find pornography, including child pornography, in methamphetamine homes.

Risky Drug Use and the Ongoing Search for Highs: Risky drug use and related behaviors continue to evolve and adapt with increasingly negative and serious costs. The consequences of detection encourage people to keep their activities underground and to avoid getting caught. This may be one of the contributory factors behind the increase in use of newer types of drugs about which little is known, including: synthetic marijuana, spice, K2, bath salts,[40] krokodil,[41] and flakka.[42] Some youths participate in other dangerous behaviors (e.g., the choking game) in the ongoing search for new highs. Such behaviors may be lethal.[43] Risks also accompany the black market. Drugs can be adulterated, or "cut," by dealers to increase quantities and profits. However, risk is not restricted to illegal drugs. Prescription drug abuse is one of the most serious problems in the United States. Overdose-related deaths have tripled since 1990.[44] An estimated 113 people die from drug overdoses each day, making it a leading cause of injury in the U.S.[45]

Drug-Related Violence: Drug-related violence is not solely carried out by transnational offenders. Rather, it is a real aspect of the underground market. The problem plagues cities across the United States. The willingness of drug traffickers to engage in increasingly violent acts to retain territory and maintain profits continues. For example, drug-related violence in Mexico is rising, as local cartels produce and supply large quantities of illicit drugs for the U.S. market.[46] This evolution has resulted in the creation of new terminology to define the brutal types of drug-related violence discovered. Rochkind explains:

> Our language adapted just as fast as these horrific actions took place, and became filled with new words fit for a dictionary of horrors. We came up with words like *encajuelado* (a person who winds up dead in a trunk), *ejecutado* (murdered by rapid gunfire), *levantado* (forced into a car and disappeared forever), *desintegrado* (a body dissolved in some kind of substance) and *encobijado* (a dead body wrapped in a blanket like a taco). The verb *sicarear* (to kill for money) quickly became a profession.[47]

It may only be a matter of time before such violent acts cross the U.S. border.

Methamphetamine is becoming one of the most serious illicit drug problems, not only within the United States but also internationally. It is the second most commonly used illicit drug[48] and the most commonly manufactured amphetamine-type stimulant (ATS) in the world today.[49] While clandestine laboratories initially declined following the implementation of precursor controls, labs have reemerged in recent years.[50] The potential for the problem to expand should not be underestimated. With lower prices and higher purity levels,[51] the potential for increases in the numbers of persons addicted to the drug is real. To mask the destruction occurring at the ground level of this problem is a disservice at best, and negligence at worst.

Communities plagued by high levels of abuse have confronted situations where nonusers purchase and sell restricted precursor chemicals, such as pseudoephedrine, to those involved with meth (i.e., smurfing).[52] Restrictions on purchasable quantities and the accompanying identification and approval requirements for pseudoephedrine products have resulted in the expansion of the number of people participating in manufacturing the drug, in one way or another. Pseudoephedrine-containing products and other controlled substances are bought and sold in the black market. The profit margins can be high, high enough to motivate even those who might never consider manufacturing to participate. For those with little disposable income, the possibility of earning fifty or a hundred dollars in minutes can be very attractive and difficult to pass up.

The methamphetamine problem has existed for decades. According to the federal Drug Enforcement Administration (DEA), between 2004 and 2012 there were 118,940 clandestine laboratory incidents in the United States.[53] The challenges inherent in stopping the supply of a drug that is highly addictive and profitable have been recognized for decades. As far back as 1996, a DEA report noted:

> Drug law enforcement efforts against clandestine methamphetamine producers constitute a "cat and mouse" game between efforts to cut off chemical supplies and efforts to obtain them from non-regulated sources. Past experience has demonstrated that methamphetamine traffickers are relentless, flexible, and creative in finding new ways to obtain chemicals by evading the network of international controls that has been established.[54]

We simultaneously know a lot about these problems and yet not nearly enough. Numerous questions remain unanswered, including the true number of laboratories, the broader societal impact, and the overall costs of methamphetamine. Even those who have dedicated years of their lives to dealing with and responding to the methamphetamine problem still have more questions than answers. Further, there is very little understanding of the problem from an insider's perspective. How can we ever hope to address the problem if we fail to examine it from the insider's perspective? How can we really know what to do about a problem, how to respond, and more importantly, why responses may or may not work, if we don't truly understand the problem itself? It is evident that while there are many *knowns*[55] and *known unknowns* with regard to methamphetamine, the number of *unknown unknowns* is uncountable. We simply do not know enough to understand the limitations of current knowledge about the problem. The dire need for the discovery of both questions and answers is undeniable.

While our criminological theories and images of crime are largely urban,[56] this problem is in many ways rural and nonmetropolitan. In places where there is little to do and limited ways to earn money legitimately, meth fills a void and serves multiple functions. It provides something "fun" to do and a sense of self-worth for people who need it. It provides those who work multiple jobs or long hours in difficult positions with the energy they need to keep going. It allows those who produce it to have methamphetamine and money.

There is no single type of user. Some use functionally and experience limited or no physical, social, or psychological dysfunctions,[57] while others progress to dysfunctional use and report significant and sometimes long-lasting effects.[58] Commonly, individuals are introduced to meth during interactions with peers or social acquaintances;[59] however, meth is not likely to be the first drug experienced.[60] Though long-term abuse increases risks for aggression and psychosis, violence is far from an inevitable outcome.[61] While similar patterns exist for male and female dealers, distinctions regarding motivations, business models, and profits earned are apparent.[62] Individuals generally learn how to "cook" the drug from friends or family members, and hierarchies have been found to exist within methamphetamine-producing groups.[63]

WHAT THIS BOOK IS ABOUT

This is a story about the lived experiences of those in the world of methamphetamine. It is an underground world hidden from view. It is a world where methamphetamine is everything, and manufacturing becomes a way to get all that you desire. Few understand. To comprehend this means knowing the dark and destructive seduction of meth. It is a life many never escape.

The journeys of the adults who participated in this study occurred in a broader context of social relationships and an external environment within which methamphetamine already existed. They did what they did because they wanted to and they could. Their journeys were not solitary ones. There were always others around similarly engaged in these behaviors. The people, their activities, and the broader environment all contribute to explaining what happened and why.

These adults were, for the most part, heavily engaged with methamphetamine, some for years and others for decades. For them, meth was not simply a drug they used, it became their life. They understand all too well how easy it is to become immersed, the lure of methamphetamine, and the high price it exacts. What starts out as just having fun ends as a life-and-death battle. They intimately understand what it's like to straddle two acutely incompatible worlds; each with very different things to offer. They know, better than anyone, the intense and ongoing struggles of getting out and staying out.

Each individual, at the time of the interview, had successfully navigated his or her way out. Their stories put a face to the problem and serve as a testament to the fact that people can and do break free. Even those most heavily engaged in a lifestyle that revolves around the consumption, distribution, and manufacture of meth can escape.

To understand the lived experience of methamphetamine you cannot think the same way that you do when the drug is not a factor. Its powerful effects and the lifestyle that develops around it distort individual thought processes and perceptions of costs, benefits, and risks. It is an altered reality. In this world, everything comes second to the drug. Using the drug and maintaining the life become more important than anything else, including children, family, and even oneself. While some call this addiction, it seems to be more than that. It is more than just a physical addiction to the stimulant drug. Those who become entrapped in this world risk anything and everything for methamphetamine, putting their own lives and those of their loved ones in peril over and over again.

To enter this world is to enter a danger zone, a zone of illusion. It is an altered reality where everything seems perfect, but where nothing is what it seems. It is a reality in which cooking meth under the bed where a young child sleeps seems alright. It is a reality where spending the entire day making the drug or being high while your children go unfed and neglected seems like the right thing to do. It is a zone where doing anything for meth becomes normal.

This book describes the world of methamphetamine from an insider's perspective. It is for anyone who wants to understand. The journey into a life that revolves around methamphetamine and the soul-wrenching reality of what it means to be in this world will be shown for all that it is, good and bad.

The stories presented here will illuminate this dark world. The journeys and experiences exposed will elucidate what drives people into this world and what pulls them back out. As their experiences will reveal, getting out is only the beginning of the challenges that lie ahead for each of them.

The in-depth descriptions of the lived experience will reveal why acknowledging the attractions of the drug and associated lifestyle is crucial for understanding the challenges inherent in responding to the problem. Through these stories you will come to better understand why those immersed in methamphetamine do some of the things they do, much to the horror of everyone else.

The story is one of illusion. The illusion of having everything you ever wanted right in front of you—the power that comes from having lots of money, the seduction of being able to create the one thing you desire most in the world, the control that comes with having something that everyone around you desperately wants and will do anything to get.

The path that leads to a methamphetamine-immersed life is a slippery slope that is much easier to travel than the one that leads out of it. The decisions and behaviors sprinkled along the path leading in, at least in retrospect, are less thought through than the ones associated with getting out. It is an understatement to say that for those most heavily engaged, having the desire to exit the life is crucial, if not essential, for any chance of escape to exist. The journey out is difficult, challenging, and arduous. Getting out and getting clean are only the first steps to successful reentrance into the conventional world. Like a slide that is easy and fun to go down, but difficult to run up, or like a hole that is easy to fall into but hard to get out of, so too is the journey through the world of methamphetamine.

These adults vividly described the all-encompassing world that had once captivated them. It is a world they understand better than any of us who attempt to do so from the outside. They spoke of their experiences using, dealing, and manufacturing. They told their stories so that others might be able to comprehend without having to personally "live it" themselves. It was essential to them that their experiences and journeys be shared, that lessons learned and challenges overcome be documented, and most importantly, that the truth be told. It was with this understanding that each of them came to be interviewed. It is with this understanding and commitment that I tell their stories.

They shared their stories because they had made it. They struggled. Some are still struggling. They had lived an existence where all control was lost to methamphetamine. Some of them came closer to the edge than others. Some of them went to darker corners of reality than others. Some came within minutes or days of the end of their lives. And yet they came to be interviewed. They came to tell their tales so that we could learn from their mistakes. Their stories serve as a warning of the dangers that lurk in the darkness of methamphetamine. They came to inform those who seek to solve the problem without understanding it of why their efforts are destined to fail. They came to explain what it was like to live a life that revolves around the drug and the challenges of getting out to anyone who may listen—including those who try to help, those who know someone involved, and those who need a reminder that there is a way out.

The stories of those who escape, especially those once most heavily captivated by meth, rarely get told. The seriousness and intensity with which my participants approached their interviews was unexpected. Some arrived with artifacts. One individual brought a copy of his court records as proof of the high quantities of meth he manufactured. A few carried pictures of what they looked like at the height of their addiction, or photos of family members so that I could see the people they love and now live for. I was reminded over and over again that although most of these people had been methamphetamine cooks, they were first and foremost just people, like you and me. They were parents. They were siblings. They were sons and daughters. They were people now struggling to regain a steady foothold in the conventional life they once exchanged for the drug. It was a life they now desperately craved.

Each story was unique and contributed to my understanding of what it is like to be in a world that revolves around the drug. Stories of loss and destruction were repeated time and time again. These different stories merged into an overarching descriptive narrative of journeys into this lifestyle and back out. The most intense interviews were with those who had been most heavily addicted and immersed. Like someone who has lived to tell a story that no one else knows, they spoke with the urgency of life or death, as though people's lives might depend on the accurate recording of what they had to say. They had seen things and experienced what few others ever had or ever would. They lived to tell a dark tale from the perspective of one who had been to the blackest corners of reality and back. They knew, perhaps more than anyone else, that this can be, and for some is, a life-and-death struggle. Methamphetamine leaves death and destruction in its path. People die. People know people who have died. There is a reason it has been referred to as "the most dangerous drug."[64,65]

These adults did not set out as young children with aspirations of becoming users, dealers, or manufacturers. Rather, as their experiences and journeys demonstrate, entanglement occurred progressively over time. So the question becomes: how and why does this happen? What can the experiences of those who walked this path, who lived this life, and who found their ways out tell us about the problem? What can they tell us about the experience of living in the methamphetamine world that will help us understand the seduction of it and the difficulties of getting out? What can their personal journeys tell us about the challenges of responding to this problem and the types of solutions that may be needed?

THE STUDY

Methamphetamine manufacturers don't just knock on your door ready to participate in an interview once research begins. The processes behind obtaining approval, locating participants, and gathering data were challenging, to say the least.[66] It was an experiment in and of itself. There was no way at the outset to know with any certainty whether anyone would respond or participate. The call for participants was aimed at anyone interested in taking part in a study about methamphetamine. Emphasis was always placed on manufacturing.

Manufacturing represents the deepest level of immersion. Users are easier to find. Dealers may be more difficult, as they are one step further in the illicit life. But manufacturing is different. It is a distinct level. These individuals are not just using meth. They are not just selling it in exchange for drugs or money. They are making it. They are creating the one thing that users want. They are creating the very thing that destroys the lives of those who fall prey to addiction.

It took four years to locate and interview the thirty-three people who participated in this study. Only six people were interviewed during the first year. I never knew whether the phone would ring. I jumped with anticipation and excitement each time it did. Sometimes the call resulted in an interview, other times it was simply a wrong number. The phone rarely rang. Locating subjects always seemed like something just beyond reach.

To truly appreciate the process behind this study, one has to comprehend what it's like to talk to a stranger on the phone, trying to find out if they ever manufactured methamphetamine. The delicate process involved unobtrusively asking callers if they had ever dealt or manufactured, without sounding like an undercover police officer or a complete idiot. It is difficult to describe; both parties in the conversations were equally nervous and uncertain. Although my questions were scripted, they were at times reminiscent of an illegal drug deal. Though no drugs were ever going to be exchanged, something just as valuable—or even more so—was. Information about drugs. Information about methamphetamine.

Interviews were scheduled with expediency to avoid any chance that callers might change their mind. Legitimate calls evolved into face-to-face meetings. Callers were required to provide a pseudonym in lieu of their real names. Some understood this and others did not. Some of those who had exited completely no longer had anything to hide.

Interviews were conducted at various times—some in the morning and others at night, sometimes on weekends and other times on weekdays. I did my best to make myself available at their convenience, at times driving as far as one hundred miles for an interview. Though I never really knew what they would be like or the story they would tell, I trusted that it would be worth the effort, that those who agreed to participate would know at least some of the answers to questions being asked.

It was only after reviewing each word and disclaimer of the two-page consent form with potential interviewees that would I pull out the tape recorder. There was always an underlying concern that this might make them change their mind. They maintained the right to withdraw their consent at any time. They never did.

It will always amaze me that people would let a complete stranger record their stories of crime, drugs, and methamphetamine manufacturing. For this I will always be thankful. Though the interviews were scheduled to be two hours in length, some were more extensive. In one of the longer interviews, a male with an extensive history of manufacturing and distribution talked for forty-five minutes at the beginning of the interview without being asked a single question.

I arrived at each interview extremely nervous; I left with an overwhelming sense of excitement and exhilaration. There was not a single interview that did not teach me something new about methamphetamine, manufacturing, or the methods by which the validity of the stories being told could be assessed. The information and insights gleaned were invaluable.

THE PLACE

It is surprising that so few who live outside of Oklahoma know anything about it. It sits almost in the middle of the United States, at the crossroads of two of the largest highways that cross this country, I-35, which runs north and south, and I-40, which links east and west. The well-known Route 66 runs through the state. Located approximately 506 miles[67] from the Mexican border, one can drive there from Oklahoma in less than ten hours.

According to the United States Census Bureau, the population of Oklahoma is estimated to be 3.8 million.[68] Nearly 80 percent of the population is Caucasian. Most of the state's population lives in its two largest cities, Oklahoma City, the capitol, and Tulsa. Interestingly enough, Tulsa county has the highest number of labs of any county in the U.S., according to a CNN Money report and map of DEA seizures.[69]

Oklahoma's largest cities are surrounded by smaller ones with populations ranging from forty thousand to one hundred thousand. However, most of its communities are small and rural. Those who drive through the state find mile after mile of sprawling fields of corn, wheat, and oilseed rape (i.e., canola); the few houses and barns that appear serve as reminders of the farming communities spread across the state. With a land area of more than sixty-eight thousand square miles, it is estimated that there are only 54.7 people per square mile.[70]

Those who study crime and criminal justice know about Oklahoma because it has the highest incarceration rate of women per capita in the world. The state regularly ranks at the top of lists of negative social indicators such as teen pregnancy, divorce rates, and obesity, and at the bottom of those that count positive ones (e.g., percentage with healthcare coverage). Despite pockets of ethnic, political, and religious diversity, the state is primarily Caucasian and conservative. It is part of what is known as the Bible Belt.

Why does any of this matter? Because this is the context within which this study and the majority of lives described here occurred. All of the interviews were conducted in Oklahoma, and all of the participants lived in the state at the time of the interviews.

THE PEOPLE

The diversity contained in the final sample was not planned. There is no way it could have been. This, however, is what makes the story that is presented reflective of reality. Some participants had traveled across different parts of the United States. A few moved to Oklahoma from another state. The final sample includes three truckers who spent decades of their lives living the high life of methamphetamine while driving cross-country time and time again.

Not surprisingly, most of the adults had encounters with the criminal justice system, including arrests (n = 31, 93.9 percent), convictions (n = 28, 85 percent), and even incarcerations (n = 31, 93.9 percent) in jail or prison; six had prior sentences from a drug court. Some had extensive criminal careers with upwards of fifteen or sometimes thirty arrests. A few were serving community sentences and were facing lengthy prison terms if they failed to successfully complete their probation.

Nearly two-thirds (n = 20) had some college education or were in college (n = 12) at the time of the interview. Eight had a high school diploma or general equivalency degree; five reported the highest level of education achieved as less than high school.

The majority (n = 26, 78.8 percent) were employed; some were full-time college students, and a few were on disability or were receiving veterans benefits. They worked in various types of jobs, including some in the area of heating and air-conditioning, and some in treatment and recovery. They were administrative assistants, painters, waitresses, and truck drivers. Thirteen were currently married,[71] eleven were divorced, eight were single and had never been married, and one was widowed. They were mothers and fathers, sons and daughters, sisters and brothers. They had anywhere from zero to seven children, including natural children and stepchildren.

All of the adults had histories of methamphetamine use. They all had some history of involvement dealing and distributing meth, and sometimes other drugs. At the most basic level, this resulted from having to buy the drug for their own consumption. At higher levels, it involved trafficking ounces or pounds of the drug.

Twenty-three were former manufacturers in the most traditional sense of the word. This included seventeen males and six females. A few described the much-debated "burying of chemicals" (i.e., burying chemicals and materials underground) said to produce an amphetamine-type drug that is consumed and sold. Others assisted local manufacturers or facilitated, financed, and organized "cooks." Some allowed methamphetamine to be manufactured in their own homes. Those on the periphery of manufacturing represent the networks involved in production and distribution of the drug.

Their histories of manufacturing span decades. Going back as early as 1984 and ending in 2010, they spoke of the various methods and processes by which methamphetamine is manufactured. Some talked about their lives as though the world in which they had used, dealt, and/or manufactured methamphetamine was different than the one they were sitting in—the one at a table, with a stranger, being recorded, and telling their tales of methamphetamine. On the basis of their own accounts, the person sitting in front of me was different from the one they spoke about. In reality they were one and the same; yet at the same time they were not. Two different people. Two different lives.

The interviews were some of the most enlightening and intellectually stimulating experiences I have ever had. They elicited a sense of excitement time and time again. Even those containing questionable substories or points, including things that could not be confirmed or ones that sounded more like fabrications or exaggerations, were revealing.

The intrinsic value of the insight provided became apparent the first time I truly understood the difference between a cold cook and a hot one. It was during my third interview, the first one with a "real" manufacturer in the most traditional sense of the word. The intensity with which Evan told his story and the danger he spoke about became real. It was as close as I would ever come to being in a room where methamphetamine is made. It was nothing short of good fortune that this experience was duplicated in other interviews.

While I never knew exactly what the end result of the project would be, I always knew, even from the very beginning, that this was a story that had to be told. The accounts that were shared and the insight provided were just too good; they illuminated a world few know much about. The story that follows is the one that was told to me. It is their story. It is the story of methamphetamine. At times the story seemed to write itself; it did not have to be forced or artificially created. They laid out the path very clearly for me to see. I just had to look at it and follow.[72]

WHAT FOLLOWS

The narratives shared here will help outsiders understand why those on the extreme end of the continuum—those immersed in the methamphetamine lifestyle—progress from using to dealing to manufacturing. The seduction of each dimension will be revealed. Through the lived experiences of these adults, insight into how and why the lifestyle eventually becomes unsustainable will be shown. The importance of people, places, and things (e.g., activities) helps explain why and how this problem exists, and more importantly, why and how it changes over time. Despite diversity within each dimension, the overall trajectory that emerged sheds light on this hidden and precarious phenomenon.

This book presents an inside view into the underground world of use, distribution, and manufacturing. Each dimension will be described through stories provided by those with the most intimate knowledge and understanding of it. The pathways that lead to a life that revolves around methamphetamine will be discussed. The challenges and difficulties of getting out will be explored. This book will help those who seek to understand the problem as it exists.

These stories illuminate what it means to be immersed in a methamphetamine lifestyle. The strengths of understanding the problem through information from those most knowledgeable about the drug and associated lifestyle will be shown. Insight into the three dimensions of involvement and interrelationships between each facet will be described. The stories that follow fill a critical gap in understanding that remains. Brownstein et al.[73] explain:

> What we've learned is that methamphetamine markets are different from other illicit drug markets, and that the organization of meth markets varies wildly. We found American towns and cities in which meth is produced and distributed in small "mom-and-pop" labs that cater to personal acquaintances, others in which meth is imported by large corporate-type organizations selling to users through locals they know and trust, and areas where both types of markets operate. Perhaps the most important thing we learned is that no matter how it is organized and operated, methamphetamine distribution is personal. To understand the dynamics of meth markets, we needed to work to understand the people who comprise them.

It is with the goal of describing the lived experiences of the methamphetamine lifestyle that this goes forward. I hope you value the journey. More importantly, I hope you begin to understand this problem and learn something new. If the research presented here provides any degree of insight into why this problem exists and the ever-present challenges of responding to it, the promises made to the research participants will have been kept.

It is my hope that you understand the attraction of a life that revolves around methamphetamine and come to understand the high price it demands. That through this journey you will see why developing innovative responses is no longer a luxury and why believing current responses are sufficient is no longer acceptable. The problem and the accompanying destruction of lives described here flourished under the policies of prohibition and the war on drugs. This story aims to lay the foundation for understanding why this matters, not just for those directly involved with methamphetamine, but for anyone who is or may be impacted in one way or another by the problem. This includes the policymakers charged with developing responses and the treatment providers working on the front lines to assist those in need. Closer to home this includes the friends and family members of those struggling with methamphetamine, serving to remind them that there is a way out from even the most-immersed lifestyles.

CHAPTER 2

Pathways to Methamphetamine

I mean, 'cause it stems from something, nobody grows up and says, you know what, I think I'm going to be an addict when I grow up or, I think I want to be a dope cook when I grow up . . . You find ways of dealing and coping with these things that you don't know what's missing in your life.

—Lucy

INTRODUCTION

Their journeys began with early childhood experiences and initial encounters with drugs. The adults came from varied backgrounds, sharing in some experiences and differing in others. Understanding the circumstances that characterized their early lives is important for placing their later life trajectories and choices into context. Their journeys began as many do, with experimentation and the use of drugs in adolescence.

These stories shed light on the early experiences and encounters that shaped the adults in this study early on in their lives. Their childhood environments were composed of social networks and relationships that in many ways were forced upon them. Children do not choose the families they are brought up in nor the early circumstances they are exposed to. It is only later, as young adults, that they begin to play a more active role in the encounters and experiences that occur. The stories that follow highlight the events, relationships, and experiences that framed the childhoods of these adults and foreshadowed the immersion that later followed.

The experiences that preceded initial encounters with drugs included some events that could be controlled and others that could not. While the journeys were not always consciously chosen with a specific and known outcome in mind, they were not as simple as "just making a mistake."[1] Rather, the path into this world plays out like a delicate dance between people and those in their networks, between seemingly important and fleeting desires for excitement, rebellion, curiosity, and new experiences, and between choices, decisions, opportunities, and encounters that eventually prove to be life-altering. It is a dance with life that eventually becomes a dance with drugs—specifically methamphetamine.

BACKGROUND EXPERIENCES

Katie, a forty-three-year-old former dealer and manufacturer, first used meth at age fourteen. While her use did not progress for years, by twenty-six she was manufacturing. At the time of her interview, she had been clean for two years. Katie had survived a childhood filled with instability, abuse, and neglect. She talked about what it was like to grow up in an impoverished environment characterized by chaos, drugs, and abuse.

Katie: Everywhere I'd go somebody was doing something. It's pretty much the poverty level though, you know what I mean?

Q: Did you grow up in a rural area?

Katie: Well, I grew up in a really small town, but my mom lived in the city part of the town, and at times I'd go stay with my dad and I did really well. I mean, I drank, sure, but I'd go back to the city and then it's just like people in the neighborhood, it's like "Hey come on, let's go do this."

Her mother abused pharmaceutical drugs. It would be one of the reasons Katie believed she would refrain from abusing pills herself. She continued to explain.

Katie: There was times I went to bed, starvin' to death, 'cause she'd spent all the welfare check or food stamps on drugs, alcohol, so when I say poverty I mean there was literally nights that I would have to cry myself to sleep because I was hungry, and I can remember back times when I was like seven and eight years old, we didn't have food. And I'd have to get up and go next door in the mornings and ask the neighbors if I could eat with them.

She detailed the severe sexual abuse she endured as a child.

Katie: I was sexually molested . . . First time I was sexually molested was by a friend of the family. I was like five. And then, seven, my two uncles started molesting me, up until I was about twelve. And they used to tell me all the time, "Well, if you tell anybody or you tell your grandma, you know she's going to die." And that just petrified me, because she was the only one I really, ever, loved. I mean, she was always there for me. She loved me unconditionally. Where my mom, I'm sure she tried, but, being a drug addict . . . So they used that against me and that played on me, so that's why I started drinking at a very early age.

The trauma would not end there. She hadn't spoken to her father, whom she described as a "full-blown alcoholic," in twenty years. The revolving door of stepfathers placed her at risk in subsequent years. She continued:

Katie: I did tell someone. I told my mom, but she didn't believe me. But . . . my mom was married ten times . . . I had several stepfathers that tried things with me and I'd tell her about it and, I remember one time when me and my sister told her that he tried to molest us while she was in the hospital, and she threw me out of the house, at twelve, with no place to go . . . and, yeah I went to stay with the neighbors for three days until my dad came and got me from [state].

The diversity in backgrounds with regard to exposure, or lack of, to abuse, trauma, drugs, and crime complicates attempts to understand personal journeys. There are commonalities and patterns among the background experiences of the adults in this study. And yet no single factor, condition, or set of circumstances explains why they eventually would come to live the lives they did.

Early experiences shape young children, providing them with knowledge they might not otherwise have had and encounters with people of various types. Social interactions with others are critical and play an important role in shaping experiences, perspectives, and opportunities that may arise. Children do not have the ability to choose who is in their social network in early years and have little impact on the types of persons in their immediate environments. However, this changes as they move into adulthood.

Though not anticipated at the outset of this research, negative childhood experiences were not uncommon. It is important to point out that no specific questions about abuse or neglect were included in the interviews. Rather, the details described here unfolded, unexpectedly, in the midst of conversations about family, backgrounds, and other life experiences. They were stories that proved invaluable for understanding all that followed; they were an integral part of their stories. The early experiences of those who emerged from extreme situations of abuse and neglect helps to understand the subsequent entanglement in the illicit world of drugs and crime.

It was only in retrospect that Vanessa, a thirty-nine-year-old former dealer who only manufactured meth for a few months, began to link her heavy involvement with drugs to her attempts to self-medicate. As she talked about her childhood, the extent of the trauma she suffered as a child became apparent.

Vanessa: At the time of my birth, my parents had just buried their firstborn child, three months prior to my birth, so the world I was born into was very different than the one that existed prior to my birth, and there's a lot of . . . indifference between my siblings and I as far as, seeing that perspective because *their childhood was not my childhood.*

Q: Right, right.

Vanessa: So I was born into two parents trying to recover from that death. My dad had went immediately into alcohol addiction because of that, alcohol addiction and woman-izing. Adultery, and this is me puttin' the pieces together, not knowing this at the time, but as a child it was very dysfunctional. I never really had a home. I know that I was put a bunch of places and as far as my memory can tell me, I mean it was never anywhere consistently. I don't know where my parents were, I know my sisters, who I see as who made sure I ate on a daily basis, well, I shouldn't say daily basis, weekly basis. Severe amounts of sexual abuse which started, my first memory is at the age of three and it, yeah just horrific, and, it's just horrific, and it's just with that displacement. So now I have identified in my own recovery, severe abandonment issues surrounding that, and lack of love, and then there was severe poverty. I actually used an outhouse until I was like eight, which, this is the eighties. This is unheard of. Tryin' to maintain that, and this is what's amazing, I continued to stay in school by the grace of God. Then severe lack of nutrition, there just, there wasn't food, there were no parents around really, and my siblings and my cousins, they were just children themselves. It was never a thought to think if I, you know, "Did she eat today?" I mean it just didn't exist and I've recognized all this in my own recovery. Those were just things . . .

Q: But you don't know where your parents were?

Vanessa: Well I can't in my memory see 'em. According to the bits and pieces that I hear, I mean, I can see the fights once in a while, when Dad would be around. I told myself mom was workin', but I don't know where she was. I really don't.

Q: And then were you put in a foster home?

Vanessa: No it was just, this is rural Oklahoma, and it's just whoever's on the hill, whatever backwoods shack that I forgot I left you at.

Vanessa endured abuse from the age of three until she was eleven. She elabo-rated on how things played out.

Vanessa: Yeah, and this was not just one person, this was various people in my life, because there was just no protection. There was no adult there to protect that situation.

Q: And was that ever reported?

Vanessa: It was reported when I was five because it had happened to my sister as well, by this certain one family member. My sister and then another distant cousin, I don't know exactly who they were, but the way that, as a five-year-old, it was asked to me was, we were put in a vehicle, and my sister was here, and my mom was here and my cousin who was, it was also happening to, was like, "This has been happenin' to us, has [it] been happenin' to you?" and "no" because you're threatened, if you tell anybody, it's your fault.

Q: Right, right.

Vanessa: "No, it's never happened." So we did actually go into the system, we had the medical examination done, which, typically you're not going to find semen, however long ago it happened, so by that they determined it didn't happen because we adamantly denied it.

Q: But you were kids.

Vanessa: I was a kid, you know, yeah . . .

Others shared in the tragedy of traumatic childhoods. Felix, a thirty-one-year-old Hispanic male was born addicted to heroin. Both of his parents had died by the time he was nine. By age ten he was using and selling cocaine. For him, becoming involved in drugs and crime was a way to survive; it would be the path he used to navigate his transition from adolescence to adulthood. Felix was a former dealer who had manufactured meth a few times, preferring to supply others with the ingredients to manufacture it for him. He described what his childhood had been like.

Felix: I've been on my own since I was twelve. I was born addicted to heroin, and my mother and father, they had a very, very abusive relationship and continued to do drugs the whole time they had us. When I was four and a half they sent me to live with my maternal grandmother. When I was seven, my father overdosed on heroin. When I was nine my mother died of AIDS. When I was twelve years old my grandmother tried to kill me, like threw a phone cord around my neck, tried to strangle me, tried to kill me, we happened to be in [state] at the time, [state] took me away, the foster homes, group homes, temp shelters, they were more abusive than the home I just left, so I would run away, and I would do it right. Like I wasn't the kid that ran away down the street and had dinner at Timmy's house, I would watch trains and jump on a train, wherever [it] stopped that's where I lived. So from the time I was twelve on, every once in a while, I'd get put in a foster home or a group home or something but for the most part I was just living out on the streets.

The fact that he was forced to survive on his own from such an early age would help explain the series of choices and events that later followed.

Evan, the thirty-two-year-old former dealer and manufacturer whose story begins this book, grew up in a home with parents who regularly and openly abused alcohol and marijuana. His family background and knowledge of his father's problematic behavior were key parts of his story.

Evan: Okay. Well, my father has had fourteen DUIs. He's been in prison, I think three times.

Q: While you were growing up?

Evan: He never went to the penitentiary while I was growing up. After my mother and father divorced when I was eighteen when I left home, I think my father, it kinda wrecked him.

Q: The divorce wrecked him?

Evan: Yeah, he didn't really care about anything anymore, and his quality of life has really went down since then. And he's got two brothers, and they've both been in the penitentiary for beating women. And my mother and her side of the family has never, they never get arrested or have done any criminal offenses on her side, but my father's side.

Q: Okay. And that's it. Mostly domestic violence?

Evan: My, my dad and his brothers.

Q: When you were growing up was any of it around you or . . . ?

Evan: No, my, my dad beat my mother.

Q: Was that ever brought to the attention of the police?

Evan: Did she did she ever call the police? No. No, she was afraid to. [Laughs nervously]

When asked if he thought his childhood experiences had influenced his own choices, he said:

Evan: Well, they say a lot of children learn everything at father's knee, and sure, I learned how to behave from him, but it's taking me a long time to realize that, my father doesn't have a very good quality of life. He doesn't have any friends or anybody that cares about him, and I don't mean to be rude or anything but he's probably going to die alone. And he probably has a pretty unhappy life, and I don't want that for myself, so I'm not going to behave that way.

He pondered the potential impact of his childhood exposure to alcohol and marijuana use in the home. When asked if he thought it had affected him, he responded:

Evan: I don't know. I think back a lot, and I wonder if I would have made the same choices if that hadn't been what was normal to me. Because I think maybe if you grew up in a home where drug use was really frowned on and that's a "no, no, don't do that ever," I think that maybe I would have made some different choices.

Wes, a twenty-eight-year-old former manufacturer who only dealt drugs when he "needed the money," similarly grew up with drug-using and alcoholic parents. After his parent's divorce, his father "got clean" while his mother continued to use. At an early age, Wes knew a lot about drugs, more than a young child should know.

Wes: At age five, I want to say age five, but my dad says later, my parents got divorced. My mom and dad both were alcoholics, addicts, and I think at age five my dad left and went into inpatient treatment. To me, I thought he was just gone forever. I was just a kid. And I lived with my mom in that addict home. There was parties every weekend. There was cocaine and alcohol, nicotine, LSD, things like that that were always around.

Q: And you knew what that was a little bit?

Wes: Yeah, when I was probably six, six or seven, I had a friend spending the night, one of my mom's friends offered us this, it looked like a rub-on tattoo, and it was LSD. It was in the shape of Mickey Mouse, so I watched my mom drag her out of the house . . . so there was a lot of that. When I went to work with my mom, my mom was a bartender, and so we would hang out in the bar, and just, hang out. I learned how to play pool, darts, and stuff like that. Shortly after that, a year to the day, my dad was granted a divorce, he was granted custody of my sister and I. I have a sister that's two years older than me, and then a half-sister, who's not my dad's, that is probably four or five years older than me. So when my dad got custody of us, he was already in recovery. He stopped using. My dad's been clean now for twenty-three years. Yeah, it's pretty amazing. He eventually married, remarried my stepmom I think in [year]. And so I was raised mainly by my dad and my stepmom.

Q: After five years?

Wes: Well, it was in between, I was in between, but my dad had custody of us. I liked going to my mom's because I didn't like the rules. My mom . . . there were no rules. It was just hang out, party and drink and watch cops, which is very odd. But at any rate we would bounce in between and when it got to a point where my mom was losing jobs, and things like that, I stayed mainly with my dad. My mom tended to talk bad about my dad. My dad never spoke a bad word about my mom. To a kid at the time, I didn't know what was going on, but now I guess I'm more distant from my mom because she still uses, but, so I lived mainly with my dad and my stepmom until eighteen when I joined the military and moved to [military base].

On whether he thought his exposure to drugs had influenced his path, he said:

Wes: Being exposed to it, I was aware of the consequences, also. I mean, my dad's side of the family are all cops, well, mainly cops and alcoholics. My mom's side are the addicts, and the thieving, and the stealing, and they're kind of to that point, but I think it had an influence on how I interact with other people in my relationship building with other people. I have a hard time with women. That's obvious with the divorces and stuff and I have a hard time just trusting people in general. I think that growing up in that is passive watchfulness, is what I have learned. I based my emotions and feelings and stuff on what's going on in the environment. So I think I learned that, which can be either a positive or a negative. But the using was definitely my choice. I was responsible for what I did, because a majority of my life I was raised in recovery. My dad did not use and he also told us the consequences of using it and so it was just easier to do it.

By the time he first encountered methamphetamine at a strip club at age eighteen, he knew quite a bit about cocaine, but nothing about meth.

Wes: I didn't know anything. I knew about cocaine because that's what my mom and dad and stuff did, and my mom's friends and stuff, so I knew what the white powder was. I knew what crack was. I knew how to [turn] rock cocaine into crack at a very young age, too.

Such early experiences in the home and environment provide direct information about specific substances being consumed. As a result, children and young adults emerge with quite a bit of knowledge about these substances. Wes reflected on his mother's use and her ongoing problems.

Wes: My mom was a crack smoker mainly. And so were my mom's friends. So I was around it. That was a natural thing but I didn't like it because I know how it destroyed and still continues to destroy my mom and her life.

It was a cycle he and many of the others were now trying to break. Lucy, a thirty-three-year-old former dealer and manufacturer, described the familial, multigenerational cycle of alcoholism that plagued her family for decades.

Lucy: My mom broke six generations of alcoholism, so my mom, she had a really rough life because of alcoholism, my grandmother was an alcoholic and she actually quit drinking when I was eight, so my mom had a chance to repair the relationship, or they had a chance to repair the relationship after the alcoholism. So alcohol has really kind of been a little scary.

Her uncle, a violent alcoholic and addict himself, had an extensive criminal history and spent much of his adulthood in and out of prison.

Lucy: Actually his son ended up committing suicide last year. Yeah and his daughter tried committing suicide. Well in [year] is when [son] died, and his daughter tried committing suicide last year and I think it was . . . when you don't get that structure at home. When you don't get that stuff you need as a child, and that was her dad, my uncle, my mom's brother, that was her dad, so she grew up, him in and out of prison, and that sort of thing.

Lucy's mother had also struggled for most of her own life.

Lucy: My mom on the other hand, she has attempted suicide many, many, many times . . . and that's a lot of what I got from my parents, what not to be in life. I didn't get role models, and "this is what you need to be doing." My parents separated and my mom always felt guilty like she had things to make up for, and her idea of parenting was, "If you like it I love it, if it makes you happy I'm for it." Well by the time I was eighteen I was pregnant with my third child. At what point were you ready to put my butt between my shoulder blades? That's what you should've done as a parent!

With seven children of her own, Lucy herself was now struggling to regain her foothold in conventional society.

Most of the adults in this study came from families where one or more persons had some history with crime, drugs, or both; this included parents, aunts and uncles, in-laws, cousins, siblings, and children. Seventeen individuals (51 percent) mentioned having family members who specifically used meth.

This included eleven persons with an immediate family member (i.e., brother/ sister, parent, child, or spouse) and six with more distant family members (e.g., aunts/uncles, cousins) who used. Four others had one or more family members with a history of other drug use.

The number of drug-using family members varied. At one extreme, it was only one other family member; at the other extreme, seemingly everyone in an individual's family had some involvement with drugs and/or crime. The latter was rare. According to Ray, a thirty-five-year-old former dealer and manufacturer, "Everybody in the family pretty much, except for grandpa" had used meth. His aunt would be the only one who had ever gotten in trouble for it. In addition to his own family, he had seen other families become heavily involved in meth. He provided insight into how this happens:

Ray: Yeah, I believe it all starts with one person, and then that's how you meet your contacts. You meet that person over at a relative's house, you get interested, and maybe get a supply from him, and he ends up supplying the family.

At the time of his interview, none of Ray's family members were still using. Ray was the only one who had become heavily engaged in dealing and manufacturing the drug. In some cases, having other family members involved with drugs and crime was not viewed as significant. Ava, a thirty-year-old former dealer and manufacturer, took responsibility for negatively impacting her own path. Although her uncle and stepdad had been involved with drugs and crime, they had overcome their problems; she described her mother as being a "very straight-laced" person. Ava believed she had been provided with every opportunity to succeed, saying:

Ava: It's been really hard. I made my life miserable, when I never had to. I had a great family and I was the only child and well-off financially and I just . . .

Negative background experiences and early exposure to drugs were not necessary antecedents for involvement with meth. Not everyone had a difficult or abusive childhood. Not everyone had parents or other family members who used drugs or committed crimes. Ten adults reported coming from families where no one else used drugs or participated in criminal activity. When asked about her family, Allie, a thirty-four-year-old dealer who sold meth manufactured by her friends, laughingly declared, "No it was *just me.*"

According to Emme, a twenty-five-year-old former dealer who had briefly participated in the burying of chemicals and been present while others manufactured, her own path went against the stability her family had provided. In her case, a traumatic rape contributed to her association with the group of peers who eventually introduced her to methamphetamine.

Emme: At that time I kinda went through a, a really traumatic thing. So I was raped, that's how I lost my virginity and I ended up having to have an abortion . . . So I had to go to school with these people, and I was harassed and it was just not a good thing. I've always been very popular. I'm still very popular, when it comes to my school, and a lot of people don't know, but I did file charges and stuff but it was just, insufficient evidence because it took me awhile to come forward. When that kinda came around, I just was, I went through a lot of different phases. I started *cutting myself.* Nobody taught me how to do that. I don't even know how I figured out how to do it. Never tried to kill myself at that time but I just wanted to run away.

Q: So you started using different drugs?

Emme: I started using different drugs. I started hanging around really, *different people.* My family is very middle class, very, I was brought up to be very different. I never had [a] really traumatic childhood. My family has money. I've been with, wealthy school, wealthy people, but I felt that they couldn't protect me and that class couldn't protect me, so I went towards more the gang bangin'. Because I thought that if anybody is going to mess with me, that'd be it . . . They would protect me, plus they understood me because I felt as low as they did. I felt that people in my class wouldn't understand.

Though not a requirement for later immersion, a majority of adults in this study came from backgrounds where they had been exposed to others involved in crime, drugs, and in some cases methamphetamine. While the direct link between past experiences and future behaviors is unknown, early experiences set the stage for what would follow.

EARLY DRUG EXPERIENCES

None of these adults initiated their drug use experiences with meth. Most started with alcohol (n = 13, 39 percent) and tobacco (n = 18, 54 percent). One individual initiated drug use with marijuana and one with inhalants. It is interesting that overall most individuals began using drugs before their teenage years. Eleven initiated drug use before the age of ten, eight between ages eleven and twelve years old (i.e., preteen), and fourteen (42 percent) during their teenage years. A few began using drugs as young as six years old. Olivia, a thirty-one-year-old former manufacturer who only sold drugs to a small number of lower-level dealers, talked about her earliest drug experiences.

Olivia: I started huffing gas when I was like, six . . . We would do it at least three times a week.

Q: For how long?
Olivia: Four or five years . . . Yeah, until we [started to] smoke weed, yeah.

While such early initiation was not common, it was not unique. Matthew, a thirty-three-year-old former dealer and manufacturer, started using tobacco and alcohol around the ages of eight and nine; he became a regular, daily user of marijuana after first trying it at age nine. He elaborated the dependence on alcohol that preceded his later involvement with "full time drugs."

Matthew: I guess I was nine, ten years old in alcohol and I had just, it was a, experimental thing, and by the time I was fifteen, I was drinking every day . . . and by the time I was twenty-two, I had to have a pint of whiskey to even get out of bed.
Q: How long did your use at that level last for?
Matthew: I was drinking a pint in the morning, and a fifth through the day and a pint right before I went to bed, or about a half a pint or so right before I went to bed, and that lasted about three good strong years. And I got real bad sick and drinking, I didn't never get any DUIs or nothin', but I was watchin' people get in a lot of trouble. So I just put it down and went to drugs, full-time drugs

Though Matthew clearly had a serious drug problem before he initiated methamphetamine use at age eighteen, his drug use progressed and became worse once he began using harder drugs. He would later become heavily immersed in a drug lifestyle.

The number of drugs initiated prior to methamphetamine ranged from a low of two to a high of ten.[2] Only one person had used only two other drugs before ever trying it; more commonly, individuals used several substances before trying meth the first time. In eight cases, methamphetamine was the last drug initiated; in all other cases, one or more other drugs were initiated afterwards.

Before methamphetamine, and sometimes long before, these individuals were using drugs; they were just using *other* drugs. In some cases early drug experiences were primarily experimental or social, in others, regular and sometimes even heavy use of other drugs preceded methamphetamine. Pre-methamphetamine patterns of drug use varied and set the stage for initial encounters with the drug. When it came to methamphetamine, Ava's first experience was characteristic.

Ava: We were just at a, like I don't know if you call it a party, get together, just occasional, hangin' out on the weekend, and I guess that's just the thing to do in junior high or when you're young and you go to people's houses and there's drugs.

Though not always in a group setting, all first encounters occurred with someone known to the initiate—a friend, social acquaintance, or other person in one's social network. Individuals were more likely to be introduced by friends (n = 16), than by a boyfriend or girlfriend (n = 6), family member (n = 4)[3] or other social acquaintance (n = 6), including older peers. In most cases, others presented individuals with their first opportunity to use meth. In a small number of cases, social contacts served as a link to others with access to it. In the majority of instances people were already using drugs with the person who first offered meth to them.

Not everyone was seeking out or planning to use the first time. Max, a twenty-three-year-old former dealer and manufacturer described how his introduction occurred.

Max: Me and a couple buddies were going on a trip for spring break, and we wanted to get some cocaine but we couldn't get any . . . we found somebody that had meth and I never tried it so we just got some of that and then went for our whole week of our spring break and was like "oh wow."

With regard to family, individuals were introduced by cousins, siblings, or other members. No one had been introduced by a parent. One had stolen prescription methamphetamine tablets[4] from his father the first time he used the drug, and a few later influenced their own children's interactions with meth. In some families meth use is part of the transition to adulthood. Vanessa came from a family where her sibling and cousins used. Her first experience occurred during a family trip.

Vanessa: It was a family member and we were actually in [state] and that's what they were doin' and that kind of the generationally, "It's your time, here you go, if you want to try it."

She was introduced by a sibling when she was sixteen. When asked what she remembered, she responded:

Vanessa: I remember it perfectly, because they were all usin' it and they just came up to me and said, "Do you wanna get high?" and I was like, "I'm not snortin' it," 'cause it was openly used, it wasn't like it was something that was hidden. And they said, "Well okay, you can drink it out of a shot glass," and I was like "Okay."

She described her first experience.

Vanessa: Yeah and it was pure, I should say. So I can remember it, I was so amped out, that I literally thought I was gonna die at the age of sixteen. And this is two days after they gave it to me. I couldn't come down, I couldn't go to sleep. I didn't understand, and you don't go ask, "What is wrong with me?" And you don't want more. So it was a really traumatic experience to go through on my own because they're still high and they're still okay because they're adults and they know what's happening, and I didn't, so I was like, I don't know what that was, and now I just remembered, I used to take white crosses, that's what I went to after that initial use because that high was still there, initially an amazing euphoric feeling, it was the comedown that was so hard.

She did not use again for three years.

In Olivia's case, her brothers adamantly refused her requests to try meth-amphetamine. Her first encounter would come from a boyfriend. She described how her introduction occurred.

Olivia: I was fourteen, and my boyfriend at the time, which would soon be my husband, I asked him about it, he's like "Why? Would you like some?" I'm like "Yeah, sure." So I went to [city] and I even remember the ride because we didn't have no brakes so we had to Flintstone it out the door ... We got it and then I went back to my friend's house and we did it.

Though she knew her boyfriend was already using, when asked if it bothered her she responded, "No, I thought it was cool." She explained why she wanted to try it:

Olivia: I'd been watching my brothers, they live this life where it's always money and always exciting and that's what it seemed at the time. I asked my oldest brother if I could get some from him and he told me "never ever ever" and ...

While she expressed a specific desire to try the drug and knew she would be trying it sometime, like many others, she did not know how addictive it would be. When asked about her experiences she declared, "I married into meth." The family she married into, including her husband and his father, used the drug. As her recollection demonstrates, initial encounters can be purposive and delib-erate despite the lack of specific knowledge about the drug and its effects.

Individuals in this study initiated meth between the ages of fourteen and forty-nine, with the average age being nineteen. Eleven people first tried it after the age of eighteen. A majority indicated that they tried it the first time it was offered to them; a few watched others use for a period of time prior to initiating the drug themselves. Those who knew that their peers or others in their social networks used the drug demonstrated a willingness to socialize in circles of users.

Bryant, a forty-one-year-old former longtime dealer who manufactured almost daily for a period of eight years, described his first encounter at age fourteen.

Bryant: I'm just gonna say the name "Jay," okay? We used to always party out north of town with a guy named [name], [a] trailer house, that's where all the beer, all the drugs, I mean everything happened. And a guy by the name [name], he used to take me out there all the time. He wasn't with me one night and I went out to that trailer house, stupid me but I was sitting in the living room, we done smoked some weed and I kept watching these guys go in and out and I asked Jay what they were doing, and he says, "Hey, why don't you come in here and try this?" I was going up fourteen years old and I mean getting this big head about whoopin' on people. I was whoopin' on eighteen-, nineteen-year-old kids that would come out to the party and start crap, I'd whoop on 'em and it was a physical deal and so I got a lot of respect real quick in that area, and anyways Jay says, "Why don't you come in here and try this?" and I knew when I first walked in there, he says, "Hey, you wanna do this?" Hell, I don't know how you supposed to do it. He says, "Well I shoot it." My minds like *okay let's shoot it,* I'm not thinking in my head you'll use a needle. Well I was brave, needles didn't scare me. "Hell, flip it out there, let's do it," and he did that and like I said it went from a thirty-unit cc shot, which is . . . about a third of the syringe . . . He said, "Do you hear bells and whistles?" "No, what kind of bells or whistles?" He said, "Well, let's do some more, apparently that's not very good," so he got out another sack and we tried a different deal, I still didn't hear 'em, but I was high, okay. I felt different and he said, "I better not give you no more 'cause you're pretty high," so I knew I was high, because he told me I was, and after two or three days of being awake I really knew I was.

Q: You stayed awake two or three days that first time?

Bryant: Oh yeah, oh yeah. And then you know from that point there it didn't go up it went straight down and I watched a lot of things go by that I probably could've changed differently had I not been in that room.

He described the events that occurred:

Bryant: Oh, he mixed it up in the spoon, he held my arm down, or didn't held it, I mean . . . he did the work for me. He stuck it in my arm, he did everything for me. I wasn't too smart at the time to know how to stick it and where to stick it and all that so yeah, he did it for me.

Q: Is that unusual to start with shooting up?

Bryant: Absolutely. Most of your people these days don't know anything about it, in that era then it was always eat. First thing you did was put a little in your hand and you eat it or wrap it up in toilet tissue or somethin' and eat it. You just never did just shoot it and the guy I'm talking about he done killed one woman, he got her in a truck wreck, I mean half of his face was gone, so he didn't really have a whole lot to live for. The way he looked at it . . . I'm glad to say Jay is clean and sober now. He's very churchgoing.

Bryant's first encounter was different from most, in that he had used intravenously, shooting up the very first time. However, two others also used intravenously the first time.[5] Intravenous use is atypical; especially the first time. More commonly, people smoke, snort, or eat the drug initially. Intravenous use of any drug is considered more "hard core" than other modes of consumption. It requires specialized knowledge, injection skills, and specific equipment (e.g., needles). Effects can be more powerful and immediate. Those who used intravenously the first time demonstrated a willingness not only to try the drug, but to inject it into their body.

Katie, whose story begins this chapter, also used intravenously her first time during an encounter with her stepfather's sister and brother. She engaged in sexual relations with the older woman. The night ended with her shooting meth intravenously. When she first used cocaine at age eighteen, she used crack; her neighbor was a crack dealer. While most people don't shoot up intravenously the first time they use meth, or initiate cocaine with crack, Katie did. While her experiences may seem extreme, she was not alone.

Emme's description of her motivations behind and the circumstances of her first encounter illustrate the complexities and contradictions often existent in experiences and decisions made during adolescence. She initiated methamphetamine at sixteen. When asked who had introduced her to it, she responded:

Emme: One of my boyfriends did. I was hanging with the crowd, and I was never into doin' the drug thing, I did the marijuana kinda to fit in. I was more into drinking, and I had lost a couple boyfriends because of it. They thought I was too prude or just wasn't into it. So I said, screw this shit. I'm not doin' this crap anymore. And had found somebody I really, really, really liked, and he introduced me to cocaine first and I tried it, and I didn't really like it. I didn't really care. I'm just like whatever. And then he introduced me to the meth, probably about a week later. And that was a different story. I mean I cried before I did, I cried after I did it 'cause I was terrified you know, 'cause [what] people say about meth, I was terrified. And then that just kinda went away.

When asked if she had felt pressured to try it at the time, she said:

Emme: Kinda, but nobody put a gun to my head. I'm my own person. I make my own decisions. I didn't have to do it . . . It was kinda like, everybody was doin' it. I never did it. I was always the one that sat on the outside. I was tired of sitting on the outside. I wanted to do what everybody else did. I'm my own person. I'm not a very big follower, but I was just kinda like "I'm gonna do it." If I do it, I don't, I don't . . . I mean he [boyfriend] kinda pressured me into it a little bit. He kinda was persuading me to do it but he didn't put a gun to my head. I coulda said no.

Q: Tell me about that first time.

Emme: I was sixteen and he had his own apartment. We always partied there. It was a big thing and a bunch of people had it. Everybody was having a good time. It was his sister's birthday if I remember correctly . . . they had a line, so I did it. Everybody kinda pressured me and I did it, and I ended up havin' probably *the best time in my life that night,* honestly.

While her initial use seemed to be strongly influenced by her boyfriend and peers, she insisted that the decision she made that night was hers and hers alone, even now describing her first experience as positive.

Despite prior drug-using experiences people knew very little about methamphetamine and its effect the first time they used. Even those with seemingly extensive drug experiences with cocaine, a drug considered similar to methamphetamine, learned through experimentation. This is illustrated by Daphne's first encounter. A forty-seven-year-old former dealer, she had helped her brother cook one time. Her initial experience followed an encounter with crack cocaine. She described the first time she used.

Daphne: The first time was in October 1997, okay, and March of 1997, my husband, who I had been with for ten years . . . okay, from 1976 we started going steady, yeah all through junior on through high school, we graduated high school and six years later we got married, so in 1976 I met him, in '89 we got married, and in '97 I filed for divorce because he hit me in a drunken stupor. That year I decided I'm gonna do something different, and I lost fifty pounds without using drugs, I just exercised every day, I was finally able to play my own music, and not his stupid heavy metal crud, and I could play my own good music that I wanted and I danced and exercised every day, I had temporary custody of the kids, I did all kinds of neat things, and then one day somebody, I don't know what it was but I had a crappy, crappy day in October and I was crying and I was sad about this and "this person is stupid" and all this drama going in my head and I went to visit a relative, one of my brothers, and he says "I really don't want to hear about the drama," and I said "Well I need to talk to someone," "Just here, smoke this," handed me a pipe and I had just recently learned that within the prior year or two that cocaine came in a different form other than snorting, you could smoke it.

Q: Like the rock?

Daphne: Crack, crack, yeah, that you could smoke rock cocaine, and I liked that but it was very expensive and I couldn't afford it, so when he handed me that pipe that's what I thought it was, and when you smoke rock cocaine, you put the flame to the glass pipe and you suck very hard, very fast cause it goes through a little steel wool and you have to get it through there to put the smoke to start coming to your lungs. I started sucking very hard on this glass pipe he handed me and he goes, "What are you doing, stop it, slow down," I said, "What do you mean, I'm just trying to get a hit," and he says, "That's not how to do it, what do you think you're smoking, crack?" I said, "Well, yeah," and he's like, "Oh this is meth." Now as much as I am aware of the drug world, I thought he was talking about methadone because I had never heard of methamphetamines, and he explained to me, and I thought the pipe looked funny 'cause it wasn't just a straight tube, there was a bubble of glass at the end and so he said, "You hold the flame under, you warm it up, you don't hold the flame right on there because it burns it, you hold it under there and warm it up, and when that starts getting warm, you pull the flame away and as it's cooling off, that's when the smoke comes off," and he taught me instantly how to smoke meth, and the first hit, the very first puff of smoke that hit my lungs, I was like "Whoa! I like this!" And I was gone, that was it. I was hooked, hook, line, and sinker, done.

Q: Was it different from the other drugs you had tried?

Daphne: It was, I hate to say heaven because I don't want to belittle my God, but that's what it was to me at that time, it was just, I found where I want to be forever, this feeling, I never want to leave this feeling, ever . . .

To put Daphne's initiation into context, she had already experimented with or used tobacco, marijuana, alcohol, cocaine, mushrooms, LSD, and mescaline before trying meth.

The descriptions of initial encounters with meth suggest a few patterns: people are generally unaware that they will be using on the day they try it, they are offered the drug by someone they know, they seize the opportunity to use it, and they have little knowledge about the drug and its effects or addictiveness the first time they use it. Though the social situations may include underlying social and peer pressures to use, most acknowledged that the decision to use was one that they had made themselves.

CONCLUSIONS

A number of these adults had come from backgrounds with various unique experiences and encounters. Some had been exposed to trauma, neglect, and abuse. While these experiences did not necessarily facilitate later methamphetamine use, they did shape these young children and potentially impacted them physically, emotionally, and mentally.

Two patterns emerge with regard to early drug use experiences. First, everyone in this study had experimented with or used other drugs prior to initiating methamphetamine. No one began their drug use with this drug. The fact that early drug experiences began with alcohol and tobacco is not unique to this sample or to this study. Similar findings have been shown in other studies of drug use. A majority of individuals here initiated their drug-using experiences before the age of thirteen. This was unexpected. By their own accounts, many engaged in drug use at an early age, sometimes even before they were ten years old. This speaks at least in part to their early exposure to drug using behaviors and accompanying opportunities to use drugs.

The second main pattern emerged in the analysis of initial encounters. Methamphetamine was always initiated during the course of an encounter with peers, family members, or other social acquaintances. In every case, initial opportunities to use occur within social situations and interactions with people individuals knew, and occasionally with whom they had previously used drugs. In some cases the initiators are close friends or family members, people one trusts and knows. This runs contrary to images of the devious drug pusher, who entices an unwitting person to try something they otherwise would not.

Few of these adults indicated that they had knowledge about what methamphetamine was or what the drug did the first time they tried it. Their recollections reaffirm the fact that they were unaware of its potential addictiveness or how this drug might differ from the previous experiences they had had. Individuals lacked information about the drug and its effects.

The data on adolescent and early adulthood drug use fits within what is known about adolescence as a time of transition often characterized in terms of rebellion, curiosity, and the search for new experiences. Those engaged in drug use and experimentation pre-, during, and postadolescence have demonstrated a willingness to take risks and participate in social groups where risk taking and drug use may be viewed as acceptable and may even be rewarded. Those seeking alternative experiences through drugs demonstrate an attraction to things that are outside of social norms. Engaging in prohibited and risky behaviors can be associated with social status within peer networks at least for a period of time.

Most early drug experiences are not based on foundations of knowledge and information. Rather, individuals learn about the different drugs and their effects by watching others, learning from those around them, and experimenting themselves. This helps to explain in part why most of the individuals did not know anything about meth when they first encountered the drug; this was true even for the ones who already heavily used cocaine at the time. The lack of information about methamphetamine when first encountered is somewhat shocking given the extent of prior drug use.

The fact that initiates did not inquire about what methamphetamine was or what it would do to them before using it is particularly surprising given that most initiated it in the company of friends, family members, or others in their social networks. On the basis of their own retrospective recollections, conversations regarding use tended to be geared more toward "Do you want to try this?" rather than on obtaining any details about the drug offered. The fact that even the few people who were already using cocaine before they tried methamphetamine were somewhat blindsided by the drug and its effects suggests that more needs to be done in terms of education about different drugs.

Despite identified patterns and anomalies, all paths converged at the point of initiating meth. It is from here that their journeys into the world of methamphetamine began, immediately for some, and over time for others.

Initial drug experiences encompass an interplay between decision-making processes and opportunities to use drugs. This arises within the social contexts where opportunities to use drugs occur. In particular, those who were older acknowledged and described the role their own decision making played in their drug-use experiences. As will be shown, this decision making continues throughout involvement with methamphetamine, even during times of heavy use and abuse. The fact that they were willing to try drugs and use substances they knew little about reiterates their willingness to engage in unknown and risky behaviors. Even under pressure, they were making choices about their drug-use experiences.

"Learning by experimentation" is a precarious way to figure things out, especially when it comes to obtaining information and knowledge about the effects and side effects, and benefits and risks of drugs. The fact that no one in this study knew anything about methamphetamine when they first tried it speaks to the failures of prevention and education efforts. At least for them, the knowledge was not there.

Early experiences with drugs in general and methamphetamine more specifically are important antecedents to the path leading to manufacturing and immersion in the drug lifestyle. They establish a willingness, no matter how potentially dangerous or risky, to experience new things, to engage in behaviors that are frowned upon at a minimum and that may cross the lines of legality, and to participate in groups in settings on the fringes of conventional society. This willingness is not limited just to their consumption of drugs; it eventually extends to other aspects of the drug lifestyle.

The chapters that follow illuminate the main dimensions—use, distribution, and manufacturing. Each dimension represents a deeper level of involvement in the lifestyle. Each is necessary, but not sufficient, for full immersion in the world of methamphetamine.

CHAPTER 3

Loving Meth

Q: And you said you have tried methamphetamine?
Patrick: That was my true love.
Q: That was your true love?
Patrick: Yes . . . . I built a life around it. I loved the stuff.
My drug of choice was methamphetamine, period.
Q: Okay. So once you started using the meth . . .
Patrick: There wasn't nothin' else there . . .
When I started doing meth, everything else didn't matter anymore.

INTRODUCTION

Everything changes when methamphetamine becomes more important than everything else. They described how they felt as *love*. This wasn't just another drug they would experiment with and use. It was *the drug*, the one that would eventually change it all; the one that would change their lives. Loving meth is *the Rubicon*. It is the line that once crossed—committed them irrevocably.[1] As Patrick, a fifty-five-year-old former manufacturer who transported large quantities of drugs but rarely dealt them, explains above, once he loved meth there was nothing else.

Why would anyone talk about loving methamphetamine? Because it gave them everything they wanted. It is a storyline captured by a research assistant early on when in large, bold, lettering she wrote: "Meth: A Love Story . . . THEY STILL LOVE IT! . . . Do anything to get it. It is their life, not a part of it. What is more powerful than money? Love. And meth is love."

Insight into motivations for use, personal preferences, and patterns of consumption will be presented. Understanding why people use and why their use progresses over time is essential for understanding subsequent immersion, including involvement in dealing and manufacturing. Daphne explained how her use of other drugs changed after she tried meth: *"Meth became my, my only reason for living."*

WHY METHAMPHETAMINE?

Use is the first dimension of the lifestyle. Users will tell you why they use. Even those no longer using explained what they liked and disliked about the drug and why they preferred it over others. Methamphetamine provides users with a sense of well-being and high levels of energy incomparable to anything attainable naturally. Surges of dopamine flood the body with endorphins. Sensitivities are heightened and users experience overwhelmingly powerful highs; the euphoria and energy can last for hours.[2]

The drug is, by design, a central nervous system stimulant. It is a synthetic drug that does exactly what it was created to do. It makes people feel good. It gives them energy. It enhances sexual desire and brings excitement and pleasure to daily life. This is why people use it. This is why they want more and more as time goes on.[3] This is also why some eventually progress to the point of doing whatever they can to get more. Loving methamphetamine is the first step. When asked why he used the drug, Wes replied, "I think that for me, my choice in using meth, was because it worked." Lucas, a thirty-nine-year-old former dealer who manufactured meth from the age of sixteen until he was thirty-eight, similarly spoke about his preference for methamphetamine, saying:

Lucas: If the ground don't open up and the devil don't call you down to the ground, you smoke something [else] . . . I'm a speed freak. I'm gonna tell you right now. I'm a speed freak. If it [gave] me energies where I could go and get things done, I was in love with it. There is no other drug in the world like methamphetamine. There is no other drug.

Even among all the different drugs he used, methamphetamine proved to be exceptional. It was different.

Initial experiences can be extraordinarily intense and transformative. For some, first encounters are life altering; lives instantaneously become subdivided into "pre-" and "post"-methamphetamine. This first became evident as Evan described his progression of use.

Evan: At first, it was just available to me, social use. And then, when I first used it, I'll just tell you how I felt, honestly, "My, where have you been all my life?" "That's the best thing I've ever done," and I wanted more of it immediately.

He emphasized the word *immediately*, seeming to change what he was saying mid-sentence. He continued.

Evan: Immediately I wanted more, and I stayed up all night, and I didn't have any more, and I felt terrible the next day. I hadn't slept. I hadn't eaten. I just wanted to lay there. I felt sick. And I thought right then, "Well, if that's what that's like, the aftereffects of it, then I'm not really interested in it." Well, about a month later, a friend of mine had some again and he said, "Let's do some again." And I said, "Well, I felt so bad last time." And he said, "If you just do a little bit in the morning, again, you'll feel fine again." And I found out that was true. And if I kept using it, then I would never feel bad. I wouldn't feel bad. I would just stay high.

This time, he emphasized the word *high*. In less than a month, he was using daily. When asked if his experiences with meth differed from those with other drugs, he responded:

Evan: Yes. Yes. Yes. Methamphetamine has been different for me than any other drug.

He would be the first to use the word "love" to describe his relationship with meth. However, he would not be the last. He continued:

Evan: And it was really, I don't want to sound, I guess I'll sound however it sounds, but it's the truth. It was *a love story for me,* because I loved it more than anything else, myself, more than anybody else, more than anything else, more than my children, more than my wife, more than my job, more than my home, any of my possessions.

While this type of experience does not always occur, the dangers of such powerful encounters should not be underestimated. In the moment, the drug seems to provide users with everything they want. The description provided by Patrick, the former manufacturer whose words begin this chapter, could be attractive to almost anyone.

Patrick: It fixes everything. You don't worry, you don't. You don't get tired. You don't get sick. It always wants to go. It never tells you no. It answers everything. To help you understand what it's like . . . gosh . . . have you ever imagined not having another bad day? Always being happy? Always being well? Always having energy to go do something else? Go home and maybe spend half the night wanting something to do? Clean your house or something? Your house'll be spotless, your cars are spotless. You're never out of energy. It's totally for ya.

For some, meth fit into their otherwise conventional lifestyles. Patrick, one of the truckers in the study, injected multiple times a day for decades. At his height, he was driving cross country and shooting up an eightball (i.e., 3 1/2 grams) each day. He was also not alone in this length or level of use, nor was he alone in that he functioned for awhile on the drug. There are those able to successfully straddle the worlds of methamphetamine and conventional society simultaneously for a period of time. Meth allowed Patrick to stay awake for long periods of time and maintain high levels of energy. As he talked, however, it became apparent that there was also something more.

Patrick: It was just something that, *it was the answer to everything.* It made . . . I don't know how to explain it. It's total euphoria. It was . . .

Q: Euphoria?

Patrick: Euphoria, and I would be tired as hell in the truck and I'd say, "Come go with me" [to my wife]. "No, I don't want to." Dope never told me no. You know?

Q: So always made you feel good and . . . ?

Patrick: Always felt good, always could get another mile or two. You heard all them stories about this and that, I wanna do those too and I did. I used to run from [east coast state] to [west coast state], load cattle in swamps in [east coast state] . . . I know there's south of [west coast city] to [the] feed yards, and I could do it by myself once a week . . . That's about six thousand miles, 6,400 miles.

Meth would become a significant part of his existence, leading him to build a life around it.

Part of the attraction of meth is that it fits into the busy and hectic lifestyles people lead. This was discussed by Vanessa.

Vanessa: Well, it used to be what I would define as fun. And it gave me a feeling of power, it was so euphoric initially, with that use, there was nothing I couldn't accomplish. It brought me up out of everything that was bringing me down in that moment, and I could go nonstop, and I'm a Type A personality, by nature, so it gave me the ability to accomplish everything that I felt I needed to accomplish to make me a complete person, which was all external, so it, that's what it provided for me. It gave me . . .

Q: So it seemed liked the perfect fit.

Vanessa: Oh it *fit me perfectly,* yeah! I walked right into that suit, it was me, you know, it was like, this is me. I'm OCD, I'm wrecked out, I can keep everything in order, and everything was external, everything is organized so my life is good, and I've got everything in place and I've got a hyper personality anyway and, this fits, 'cause when I run out of my natural energy I can just take this and continue on.

For years she maintained an outwardly conventional existence, hiding her use from even those closest to her.

Vanessa: No one did ever know [laughs]. Yeah, I was a highly functioning addict, 'cause I ran a business. I took care of children. Children who had straight As in school. At one point I had my mother, all three of my children, a four-bedroom home, I was a full-time college student and I worked . . . and high the whole time. Yeah. Yeah.

While meth was not the only drug she used, it was the main one.

Vanessa: Completely functioning addict. No one ever asked me. No one ever questioned me. It was a daily routine, I was so OCD with my use, it was daily. It was exactly this amount at exactly this time, every single day. I committed to make myself go to sleep at night. I committed to make myself eat, somewhat, during the days. I always maintained my hygiene, because I had small children.

Mia, a thirty-nine-year-old former dealer who organized and facilitated cooks for manufacturers, talked about the beneficial side effect of weight loss.

Mia: You can really maintain your weight, and I'm the largest I've ever been and it was just an issue with me, and it seemed like, "I'm on top of things and in control and can do a lot."

Weight control is one of the socially desirable effects of the drug. Enhanced sexuality is yet another. Sex is one of life's most pleasurable, instinctual, primitive, and visceral experiences. Sexual experiences on meth are referred to as the best experiences one can ever have; fueled by the drug, they are unmatched in the natural world. Surges of dopamine and endorphins intensify sexual stimulation and combine with abnormally high levels of energy to allow for long sessions of sexual activity. This can become one of the most powerful attractions of meth. It is a very real part of the seduction. Lucas reminisced about the enhancement it brought to him and his relationships.

Lucas: I mean you get everything done you want to get done, your sex life's awesome. That's the main reason I stuck with it for as long as I did was for the sex, because honestly, you're pleasing your woman. No problem, so I mean there's no "Honey I'm tired." There's none of that. You come home from working eight hours, make love for two hours, go to sleep, eat your supper, your wife smiles every day. She doesn't complain. Everything's good.

Evan agreed, saying:

Evan: Oh, oh, there's something, something that I really did like about using methamphetamine . . . It's, the sex is incredible. It's like, I don't know. It adds somethin' to it. It adds something to it. It's something primal, I don't know, it's very intense . . . It makes it to where a man can have sex for, all night long, and, it's, it's something.

Is the love of methamphetamine addiction or something more? The question did not have a simple and specific answer. While not everyone spoke of loving meth, many did. Additional variations existed with regard to whether meth was viewed as addictive. Steven, a twenty-four-year-old former low-level dealer, elaborated on why his progression occurred.

Steven: It wasn't because the high wasn't there anymore. It was just because I wanted to be high all the time, every day because I liked the way that it made me feel and the way I acted towards other people. All your negativity went away when you were on it. You were nothin' but "Hey, how you doin' today?" And you always had a smile on your face, because of the way you felt, whether anyone said anything bad about you or not, you were still happy for who you were.

Q: When you say you were addicted the first time, what does that mean?

Steven: Well, whenever I said I fell in love with it the first time I tried it?

Q: Or that you say "I was immediately addicted?" What does that mean?

Steven: Physically and mentally. I was in love with the effect.

Q: It was just good.

Steven: It was awesome. Best thing I'd ever done in my life.

As Steven's words demonstrate, personal experiences were intermingled with social ones. Being high not only changed the way he felt, but it altered his experiences and interactions with others around him. Though he was using multiple times a day within six months of first trying meth, he insisted there was a distinction between his desire for methamphetamine and addiction. He tried to explain.

Steven: Addictiveness? Meth isn't addictive. But I didn't know how I would feel after I smoked it, no, but because of the effect that it had on my body, I wanted more and more. It wasn't an addiction at all. It was a want.

Emme similarly questioned the notion that her heavy use of meth was addiction:

Emme: I still don't understand how people can be addicted. In a way I have a problem with that because I was never addicted. I don't understand how people are alcoholics.

Q: You think it was a choice?

Emme: It's always a choice. It's a choice for them. It's a choice for somebody that's smoking. Yeah, you're addicted, but you can choose to stop if you really want to stop. You can stop. You're not having a gun to your head. You're doing it 'cause you're choosing to do it. I understand you need help. A lot of people do need help to quit. I do understand that, but I don't understand a lot of the addictiveness part of it.

Such perceptions, however, were not common, nor were they shared by everyone. Addictiveness was a common theme in most discussions. Conner, a twenty-four-year-old former dealer and manufacturer, referred to meth as "the most addictive thing on the planet." For him and many others the idea that methamphetamine is highly addictive was indisputable.

PATTERNS OF CONSUMPTION

Users vary in their patterns of consumption and preferences are subject to change over time. As people experiment and use, they develop preferences for what they consider the most enjoyable experiences and the social contexts within which they prefer to use. Some prefer smoking it while others prefer snorting, eating, or injecting it intravenously. Some people used meth primarily in social settings while others prefer to use it while alone; still others didn't express having specific preferences. Decisions about use did not occur in a vacuum. Rather, social networks had the potential to influence personal preferences and patterns of use.

Jessica, a thirty-seven-year-old former dealer who once lived with a boyfriend who manufactured meth, explained how her use progressed over a period of several years after she first tried meth at age twenty-four.

Jessica: I didn't like it very much. I didn't do it very much. And after the first time I did it, I didn't do it again for probably six months. And then I would do it for a couple of days, well, for like once, and then a couple of days later I'd do it again. Just a few times a week. And then, when I was probably about thirty, twenty-nine or thirty, is when I started using on a daily basis up until about a month ago.

She learned to inconspicuously consume the drug—by adding it to her coffee.

Jessica: Well, it's funny. I used to swallow it. I'd wrap it up in a big capsule or a piece of paper and I would swallow it, because I never was a smoker. And I was with a different boyfriend at the time who did not use and I had quit for a long time and he didn't know I had started using again, and we were camping, and I didn't have a way to swallow it and I didn't want to just put it in my mouth, so I dumped it in my coffee, and about two weeks of that, and after that I was ruined for eating it anymore. I couldn't get off eating it. And so I put it in my coffee. That's the only way I could ever really get off on it.

Q: When you swallowed it . . . how long did it take?

Jessica: About thirty minutes. Yeah, the coffee was about instantly. Yeah, it would last all day. So I only had to do it just that one time.

At her height, she was consuming one-fourth of a gram a day. Like others, her preferences changed over time. While she initially used the drug socially, by the end she was using it alone.

Personal preferences do not exist in a vacuum; rather, they exist within personal and social contexts. People often associate with others who engage in similar behaviors. In many cases, the social aspects cannot be separated from the personal ones. People use not only because of how meth makes them feel and how they experience the drug, but because of the social nature of drug-using activities. Typically, users consume the drug with others within a social setting that is viewed as positive and fun. In some cases, preferences and patterns of consumption model those occurring with the social network within which the drug is used. Steven's preferred method of use—hot railing—aligned with that of his peers.

Steven: Hot railing. You have a glass pipe. They all had, they had a ball on the end of it, a bowl, right, and the regular name for a pipe like that would be a glass dick, that's what we would call 'em. You'd break off the bulb on the end of it, you would line the meth, heat up your pipe, real hot, on one side because you're gonna have to hold it right here and then you heat up the rest of the pipe as hot as it can possibly get. 'Cause it melts it all in the same time, and you get the liquids in your . . .

Q: Now are you inhaling it? Snorting it? And it's hot?

Steven: You snort it while it's hot, yeah.

Q: It's like vapors? Does it vaporize it?

Steven: It'll be vapors and liquid at the same time. And as you did that, you'd feel the burn as it hit, but it'd evaporate so quickly and it never burnt the back of your nose. You just inhale it and whooosssh.

He preferred the crystal form of the drug to powder because crystals were easier to burn. It was a personal preference built within a social one. He elaborated on hot railing crystalized meth.

Steven: It's so much harder to burn a powder then it is a crystal . . . You wanted it crystallized so whenever you put it in that little ball that's at the top of the bowl, you put it in there and you start to watch it form a liquid, then you roll it, so it'll hit every side of the bowl so that the meth will last a whole lot longer that way. You can smoke it from different angles to get all of it out instead of it just bein' in the one spot, because you can burn your pipe real bad if you just have it in that one spot and if [you] keep the torch on it too long, it starts to burn the meth and it burnt the glass at the same time to where it turns black and you can't get the black out, but a lot of times you can use rubbing alcohol on a Q-tip, put it in there, but sometimes you burn it too much and you can never get it out.

In this and other drug worlds, there are *subcultures within subcultures.* The term was originally introduced by Zach, a thirty-five-year-old former dealer who indirectly participated in manufacturing for a short period of time, while referencing differences between types of drug users (e.g., heroin versus methamphetamine). The notion applies to variances between those using the same type of drug as well. One of the most concrete lines of distinction exists between those who inject intravenously and those who do not. It is a line that differentiates the more hard-core users from everyone else. The adults in this study included both.

Sometimes, personal preferences take precedence over social considerations. Here Nicholas, a twenty-seven-year-old former dealer and cook, describes why he preferred to smoke over injecting despite the fact that most of his peers were IV users.

Nicholas: I liked to smoke it . . . The injection, I always felt guilty about the injection. It was just something inside me that told me it was wrong, where with the smoking it was a lot easier to hide. I can't really explain but the smoking, I could always just throw the pipe on the ground and smash it and it wouldn't mean nothing. Whenever you have your little junkie kit, that's what I always called 'em, when you got your needle, you got your spoon . . . .

Q: Junkie kit?

Nicholas: Yeah that's what I always called it, a junkie kit. Anybody I knew that shoots up, they have a needle, they have a spoon, they have Q-tips in a little bag and you can't just throw that away.

While not all who used intravenously ended up preferring this method of use, the overwhelming majority of IV users did.

For many, progression to IV use represents the deepest level of immersion with regard to use. Wes spoke about how his method of use progressed over time as he became more heavily involved.

Wes: I guess the progression went from snorting lines to snorting and eating it in the pill capsules, and then from doing that to smoking it, because then I realized you can do that, too. That was probably two, gosh, I probably spent two years or so just smoking it. And then the last two years of my addiction was IV use.

Ray similarly used for years before becoming an IV user. The change in his pattern of use coincided with his increasing participation in the lifestyle and interactions with other IV users of the drug. When asked if the people he was using with were injecting too, he referenced the name they had come up with for their behavior—"We called it the shooting gallery." *The shooting gallery*— the words referenced who they were and what they did.

Though the high number of people who injected was unexpected, in retrospect it should not have been. Intravenous use seemed to be the preferred method for many. As he reminisced about his preference for injecting, Evan started breathing very heavily, almost seeming to hyperventilate. The feelings and experiences were so powerful that even now, years later, talking about them seemed to affect him physically.

Evan: Yeah, if it's good, like that, when you inject it, right away, you can taste it in the back of your throat, if it is good and when you inject it, there's something called the rush, and that is probably for the first eight or nine minutes after you take a hit of it in your vein . . . the only way to describe it I think is if you were in standing in a train tunnel and there was a train going through, it's so loud it just, it overtakes you and, I mean, I can't see anything. I can hear someone, I can see someone movin' their mouth and everything but I think I can't, it takes your breath and you just . . .

During the course of his involvement, Evan had used in different ways. He had eaten, smoked, snorted, and injected. His preference for intravenous use was in part based on the positive and negative aspects of the different using experiences he had had. He attempted to explain.

Evan: No, I never really liked eatin' it. Hurts my stomach. I never really liked snortin' it, either, because it hurts my head. And it hurts real bad, it burns, real bad. It's, it's a real nasty raunchy drug. And, smokin' it's pretty good. I really liked that. I, I smoked it longer than I shot it. But, once I started shootin' it after smokin' it, that was it.

Meth users typically used other drugs as well. Poly-drug use experiences ranged from using meth with one or more drugs including alcohol, tobacco, and marijuana to injecting combinations of illicit drugs together. Heavy methamphetamine users commonly preferred it to other drugs. Jackson, a thirty-eight-year-old former dealer and manufacturer, injected it for more than ten years. His progression occurred over a period of time.

Jackson: I smoked pot first and then . . . I took downers for a while, and then went to methamphetamines, and methamphetamine and pot is all I done for twenty years . . . Yeah, yeah, once I started doing methamphetamines it got to where I didn't want to do nothin' else but methamphetamines and smoke pot.

For Troy, a thirty-four-year-old former dealer and cook, the change in his method of consumption coincided with the progression of his use and immersion into the drug lifestyle. Only clean for a month at the time of his interview, he described the impact of becoming an IV user on his involvement with methamphetamine.

Troy: The alcohol first, and I liked the marijuana, I didn't care for alcohol, though, at the time. And then when I started messing with the methamphetamine I really liked it, a lot more than anything.

He elaborated on the progression that followed.

Troy: When I first started it, I was just sniffing it, and then, probably when I got about seventeen years old I started usin', I [just] become an IV drug user, and that's really when it progressed from like a weekend thing, to where I was just like a blown-out junkie by then . . .

Q: By the time you started injecting it?

Troy: Yeah when I started injectin', that's when it really really progressed, from that point on, to this time right now.

His progression followed a four-year period during which time he mostly smoked and snorted meth on weekends. At his height, he was injecting more than ten times each day.

It was not just about getting high. Rather, these adults were engaging in experiences aimed at getting higher than high. Wes explained his preference for mixing drugs when he shot up intravenously:

Wes: The cocaine only lasts you usually if you do it intravenously. It doesn't last very long, twenty minutes, you get the echo, you feel high, and then you feel like punching somebody. If you just did cocaine. Mixing the two, I'd get the same starting effects, the echoing, the train noise, and then I'd feel high, and then with the meth it would just kick it up another notch, yeah, kick it up another notch and at that point you're an astronaut. And that's where the audible, visual hallucinations kick in.

At his height, he was injecting every three hours. He developed an innovative way to manage his heavy IV use and minimize the risks associated with this method of consumption.

Wes: Every three hours. I was an IV drug user. At one point in my addiction, I actually put in, because in the military they taught us how to be combat life savers and how to stick somebody, how to put in an IV. At one point I put in a catheter, because I got tired of sticking myself. So I would use that. At that point, I would use every couple hours and at least a quarter bag, which is a lot. At that point, I was spending a lot of money and that's when I started to learn the process of manufacturing that stuff.

He discussed his progression and the specific experiences that influenced him to begin shooting up himself. The influence of others similarly partaking in drug-related activities was apparent.

Wes: I tried to do it every weekend, but it became probably an every other day thing. What happened is I stopped going to the club with my girlfriend or wife at the time. I would have to stay home and take care of her son and so I wouldn't do it around him that much. I would just do it to maintain. It wasn't getting me high enough and that's when switching over, because [it] eventually got to the point where the kids were always at the grandparents' house. So we were able to smoke it. We'd have a bunch of people over. We'd be passing the pipe. There'd be five-six-seven different pipes and just a spread of stuff on the table. After smoking it, and there again, it gave a different effect. It felt different than just snorting it. I think after smoking it, it is also on a constant basis, when it progressed to smoking it every day, just smoking it to go to sleep even; it was always there. I'd smoke it when I woke up, smoke it when I'd try to go to sleep, just whatever. It was an everyday thing. Like lighting up a cigarette, I might have a pipe in the car. I'd have a pipe in the house; I'd have one in the living room, and this is when the kids were always staying at the grandparents' house. And then I would rent motel rooms and smoke it all the time.

His increasing consumption was, at least in part, influenced by his desire to maintain the partying atmosphere. Over time, the types of users he partied with started to change.

Wes: When that started happening, when smoking it more started happening, we started to be around people who just wanted to, well, they would leave the room, and just come back totally blitzed. Their eyes, you wouldn't see any color or anything. I'm like, "What the heck is that all about? Did you take some to the bathroom with you?" And they're like "no, I shot up." Then they would just . . . they'd sit there and smoke, just for the taste. But then they'd be off the charts. I'm like, "I'm not getting the same effect; I'm not getting as high. I can still function." These guys are bouncing off the walls. It seemed like they were having more fun.

Katie had used meth a few times before progressing to heavy intravenous use at the age of nineteen. By her own account, this time it was different. Her level of use was self-described as "full force" until she would later get busted at age twenty-five. She eventually developed a $1,000- to $1,500-a-day habit, and described her pattern of use as: "All day. As soon as the rush was gone I was puttin' some more in my arm." At her height, she was shooting up twelve to fifteen times per day.

Not everyone who uses intravenously ends up becoming a regular IV user. Mia referred to the two-week period she injected as one of her darkest times.

Mia: I did try it for like about two weeks. A lot of people around me did it and I thought it was something I had never experienced and I can remember, though I didn't think you could reach a new low, and I remember just hating and loathing myself because I can't believe . . . well, you have a line in the sand and "Oh, I will never do this" or "I will never do this."

Q: You crossed the line?

Mia: Yeah, I did and I just remember that was one of the points of just totally hating myself and I'm type 1 diabetic so I had access to syringes my whole life since I was ten. I just never ever wanted to do that and I'm really fortunate, I'm glad that I could never really do it like that . . . I'm very glad about that.

In her case, personal preferences also eclipsed social ones.

There are contradictions and complexities in the ways people explain their relationship with methamphetamine; some decisions only seem to make sense when examined from the perspective of those involved. Here, Lucas describes his preference for smoking and the reason he never ate the drug:

Lucas: No. Hell, no. I'm not eating nothing. I made it so I know what went in it. I'm not putting no muriatic acid in my mouth. But I'm smoking it like an idiot. I don't know why. It smokes, I'm smoking it.

He elaborated about the contradictions inherent in having such powerful drug experiences.

Lucas: Yeah, it's the mixture of the chemicals that makes it so powerful, because if you get up in the morning on a normal routine like you sitting here yawning. When you wake up in the morning and you snort a little line this long of methamphetamine, the rest of the day all your paperwork got done, all your job got done, everything at the house got done. Everybody's happy. When you go to bed tonight, you make love for an hour and a half, two hours, your wife's happy. You wake up in the morning. Everything makes, it's like the devil . . . Everything works perfect on methamphetamine.

A final point is worth mentioning. When they talked about methamphetamine they were not always talking about the same thing. There are as many different types of methamphetamine as there are manufacturing processes and manufacturers of the drug. The importance of this point became evident during the conversation with Holly, a fifty-four-year-old former dealer who participated in the burying of chemicals for a short period of time. In response to a question about her likes and dislikes, she laughingly stated, "Which one of 'em? There's different kinds." She preferred one type over others, comparing and contrasting the anhydrous ammonia-based version with the newer form, ice. As she spoke, it became clear that in any discussion of methamphetamine one must be very specific. Allie elaborated on the different types of meth she had seen.

Allie: Oh lord, it came in all different forms, and all different colors, and all different, oh wow.
Q: Is that because of the way people make it?
Allie: Yes.
Q: It's so it can look different?
Allie: It can look different, it could be more potent, they had peanut butter crank.
Q: I never heard of that one.
Allie: Peanut butter crank is kind of an old-time, sometimes it would be a little bit more wet, you'd have to eat it, I mean blue, red, purple, pink, yellow, white, now the crystals, the crystal meth I think I actually only did real crystal meth once, and it's probably, best cleanest stuff I ever did. The worst thing I ever did was ice. Ice started coming around, ice was in big, big chunks, ice lookin', it messed my head up really bad . . . Ice is probably the worst stuff to come around, it's very, very potent.

Though the term "ice" was mentioned many times throughout the interviews, the meaning of the term was not always consistent or clear. Matthew,

one of the more experienced former cooks, commented on the various mean-
ings of "ice." His response followed a set of questions aimed at obtaining
clarification about whether or not he had ever heard about people "burying"
chemicals to produce a methlike stimulant.

Matthew: They bury em, you talkin' about the ice?

Q: Well, I'm trying to figure out what ice is. I thought ice was what comes in from
Mexico, but that's not what people that I'm interviewing are telling me.

Matthew: Yeah, it comes in from Mexico.

Q: But they also make ice here?

Matthew: It's being made right here, right now. It could be made within two hundred
foot of you at any point in time, and you'd never know. You'd be standing on top of it.

Q: What is ice, then?

Matthew: Okay, ice is an algae. It is a fungus. And what they do, one of the ways of
doing it, you can take gun bluing, you can take ammonia, pure ammonia, clean ammonia, you got to freeze it and filter it, and let's see, gun bluing, ammonia, see it's been so
long, gun bluing, ammonia, there's another one. I got to think of it. There's three . . .

He talked about what he knew about the "ice" being produced locally. The
confusion in terminology, particularly when it came to the meaning of "ice,"
continued throughout the study.

The lack of consistency in wording added to the diversity of production
processes and finished product and illuminates why it is difficult as an outsider
to understand exactly what types of drugs are being consumed in the underground world of methamphetamine. The fact that many different types of the
drug are being consumed complicates efforts to understand the problem and
develop effective responses.

CONCLUSIONS

Understanding use is critical for comprehending subsequent progression to
dealing and manufacturing. Progression of use and the associated inability to
maintain increasingly high levels of consumption help explain why some users
advance to dealing and later, making the drug themselves.

People use for specific reasons and in different ways. There is variability in
patterns of consumption, including the social contexts within which the drug
is consumed. Users develop personal preferences with regard to types and
methods of use. For those who become heavily involved, patterns of consumption progress and change over time, becoming increasingly difficult to maintain.

They used, at least at first, for specific reasons and to obtain desired effects. Initial experiences are influenced by peers already engaging in the lifestyle. There is a seduction and attraction to their experiences early on.

Methods of consumption relate to functionability. Ingesting methamphetamine or sipping it in a drink is a less conspicuous method of use than smoking the drug. Injecting it requires specific knowledge and equipment, and leaves potentially detectable track marks and scars. Persons who inject methamphetamine are viewed as more hard-core users in part due to the intrusiveness of this mode of consumption. Personal preferences are based on individualized perceptions about what is and is not acceptable, as well as differential effects. They are also influenced by, and sometimes based on, the activities of drug-using peers and the social groups within which use occurs. With specific regard to method of consumption, they necessitate that some methods of use be more hidden, clandestine, and risky than others.

Specificity is needed when discussing methamphetamine use, for variations abound. Individuals develop preferences for patterns of use, modes of consumption, types, and forms of methamphetamine. This diversity, also known as heterogeneity, refers to "the quality or state of being heterogeneous."[4] The phenomena are heterogeneous, which means "consisting of dissimilar or diverse ingredients or constituents: MIXED."

Understanding how users viewed and experienced meth, and why they used, are essential pieces of the puzzle. Learning from their experiences is the closest those who have never used can get to understanding the drug's attraction and manner in which it subsequently fuels a lifestyle that revolves around meth. For those who have never used, trying methamphetamine is not an option. Trying the drug, even once, is a dance with chance. It is an activity with the potential of becoming a defining event that alters the course of one's life. Initiation is a necessary step for immersion; however, it is not, in and of itself, sufficient.

There is no scale with which to gauge who can use experimentally or socially and who cannot. While users as a whole are a diverse and heterogeneous group, there is no way to assess how the drug will affect one individually. Trying the drug to understand should never be an option. The risks are just too high.

The experiences of these adults did not take place in a vacuum. In their social worlds, they were not the only ones using meth. Rather, they lived in the midst of communities where others were using, dealing, and sometimes even manufacturing the drug. And this, at least in part, helps to explain what followed next.

As users become further engrossed, social networks begin to reflect the progression that follows. Users and others similarly situated dominate social spheres, as they are the only ones who truly understand what it means to love meth. As all of these individuals attempt to maintain the benefits associated with the drug, consumption both increases and progresses. Ultimately, those involved influence one another into a more heavily immersed lifestyle.

The truth is that progressively increasing habits are difficult, if not impossible, to sustain over time. At one hundred dollars a gram, habits are difficult to support financially. It is not unusual for heavy users to spend upward of hundreds or thousands of dollars each day. There are few ways to legitimately support such costly habits without becoming increasingly engaged in the drug lifestyle or other illicit activities. In the midst of their desire to maintain the experiences they discovered, they find ways to continue.

While addiction may result in life-altering and dire consequences, there is a reason methamphetamine captivates users and ensnares their lives. Loving methamphetamine is the Rubicon that leads into the world of methamphetamine and the progression that follows. A Rubicon is "a bounding or limiting line; *especially*: one that when crossed commits a person irrevocably."[5] It is a line that many come near and never cross; for others it becomes a point of no return. Once they love it, there is nothing else. It is the essential base truth captured in the introductory paragraph of chapter 3 of the book *Iced*:

> Everything you need to know about why people take meth can be summed up in a quote by one of its most ardent and vociferous enemies. Paul Laymon, assistant U.S. attorney for Chattanooga, Tennessee, and an expert at prosecuting meth cases, described its allure to a collection of cops and lawyers. "Who wouldn't want to use it?" he asked rhetorically. "You lose weight and you have great sex." He's right. Meth can supply almost perfect happiness—at least at first.[6]

Though loving meth is the initial step in the life, it is only the beginning.

CHAPTER 4

Dealing Meth

Most of my access was at first buying it in large quantities, and distributin' it in large
quantities, and using it in large quantities, 'cause it's hard to sell quantities of methamphetamine without using methamphetamine. People are real skittish on that.
They're not gonna buy from someone that don't use.

—Conner

INTRODUCTION

Money and methamphetamine—two of the most valued commodities in this
world. With a street value of one hundred dollars a gram, meth is expensive
to buy and lucrative to sell. Many sell to support their own habits; dealing is
a way to get meth cheaper, or for free.

As drug habits grow, dealing becomes critical for those seeking to support
progressive levels of use and maintain the lifestyle that accompanies it.
Habits can cost upwards of hundreds of dollars a day; there are few legitimate
ways to earn such large amounts of disposable cash quickly or in a sustainable
manner. As many users were already participating in the illicit market
as purchasers of the drug, the transition from user to dealer is not unexpected.
While most dealers use meth, not all do. Some are motivated by profit.
Dealing meth is a highly profitable endeavor and profit is something many
value.

In the world of methamphetamine, dealers critically link users and traffickers or producers. There are low-level street dealers who sell small quantities like quarter papers and quarter grams directly to end users. Then there
are those who "move" or sell larger quantities, including quarter pounds and
pounds. Though there are also highly organized traffickers closely linked to
large-scale producers of the drug, they are not represented here.

The majority of dealers in this study operated at the lower and middle levels of the distribution chain and used heavily themselves. A few participated in more organized activities such as trafficking and transporting large quantities across state lines. Although dealing activities are not always restricted to meth, it serves as the focus here.

At the street level, using is often necessary to facilitate sales. Among those on the periphery of one's social network, using may be the only way to validate that one is not an undercover cop. It has the added benefit of keeping dealers high. Transactions occur at different levels, and dealers employ diverse types of strategies and tactics to increase profits, maintain a consumer base, and evade detection. Typically, dealing takes place within the context of social relationships and networks with others who use.

The black market within which meth is bought, sold, and traded is a highly criminalized and paranoia-filled world. Dealers must continuously walk a fine line between maintaining their business and avoiding risks associated with the illicit black market. Dealers are wanted by those desperately craving the drug and by the law enforcement agents trying to catch them. While risk is a great part of this aspect of the life, it does not serve as the focus here. Rather, the present chapter highlights motivations for and patterns of dealing activities.

Distribution chains critically link users, or consumers, to suppliers. Dealing-related decisions are focused on getting paid and avoiding detection. Cognizant of risk and reward, dealers walk a fine line. Not everyone can be successful in this endeavor; success requires the ability to navigate through the chaos and risk of the black market.

MOTIVES FOR DEALING AND DISTRIBUTING: MAKING DOLLARS AND SENSE AND FREE METH

Understanding why people deal methamphetamine is imperative. For many, it is critical step between using the drug themselves and later manufacturing it. Most typically, individuals begin selling as a way to support their own habits and the lifestyles that accompany them. It is also a way to ensure a reliable supply to keep the party going.

Emme's progressive use coincided with the loss of her main source of access following a breakup with a boyfriend. At the time, she was "doing it every day all day. Every single day." Sustaining this level of use required that she find a new way to access the drug. By age seventeen she was associated with a group of peers who had access to it all the time. She explains how her access changed.

Emme: I mean, we all were friends, but a couple of his friends that I had met with him, met them through him, we became really good friends, and they had access to it at all times.

Q: Did you start buying it?

Emme: [Yes]. One of 'em was, I could say, I guess, he is one of my best friends at the time. He didn't want me to, but I pretty much said, "I don't give a shit, you're gonna do it. I'm my own person," and so he ended up doing it. But after a while, he stopped being a daddy and joined the party, kinda thing.

Natalie, a thirty-nine-year-old former dealer and cook, further shed light on why she and others would eventually begin dealing themselves. The fact that she was employed as a stripper provided her with important connections as well as a steady customer base. She discussed her motivations:

Natalie: Money and for their own use, because if you sell enough, you can support your own habit. You don't have to pay for it.

Q: And that's pretty big?

Natalie: Well, yeah, when you go to using two or three hundred dollars' worth of dope a day that's an expensive habit. If you can sell enough to support that, then that's a really good incentive for getting into selling it.

Dealing supported her $300-a-day habit and allowed her to earn large sums of money at the same time. At one point, she claims to have earned over $90,000 in a couple of months, though she had little to show for it now.

Daphne similarly dealt to support her habit and lifestyle. In the end, dealing meth was her only source of income.

Daphne: It progressed to the fact that in the last couple years, I was never out of it, never out of it, didn't work, I just dealt, it progressed to the dealing stage to be able to afford it.

She eventually started "hooking up" (i.e., having sex) with dealers as an alternative way to get the drug. She hinted at the attractiveness of the money and accompanying risks that went along with this level of immersion as she talked about whether she ever went without using.

Daphne: If I did, it was because either it just wasn't around, everybody was out, I knew anybody that ever had any dope, even if they hated me and I couldn't go there, I knew someone that could, so if everybody was out, not having the money was not an option because you had something, we had something of value that we could trade, "cluck off" we call it. It just wasn't an option, but I rarely got to that point of getting rid of my own things for meth. What I did was hooked up with the dealers, and became a dealer myself so that I could afford it . . . I mean there were times that we had such big wads of cash, and that was addicting too.

Mia's explanation of why she started dealing was concise and to the point.

Mia: Simply so I could get the drugs. I wanted to be able to do it and not have to pay for it.

She expanded on the importance of staying cautious as she talked about the people she dealt to. Social relationships were an important part of the story.

Mia: Just like people I knew. There was like a whole network of people, a whole community of people. I can remember going off to this one house where a dealer and I met a lot of people the second time around, and it was just like it was on the south side and it was just a lot of people. That guy right now is actually serving a lot of time.

Q: Were they mostly to people you knew or did you ever sell to strangers?

Mia: People I knew. Like maybe they would get it for somebody. New people would be integrated slowly, because I was paranoid.

Q: So strangers would become acquaintances?

Mia: Well, I'm saying like somebody I might deal with them for a while and they'd say, "Well, I know somebody."

The transiency of people coming into and out of the life was characteristic. For her, progression into dealing almost occurred nondistinctly over time.

Mia: Before, I was just buying it for me. I was buying quite a bit. Of course, I'm sharing and partying with everybody. And then I don't know what the transition was from me just buying it and partying to me getting rid of some of it. I don't really know why. Well I know why is because I didn't want to keep payin' for it.

She elaborated about why people get involved in dealing.

Mia: Because they want to do their drugs and, well, I take that back. I'd say one would be if they didn't use drugs, it was the money. For two, but if they did use drugs, then it would be to be able to get their drugs.

For Dillon, a thirty-seven-year-old former dealer and cook, his progressive consumption of meth similarly coincided with his entrance into dealing. His description of the manner by which this took place was insightful. His motivations for dealing were influenced by his partying lifestyle and the need to maintain a regular supply for himself and those he partied with at the time.

Dillon: When I was in my twenties, it started out where my stepbrother and another roommate of ours was all goin' out drinkin' on Friday nights and all, just kinda goin' to the clubs, maybe a coupla dance clubs, and they got a little bit a meth, and they snorted a little line, and we'd all go out drinkin' and I didn't do none, and they'd outdrink me, and they'd pick up the girls and all that, and I'd end up makin' a butt of myself and throwin' up and couldn't keep up with nobody. And then after about two times of that, then I was like, "Well hey, let me try a little bit of that." And then it just escalated, cause at that point it was like, "Okay, there's three of us now, we need to get a little more," and then it was like somebody else got involved in it too, so we got a little more. And I got this bright idea that I was gonna turn around and say, "Hold on, we're gettin' like, a hundred dollars' worth here," and being from the drug world I knew how the weights and measurements and all that went. And I was like, "I can put twenty-five more dollars of that, and get all mine for free," and so I got a sixteenth, and then it just . . . It blew up from there.

Vanessa elaborated on the pros and cons of staying high to sell meth as she described the height of her involvement.

Vanessa: You're sittin' around with a pipe in your mouth unless you actually have to go do something that's meth-related.

Q: So you're just using.

Vanessa: You're just nonstop using, you're high, you're sittin' there with a bong, a pipe, a razor, and a mirror. You have every form of use that you can, with all the dope that you need, in bags and just anything that you need, 'cause you're selling it in the meantime, you're not just using it, you're sellin' it, but you're staying high to sell it, which you're actually just smokin' up your own profit, it's not a bowl of fruit on the table, it's a bowl of meth, and everything that goes with it.

In the world of methamphetamine as in conventional society, easy money is viewed as a good thing. And as is sometimes the case even in legal endeavors, there can be shadiness involved. This was hinted at by Wes as he expanded on why some people deal meth while others don't.

Wes: To support their habit, I guess. And you know it's the same thing. When it's [the] quick money and instant gratification society that we are, we have the Internet and we have this speed but it has to be faster. Nothing is ever fast enough. I need it now, right now, and when it gets to that, selling was easy. It's easy money. You can take from it, too. It's all about manipulation, lying, cheating, stealing-type stuff.

Jessica elaborated on why not everyone who deals has what it takes to maintain their activities and be "successful."

Jessica: I think there's very few people who actually do deal it that can deal it. See, a lot of people probably start off that way because they can make a lot and they can make money and get theirs free, but for the most part, most people that do this, they can't not do it all themselves, and then not get either behind in money or just lose out, lose everything. That's how some people start pawning their stuff. I've never lost anything for this. But there's some people who can do it and who can do it well, and they know what they're doing. Whether they use it or not, most of them use it, though. But they know how to do it right.

There were very real benefits to dealing meth.

PATTERNS OF DISTRIBUTION

Dealers operate at different levels of the distribution network and engage in different patterns. Differences exist with regard to where the drug is coming from (e.g., local or out-of-state), proximity to and relationships with producers, and the level at which they operate.

At the lowest levels are those who sell the small quantities packaged for end-users; transactions can be for quarter- or half-papers (i.e., quarter grams or half grams) and grams. While profitability is highest at the lowest levels of distribution, the potential for detection and other ancillary risks escalate as the number of interactions and transactions increases. This was something several dealers discussed.

Steven, one of the lowest-level dealers, sold eighty to one hundred dollars' worth of meth a day to friends and acquaintances. He described his peers as "low lives . . . they weren't bums, but they were low lives." Though eighty to one hundred dollars a day seemed like a lot to him, such transactions are about as small as they get.

Allie was a middle-level dealer who started dealing after reuniting with high school friends who were making meth. It would be the beginning of a mutually interdependent relationship; they made the drug and she sold it. Her transactions differed from Steven's in that one hundred dollars was the smallest amount she would sell. She preferred selling ounces. As a self-described "direct seller," she dealt multiple times a day for almost a decade. She described how things worked.

Allie: I was the one that sold it. I was the one that did the direct selling of it. I would get it from the guy and I would weigh it up, and people would come to my house, or I would . . .
Q: And would this be like an everyday thing that you were involved in selling it?
Allie: Oh yeah, every day all day. Each person would usually buy at least a gram.

Like many others, she only sold to persons linked to others she knew.

Allie: Friends, there was some instances where I would sell to strangers because they were friends of the friends. Never sold to family members, like I said I think I'm the only one in my family that's ever done that.

Q: Were you ever worried that someone might be an undercover police officer or a narc or anything when you were selling it?

Allie: No, not usually, because the people that were with [them], if they were with some of my friends I trusted them.

As she spoke it became clear that her networks were simultaneously vast and tight. She explains.

Allie: Usually they were males, they were usually at least twenty-one [years old], because it'd be people that went to the bar with me or, and then my friends, family, and then they would have people that their people would call me and I got pretty involved, I was dealing with the KKK [Ku Klux Klan], I was dealing with a lot of people.

Whether objectively accurate or not, she claimed to have been one of the biggest dealers in the state. She explained her reasoning for saying this, stating:

Allie: How I kinda based it on was everybody, as many people as I was dealing with, I mean I was dealing from [city] to [northern state]. Here in [city] I had *so many different connections.* Everybody knew that I would always have something. Everybody knew they could always call me, it just spread.

The last time she had been arrested she had five hundred numbers programmed into her cell phone. While her activities were primarily restricted to Oklahoma, her customers were not. Truck drivers were some of her biggest customers. Though she dealt daily for more than nine years, she had only been caught twice. It was a fast life, with drugs and fast money. In the end, she had no idea how much money she earned and little if anything to show for it now.

Allie: I mean one day I could sell an ounce and the next day I maybe only sold half an ounce, there's no way, I never ever kept track of anything like that, that's a good question. I'm gonna be thinking, huh . . . I would never, I would never have less than $500 in my pocket at a time but as soon as I had $500, that would be my rent, or that would be my truck payment, or that would be the electric payment.

Q: But if you sold an ounce, how much would you make off that ounce?

Allie: Well, I'd usually spend, anywhere from $500 to $700, and I would turn around, and probably make close to $2,000.

Other than the friends who were making it, she worked alone and sold for herself, never holding more than a few ounces at a time.

Sam, a forty-four-year-old former small-scale dealer, began dealing soon after using meth for the first time, having learned how to deal drugs in high school. As he explained his motivations, he described how his dealing activities changed over time.

Sam: I did it so mine didn't cost. That's the reason why anybody does it, just like if you're dealing weed, you're dealing it so that your part doesn't cost, that's the bottom line.

He started dealing meth after the second or third time he ever used.

Sam: You're already looking for that, you're looking for your free high, the more you bought the cheaper it was, the cost went down. So you went ahead per se if each unit was twenty-five bucks and you could get six units for a hundred bucks.

Q: So you're getting money and free drugs basically if you deal?

Sam: Absolutely. That's all it was, that's why I just kept my circle small. In the first place I didn't want people running up and down. I had very nice house in a very nice neighborhood, I did not need people looking like they looked in my neighborhood. Bells go off real fast where I lived at.

While he limited the amounts he sold, he was willing to facilitate larger purchases for others if needed.

Briana, a fifty-five-year-old former dealer, had a role in the distribution chain that varied from most others. As a "runner," she moved finished product into the state, working for local producers in the United States and the Mexican cartel. Her initial access to the drug came through cousins and later a heavy-using boyfriend. She described the progression that followed.

Briana: Yeah, and we would buy it from others mostly. But then as it progressed I would go buy a large quantity and sell quarters to others, I would go buy large quantities for other people too. I was pretty trustworthy as an addict and they could give me thousands of dollars and I would go to [city] and buy ounces. The most I ever bought was a quarter pound of meth, which is a lot of meth.

She would not be the only one to deal such large quantities. She explained how things worked within these transactions.

Briana: It was some of all, you know. You trade, you, you, you . . . you buy. If you have money. You trade. You . . . Get fronted, whatever you can do, okay? It was kind of a combination of, like I said mostly I purchased and resold. I would purchase in quantity and resell but something always would happen, and I would get back down to nothing and then I might have to go have somebody front me, which you know what fronting is, right?

Q: They give it to you?

Briana: They give it to you on credit basically and then you pay them back, and I would go get it fronted and I would start over and I would build it up again and then something would happen, so.

Q: So you're always buying it to be able to get money?

Briana: And using it and yeah, its . . . Yeah, yeah, whatever you have to do, basically. I guess I would call it like hustling. Hustling would be the word I would use to describe it.

For her, there was a clear distinction between selling and transporting or running the drug.

Briana: The largest quantity that I probably sold would be like an eightball or a quarter ounce which would be, you know, two eightballs, but I fetched a lot, see . . .

Q: What does fetched mean?

Briana: Somebody would give me $2,000 and say, "Here, go get me some dope," and I would go to [city] and I would bring back two ounces, so is that selling two ounces? Not really, because it was their money. So I would just go fetch it and bring it back.

Q: Kind of like a runner?

Briana: Right, yeah, and the largest amount that I did under that was a quarter pound.

Q: What was in that for you?

Briana: Well they would give me dope out of it. They would give me dope out of it and then I would cut it a little bit and take a little bit more dope, so out of an ounce I would get probably about a quarter ounce. They would give me an eightball and then I would cut an eightball.

Her connections were critical. Though she was one of the only females who "moved product" across state lines, drug running is not unique to meth.

People varied in terms of who they were willing to deal with, where they would sell, and how. While many limited dealing to people within their networks, others sold to those on the periphery, including "friends of friends" or "acquaintances." Dillon was one of the only dealers who risked selling to strangers. He described the places he sold the drug.

Dillon: Oh, public places, mostly houses, there were just variations, you know, sometimes you would call somebody up and say, "Meet me at [restaurant]," and sometimes they'd just come over to your house, and sometimes you go to their house, sometimes you go by and meet at [store].

Q: Were they all people you knew or would you sometimes deal to strangers?

Dillon: Usually people you knew, and you tried to keep it that way, but the hunger for money, power, and drugs overrode that a lot of times and you would like, ah "they don't look like a cop" kind of thing.

Q: So sometimes you might sell to someone you don't really know?

Dillon: Yeah.

Q: Were the people you would sell to mostly family, friends, or strangers?

Dillon: Strangers. Yeah, I mean it's, it's something, you call 'em friends or acquaintances, I guess.

It is a world where friends are friends because of the drugs. He sold regularly for almost four years. For him dealing activities occurred "everyday all the time. It was twenty-four hours a day." Like the others who eventually progressed to manufacturing, his pattern of dealing would later change once he started making meth himself.

Holly started with selling sixteenths and by the end was selling ounces. Here she described how she used other people, including family members, to avoid getting caught herself.

Holly: If I didn't know them, then I would send a runner.

Q: Someone else. Who were they?

Holly: Pretty much family. Not my kids. But they were family . . . Relatives. Not my kids, but my nephew and stuff like that.

She elaborated on why runners were willing to take the risk.

Holly: It's [meth] a large percentage of it, yes, because if you got a runner you get a sixteenth, and you tell that runner, "You're to bring me back," now if it's ice, they end up cutting the ice, but because ice is like dollar for dollar. But if it was red phosphorus dope then, or crank, you tell 'em, "I just need $110 for this, the rest is yours" . . . Take what you want off of it. "You bring me $110. The rest is yours, or $120 or $130, whatever."

In Holly's case, she was the one leading others in her social network into the lifestyle.

Bryant was one of the few dealers who mentioned dealing meth to professionals.

Bryant: So you know this methamphetamine use goes a lot deeper than just average thug[s] out here, I mean there's lawyers, I was selling to lawyers. He's dead and gone now but there was a judge out of [town] I used to smoke pot with.

Q: It's not just who we think it is?

Bryant: It's not, yeah it's not just the shirt and tails, it's suit and ties too and it's, it can happen anywhere. Bankers, I've dealt with bankers with methamphetamines.

Q: I like your quote, it's not just the shirt and tails, it's the suit and ties too.

Bryant: That's what it is. I mean the bankers that we used to deal with, they would bring the bank's money and buy the stuff. I don't know what they done with it, didn't ask.

The extent of Zach's dealing activities varied according to whether or not he was manufacturing at the time. As his immersion increased, so did the quantities he dealt.

Zach: When we were manufacturing, it was pretty much low-level for the most part. When we were manufacturing we were selling ounces of methamphetamine for a thousand dollars.

Q: And when you weren't manufacturing what were you selling?

Zach: Oh maybe, six, I think I sold eightballs a couple, eighth of an ounce a couple of times . . . Yes. An eighth of an ounce, yes, an eightball.

At his height, other people would deal for him. He elaborated on differences in his own dealing patterns over time, making a clear distinction between the times he was "selling on and off" and those when he was "serious selling."

Q: How often would you sell?
Zach: I mean seriously selling or off-and-on selling?
Q: However you . . .
Zach: That's just part of it, I think . . .
Q: What do you mean between just selling and seriously selling? What's the difference?
Zach: Okay, if I was a student in high school and I had so much marijuana and I would roll up so much marijuana into marijuana cigarettes and sell those marijuana cigarettes, that wouldn't be really seriously selling. But if I was, that's all I did was bought and sold drugs, I wouldn't say . . . that would be seriously selling.

According to his own account, he heavily dealt for almost eighteen years. He elaborated on the steps he took to avoid detection.

Zach: Wouldn't use my real name and would keep it all on me so I could get rid of it at the same time, try not to stay in one spot too much.

When asked what he worried about most when dealing, he said:

Zach: I wouldn't really worry about getting caught until I was almost caught. Not getting paid was a deal, yeah, not getting it to start dealing it was probably the biggest deal.

Felix was one of the higher-level distributors in the study. He admitted to running drugs (i.e., transporting them) in several different states. He would work the system to make money even when he didn't actually have meth, saying:

Felix: It's everywhere I lived. I lived in nineteen different states between the ages of twelve and nineteen, so everywhere I went, that's what you do, like, the quickest way to make money, even if you had absolutely nothing, do you know what BC Powder is? . . . The headache stuff . . . Okay if you take BC Powder and 7 Up and baking soda, it rocks up, and looks like crack, so you take that and you sell that to somebody who doesn't know any better, you take that money, now you have money to go make a legit buy and then you just nickel-and-dime your way up.

The biggest risk he had ever taken when dealing meth was "putting two keys [kilos] on a greyhound bus and trucking across four state lines." Though he would only do this approximately twenty times, as he pointed out, "That's enough to put me in prison for the rest of my natural life and then some." He explained how he avoided getting caught over the years.

Felix: The people that get caught are stupid. I'm sorry, like plain and simple, that's all it is. If you pay attention, you'll see your way out of anything. The best way to not get caught is to do the things that nobody expects. Okay, and sometimes it's hard to talk to people you're dealing with into doing the things that nobody expects, but you pay attention. Like this was pre-9/11 so think about modes of transportation. What's the one mode of transportation that nobody ever messes with? The Greyhound bus. So how do you take twelve keys of coke from [state] back to [state]? You drive down, you fly down there, you come back on the Greyhound bus. Nobody messes with the bus, there you go. You want to figure out the best place to offload a bunch, a bunch, a large quantity of coke, do it right by the police station. Why? Nobody pays attention to that. Nobody in their right mind would think that the guy that broke down with the flat tire . . . I mean it was simple, it was really as simple as rigging your tire to blow, you let it go flat right across the street from the police station where nobody's watching, and you take out a bag of tools, somebody else, a Good Samaritan pulls up, decides to help you, switch the bags, change the tire, drive away.

Q: And that's a drug deal?

Felix: [Yes]. Also in the parking lot of a jail works really well, because nobody suspects that. Nobody thinks that hey, somebody's doing a drug deal in the parking lot of a jail. And as long as you never look around, never look shifty, just go on about your normal day, like those everyday ordinary activities, nobody ever suspects you. Why do people get caught shoplifting? Because they look around and they look all shifty and crazy. Go in there like you own the joint, like it's the most natural thing in the world and you never get caught.

As he spoke it became apparent that he seemed to think dealing meth was not a bad thing if one was smart about it. In his experience, there was a critical difference between larger-quantity deals and smaller ones; at higher levels, having a buyer set up in advance is essential. At the time, he was selling ounces of uncut meth manufactured locally for "thousands and thousands and thousands of dollars." It was something he viewed as a business.

Felix: Anybody with any business sense can make copious amounts of money selling drugs, I mean if you were gonna start a business, would you manufacture a whole warehouse full of crap before you started, before you had any buyers set up, no. You go put out your feelers, you nickel-and-dime your way until you see where your market's at, and then you, it's dangerous as shit though, because at some point you have to decide, you have to kinda make a decision to take the market over, in doing so, you're gonna piss off nineteen people who are spun out all the time.

He explained his preference for larger sales.

Felix: Nickel-and-dime hustlers get caught . . . I tried to stay away from the nickel-and-dime scene, I didn't want to sell anything less than an eightball. Because the nickel-and-dime shit gets you caught. Think about the idiots that get caught, they get caught with what, like a gram, selling it to an undercover cop. No, no sir.

They were willing to engage such activities because the profits were simply too high. Evan explains.

Evan: I would buy probably about an ounce a week. An ounce is about seven hundred dollars. I could sell an ounce a week, and probably make about two thousand dollars, and keep myself high.

He described the process of "making customers."

Evan: You buy it in a bigger amount, like an ounce, you get it cheap. Sell it off, in grams and things, and it's big money. That's what the draw of it is. It's real easy to make. Everybody wants it. You can actually make customers by giving somebody some for free a few times and everything, and then they're really wanting it, saying, "You got any more of that?," and you say, "Well, I don't have any more for free, but I've got some for sale."

Making customers was a point Sam had alluded to as well, when he said: "Oh all good dealers give it to you to start with, always."

Methamphetamine is not always the first drug that people deal. Conner was heavily engaged in selling cocaine long before meth. For him, the transition was purposeful and by design.

Conner: In selling methamphetamine? I told you that I was selling cocaine, and then a buddy of mine introduced me to it and I wanted to get away from the African American, basically, dealing of crack, or the uppity-up people, I still sold cocaine to the, kinda the upper-class people in [city] but I just seen the market value of methamphetamine out there, so . . .

Q: It was economics?

Conner: [Laughs] It was, and basically a money thing. I was like "wow," I could turn three times the amount of methamphetamine as I can cocaine, for about the same price as purchasing it.

Like many others, he was already heavily in the drug lifestyle. His familiarity with the illicit drug business facilitated the transition to this new venture.

Conner: Well, I already knew the business, 'cause I was selling cocaine, you see what I'm sayin', so I already knew the drug business, and like I said I've known the drug business, even though I didn't really, when I was using marijuana, I pretty much just sold marijuana from when I was like fifteen to eighteen, nineteen, whatever, I was always selling pot here and there, so I kinda knew the business but I was mainly just selling pot to be cool, whatever, it's cool. I kinda knew there was always money involved in drugs but then when I got split up from my first, I don't know if I should say wife or girlfriend, yeah, whatever, I started dealing marijuana then, and I said, "Wow, that's a lot of money in marijuana," so then I started, I moved over to cocaine. I don't know who introduced me to cocaine. I think I kinda just started, just kinda fell into the drug world. But the same guy that introduced me to meth is the same guy that introduced me to the Mexico connection on the pills. That's something you might, I think, might be helpful for you there, one guy that turned, you know . . .

Q: The one guy is your connection into that world?

Conner: Right. Well he wasn't a connection 'cause he didn't have no money, really. But I had the money, and he had the resources. So we pulled together, and started distribution together.

Connections were important. Before he started making it, Conner was buying and selling large quantities of meth primarily for profit. He would buy anywhere from a quarter pound to a pound of meth at a time; the prices ranged from $3,000 to $10,000. These large sums of money translated into even larger profits on the streets where meth is sold.

Conner: Well, let's see, I would get a pound and basically a pound is sixteen ounces. Then after you put, what they call a cut on it, I would put half that in cut which would make twenty-four ounces. I was selling it for $300 a quarter ounce which is $1,200 an ounce. Okay, twelve hundred times twenty-four is about twenty-eight thousand, I was giving ten thousand, so I was making eighteen thousand off of it, and I was turning that about once a week.

He broke down the quantities as they linked to weights and prices; it was specialized knowledge on a need-to-know basis.

Conner: It goes for about, anywhere from ninety to a hundred dollars a gram, to $125 for what they call a sixteenth, or two to two fifty for an eightball, which is an eighth of an ounce. And the sixteenth is a sixteenth of an ounce. A quarter of an ounce . . . I can break it down for you okay, twenty-eight grams is an ounce, right, okay. This is the money people still can make off of it, okay, look at it this way, okay, you can buy an ounce, relatively for about $1,000 right now. If you didn't cut it at all, you could break it down into grams, which is a hundred dollars a gram, twenty-eight grams is twenty-eight hundred. You spent a thousand. You made eighteen hundred. So, before you even cut it, you've made eighteen hundred dollars, if you sell it by the gram, which people buy the gram up all day long.

As profitable as it is on the street, the value of meth is even higher behind prison walls. Lucas was unique in that he spoke of dealing while in prison. According to him, he earned $28,000 selling meth during the two years he was incarcerated. He described how the scheme worked. As he spoke he alluded to the different world this took place in.

Lucas: I would bring three grams in prison, which I would give it to this big black guy, which ran the house, is what they call a house call. He was the one who took care of it.

When I got paid for the eightball, I got $3,000 each eight-ball. So you figure $1,000 a gram. And then he got a free half gram.

Q: He distributed it from there?

Lucas : He distributed it. He would sell it. I would just sit back, because I knew him from the streets. He would sell everything and he would send my wife money orders. Their people would send money orders. There wouldn't never [be] no money transaction in the prison system, whatsoever. It was always done outside the penitentiary. So I mean there's no proving.

Q: That's a whole other study in itself.

Lucas: That's a whole other world there, young lady.

Some dealers purposefully enable users by selling or giving away syringes to those seeking to use the drug intravenously. Knowing that not everyone had access to needles, Wes had developed a strategy aimed at facilitating sales.

Wes: When I would sell them their stuff and give 'em a syringe. And it's not that I was trying to be a prophet or anything, it's just that I knew that they most likely didn't have access to the syringe. So I would just give it to 'em. I have hundreds of 'em. What was the point? I didn't really like to sell, but that's kind of what people recognized was that. It was a way to get your name out there. You had to do something different than everybody else ... I was somebody you can get points from and that's the key word for a needle or syringe.

He was not alone. It was a way to keep customers coming back for more.

Roman, a thirty-nine-year-old former dealer, captured customers by selling cheap pipes as an incentive, making it hard for users to say no. He described the business strategy he employed when dealing meth. For him, using was primarily a means of acquiring customers. This was something that became evident when he responded to a question about whether he used meth alone or with others.

Roman: I would usually use, if I did do it, I would use it with people, because I sold it and it was a way to kinda get them going. You see, if it was like crack or whatever, I used to always make the joke, there's a vulgar term for it. I guess you need to know this stuff. It's called "smoking the glass dick." I don't know if you've ever heard that. They say that because it's all you want and the way you hold it and stuff, it looks like, anyway, the point is in order for me, I was the salesman, I've always been in sales when I was younger, from selling Budweiser to selling cars to selling stuff, so I used stuff I learned, educated myself with, and I gave people incentives when I sold it to them. "Hey, I'll give you this and I'll throw in a little extra for profit or for your own personal use." It never went to profit. It always went to personal use. I always made the joke, today is coupon week. But they fell for it. "Let me hook you up." "I don't want none, Roman, I ain't got no money, dude, I ain't got no money." "Well, that's cool. I'll just do some with you." And I'd get 'em baited up, get 'em smokin' and stuff and they don't want me to leave. "Man, okay dude, I'll pay you on payday."

Business was business.

CONCLUSIONS

Everyone in this study had at least some involvement with dealing methamphetamine. At some point, each had progressed from just using the drug to selling or moving large quantities of finished product. Their illicit dealing activities were not restricted to methamphetamine. Sometimes they sold multiple drugs, other times they moved from one to another.

There were clear benefits to dealing meth. Dealers often spoke of building customer bases, avoiding detection, and staying safe, demonstrating the rationality underlying this activity. For them, dealing was another way to earn money. It was also another means for obtaining the meth they consumed. Dealing took place within the context of social relationships and networks with others. Networks from the past merged with newer ones as immersion in the lifestyle progressed.

The diversity that emerged in terms of patterns and levels of involvement with distribution mirrors the variations that existed within the phenomenon of using. Some worked for themselves, while others did not. Some were close to the top of distribution and supply chains, while others sold far from the point of production. There were those who only sold to people they knew, and others who risked selling to almost anyone. The levels of participation and distribution are varied. Regardless of size or scope of distribution chains or networks, dealing is the essential and critical link between the users of methamphetamine and those who produce the drug.

The potential profitability of methamphetamine deals should not be underestimated. On the streets, it sells for one hundred dollars a gram. There are 453.592 grams in a pound. Before restrictions and controls on chemicals and products were enacted, meth was cheap and easy to make. At high levels of production, the potential profit margins can be astronomical. The street value of the fifty tons of finished methamphetamine seized in Mexico in 2012 had the potential to translate into millions. Successful dealers made lots of money. But, as they will tell you, *fast money goes fast*. For those who become immersed, it was all about the two things that mattered most: methamphetamine and money.

While not all dealers were legitimately employed, those who were worked in professions and settings (e.g., bars, strip clubs) that provided them with a consumer base. They employed business practices not unheard of in the conventional world. They would go the extra mile, making themselves available twenty-four hours a day, fronting meth and letting people try it for free. Some even gave away paraphernalia such as needles or pipes. In the midst of the increasingly dangerous world, they employed a business sense and utilized specific strategies to get and keep customers. For some, playing it smart equated to being safe. It is perhaps ironic that some of their practices emulated the traditional business model that underlies capitalism in corporate America.

Dealers who moved from selling other drugs (e.g., marijuana, cocaine) to methamphetamine were motivated in part by a desire to deal with a different type of user base as well as the profitability involved. Understanding motives for dealing is important for grasping why and how people begin to become entangled in the life.

Methamphetamine and money were the primary motivations for dealing. For those with heavy methamphetamine habits, maintaining and supporting progressive levels of personal consumption served as an important motivator. For those for whom dealing is financially driven, personal use can serve to validate that one is not an undercover cop. Dealing becomes a way to make money and obtain methamphetamine, which in and of itself translates into more money. People deal drugs because doing so is profitable. There is money to be made. When it comes to methamphetamine, there is lots of it. In this black market, methamphetamine is a commodity that translates into profit.

For these adults, initiation into dealing meth followed the progression of their own use. It preceded the initiation of their entrée into manufacturing. They were dealers who would later become manufacturers. It was a transition within which they eventually helped create the demand they had once only been trying to meet.

CHAPTER 5

Manufacturing Meth

Well, you ever made $5,000 to $25,000 in a day?

—Matthew

INTRODUCTION

Clandestine manufacturing is the riskiest dimension, existing underground, hidden from outsiders. It is risky because of the dangers and volatility of production processes and because cooks are wanted by those seeking the drug and by law enforcement. In this cat-and-mouse game, the stakes are high. No one knows more about what goes on in the homes, motel rooms, garages, and other places where meth is made than the people who were there.

They had extensive knowledge and experience. The majority (n = 23) manufactured meth; eight others assisted more indirectly.[1] Their participation spanned decades, beginning in 1984 and ending in 2010. Those with the lengthiest histories talked about various forms of the drug and its derivatives including meth tabs, white crosses, and bennies (i.e., Benzedrine). The earliest references to manufacturing included extracting the drug from nasal inhalers and breaking down pharmaceutical pills.

Their experiences varied. Cooks included men and women with diverse histories of manufacturing. Some cooked once or a few times; others cooked for years on end. There were those who only knew of one way to make the drug and others with experience making it several different ways. They shared their knowledge, albeit reluctantly, about the ways the drug is produced, describing the P2P (i.e., phenyl-2-propanone), red phosphorus, and the anhydrous ammonia, or Nazi, methods. Some talked of "burying" chemicals to produce an amphetaminelike stimulant to consume and sell. Though all the manufacturers in this study used, not everyone who makes it necessarily does.

This chapter describes manufacturing from an insider's perspective. Though risk is ever-present with manufacturing, the focus will be on the processes by which people become engaged, motives, and differences in patterns of production. Through the lens of former cooks, the choices and decisions that underlie and drive manufacturing will be revealed. The importance of social relationships, environmental context, and the availability of precursor chemicals and supplies as facilitators for manufacturing-related activities will be demonstrated. Manufacturing represents the deepest level of immersion in the world of methamphetamine.

LEARNING TO COOK

People learn to manufacture from people they know. Opportunities are seized, sought, and created. Some come upon the opportunity by chance while others purposefully create situations within which to learn intentionally and deliberately. Most are taught what to do and how to do it, progressing from observer to participant to manufacturer over a relatively short period of time.

Ian, a forty-five-year-old former dealer who manufactured meth for two decades, spoke of one of the earliest manufacturing methods. Having learned the old prison style of extracting it from nasal inhalers, he would later learn to cook using the P2P production method in the 1980s. A "buddy" of his who had spent many years in prison had taught him. He described the now uncommon process, comparing it to the newer methods emerging today.

Ian: I'm gonna put it like this: years ago, it's not like today, it took three days to set up a major lab, it took three days to gather up the glass for it, and it produced eighty to a hundred thousand, we produced [$80,000] to $100,000 worth of methamphetamine. Today they produce two to three ounces with these little ol' labs they carry, it's $3,000 or $4,000 and you're getting the same type but it wasn't like today. Today you got the Internet and this anhydrous and these little [pseudoephedrine] pills and they do it high, that's why shit blows up, and that's why people go to jail and people get hurt.

Like many others, his primary motivations were money and methamphetamine.

Those interested in manufacturing did not have to go far to find others making the drug. Social networks were key for learning how to cook. Both Ava and Max learned as teenagers living in small, rural towns from friends already making it. Ava's entrance to manufacturing occurred after she could no longer afford a heavy prescription pill habit she developed. Methamphetamine was a cheaper addiction and would be easier to obtain, especially if she made it herself. Her initiation to manufacturing coincided with her progression from smoking the drug to shooting it up intravenously. She described not knowing exactly what she was witnessing the first time she saw her friends cooking.

Ava: Well, because I was just amazed by the way it looked, how the liquid turned into . . .

Q: Did you know he cooked?

Ava: Well, actually I didn't know what they were doin' at first. I was like, "What are you guys doin'?" 'Cause I was young, I was just like thirteen, fourteen. I was just an idiot. I was like, "Wow, what are you doin'?" And then he told me, they were being sarcastic 'cause I didn't know and they were makin' fun of me 'cause they thought it was a stupid question but they like, "The stuff you were smokin' the other day, that's what I'm makin.'" I was like, "No way."

She was in high school at the time. She elaborated on her attraction to manufacturing.

Ava: Yeah, because it [manufacturing] makes, it made it exciting. I mean, to me *I was fascinated* . . . Well, I started smokin' it a lot, just with friends, and then I met somebody that knew how to cook it, and I went with him to go do it. When I saw how they did it, and just to watch it, it was amazing how the liquid turned and I was like, wow. I was just amazed, like a school experiment. So after I started cooking is when I started shootin' it, because, just like when people overdose on things, even though you don't need more, your body thinks you need more because you don't feel the same high. So you're actually always overdosing yourself when you're on drugs, even though you don't realize it. But that's why I started shootin' it, because I couldn't get high anymore smokin' it.

Max similarly became involved to support his progressive habit; he found himself using too much of the product he was planning to sell. He learned how to make anhydrous dope from a friend. It was not a difficult endeavor given that his friend lived across the street from a farming cooperative (i.e., co-op) where the chemical anhydrous ammonia was easily accessible.

Max: One of my really good friends, he actually lived across the street from a co-op in a smaller town so we'd have fun and run over across to the co-op and then run back into the woods behind it and make it and then come back to his house and be done.

Q: He taught you how to make it?

Max: Yeah, the gist of it . . . I mean if you see somebody do it so many times it's easy . . . I think like a twelve-year-old could do it, I mean honestly . . . it's really simple.

Wes was also heavily using meth when the opportunity to learn to cook presented itself. At the time he was living a chaotic and unstable life. His wife had just left him. He was being evicted from his home. He described how the opportunity arose.

Wes: Well, I started manufacturing. After I started buying it, this one guy came over to the house we were getting evicted out of actually, and he's like, "Dude, you guys are getting evicted, I want to show you something." And then I read about it. I had researched it and thought about manufacturing just to support myself. That's when I learned under somebody else. When he showed me the process, his process was kind of dangerous. It's all dangerous, don't get me wrong. But I knew, based on the research that I did, that you had to have a well-ventilated area and stuff like that. He's talking about putting towels under doors and closing vents and stuff and I was knowledgeable enough to understand that when you mix chemicals, the fumes are also very toxic. So, I took from him what I learned and started my own method.

At this point things spiraled downward and deteriorated beyond control.

Wes: This guy came to my door one day with everything to do it with. And he said, "I know she's gone; you probably don't have [meth]," because I called him once or twice to get some. He said, "I want to show you something. Can you help me? I just need a place." I said, "The kids aren't here, I'm sleepin' on the floor." The stupid cat, I wasn't taking care of the stupid cat. He was doing whatever he wanted to anywhere. So it was a terrible environment, roaches and stuff like that. It was a depiction of what one thinks a meth house to be.

Q: Kinda what you picture?

Wes: Yeah, feces and cat stuff and my water got shut off, which kinda sucked. But then, I maintained. I was able to go to the store and get water to flush the toilet and stuff like that. He came and he's like, "Dude, you're probably outta here," all this stuff was gone 'cause she [wife] took everything, so, I was just left with a pissed cat, piss-soaked futon mattress the only place to sleep. He came to the door, and he said, "You're gonna be gone anyway. You can come with me after this, and I'll drop you off wherever and I'll show you how to do this stuff," how to manufacture it, basically. His process scared the hell out of me, 'cause he was smokin' a cigarette during it and stuff and it was real nerve wracking, not to mention, it was against the law. So I was always paranoid about the cops coming.

The man showed him how to cook step by step and Wes discovered his interest in manufacturing to support his own habit. He continued to explain the situation.

Wes: I was comin' to that point where we're usin' a whole hell of a lot here. Why can't we just do it ourselves? And I lived out by a field, the corner of [city], so I could have went outside and did it, and all my neighbors used. Everybody around me used, so we were safe. Matter of fact, they could watch out, they could also help purchase the materials, so, yeah, there's a way to do it. The best way is hands on. He taught me hands on and it was an anhydrous cook.

Like most others, his desire to manufacture was influenced by the fact that he was part of a social network in a community where methamphetamine was prevalent, and by his own progressive consumption of the drug. At his height, he was injecting every three hours; learning to make it was a way to maintain what had become an otherwise unsustainable habit and support his deteriorating life. But there was more. There was a high that accompanied making the drug.

Wes: And that's another thing, just watching the process is . . . *Getting it, making it, and using it* all gives you that effect of aaahhh . . .

For Evan, the introduction to manufacturing was more proactive.

Evan: While I still smoked it, the person I was gettin' it from had it all the time, all the time, and I said, "How do you have it all the time?" And he said, "Well, me and this other guy, we make it." And I said, "No you don't." I had this image in my head of these outlaw bikers and you could smell that a mile away and he said, "Yeah, in six, eight hours we could probably get about a quarter of a pound of it." Then I said, "No, you're lyin'." He said, "Well if you just come, why don't you come this Friday, and you can help out, watch." And I thought, "Really, that's okay?" And he said, "Yeah." And so I went, and he told me to keep my mouth shut and my eyes open. And I did. And I found out how easy it was to make it, and after that I thought, well that's it. I don't need you guys anymore, and I can make it myself.

Dillon learned more indirectly from a former manufacturer he met in jail. He talked about how he learned the process and the fascination of doing so.

Dillon: I learned when, I was in my twenties, just when I went to the county jail one time, I think on my way to RID [corrections program], the first time I was incarcerated, and there was a guy there who was a known cook on the street, he was in the county jail too, and we would get out for [recreation] time, I guess you call [it], and it's just a big open pod is all it is and we would walk in circles, and I was curious, I mean back then, people who didn't cook it was fascinated by the idea, with *the power, the control.* And so he was fixin' to go away for a long time, so I talked him into teaching me how to do it, and I didn't know what anything was, I didn't know what red phosphorus was or any of that stuff, and we sit there and walked circles, and he sit there and explained to me what everything was, how you do it, and then he'd troubleshoot it, and after I learned how to do all that, then he would turn and say, "Okay now what if this happened? What would you do? Fix it," and before it was said and done with I could cook it in my sleep.

He would learn to cook via the red phosphorus method. When he started manufacturing a few years later he did so as an apprentice of sorts.

Dillon: Actually I worked with somebody else for a little while, with their help of getting them chemicals, and it's kinda like an apprentice kind of thing, and you just kinda help with the cleaning up and getting done, and every so often you get the stuff to do it yourself.

Q: How do you get involved in that?

Dillon: At that stage of the game, cooks are kinda commonly known, I knew like three or four of 'em and it's just like one of those things where you say, and sometimes it depends on how you want to approach it. Sometimes you just go up to them and say, "Hey I need to know how to do this," or "Hey, I got a pound of ephedrine, and if you go with red," a joint deal kinda thing.

Here, he elaborated on why he started manufacturing.

Dillon: More ready supply of meth, the power, the control, and just the fascination.

His motivations were similar to those of others.

Bryant similarly learned how to make meth while in prison. Already using for more than sixteen years at the time, he too found the process and prospect of being able to cook the drug himself seductive.

Bryant: I was always intrigued with the cooking. I might have went to a lab once or twice, but as far as getting my hands on. I guess when I was [in] prison the last time I learned the little things. The guy that I was telling you about, I would call him from time to time and he would tell me, "Brother," he said, "I've learned to do it, you wouldn't believe it," and he really got me excited about it. I was getting close to getting out and I wanted to learn and hell, I started researching, and I've got all these books, I've got access to computers, I mean the whole nine yards.

He explained how he learned and developed his own style.

Bryant: That's where I learned to cook methamphetamine and I learned and I studied. Well, when I got out, hell I don't know, maybe six–seven months, things were getting rough, [ex-wife] was together and I said, "Well, I've got a way I can make some money," I said "But I don't know if I'll ever be able to get out of it," and we took that chance, you know, and I went and got in it, and first place I went and cooked was with [name]. He took me out north of [city] out there, and we sat on a hill and he showed me. Well it's one of them deals you learn the basics and then you figure out. Like washing dishes, your mama showed you how to wash dishes but when you done it on your own you had to learn how to . . . You learn your style. Well I went from learning with [name] the basics, to going to [city] and learning my way of doing it. And sure, I messed up once or twice or something and then it got to, I went north of [city] at a farm that was a safe house to do it. And we had a barn, we had a lake, anything we needed, we had it.

Matthew's approach to learning was proactive and planned. He paid some-one to teach him. He described how he initiated manufacturing.

Matthew: When I first got started on meth, a friend of mine told me what kind of money was to be made in it, and I was runnin' low on money and lookin' for a fast way to make a lot of cash . . . Money is a big part of it. I like money. I never worried about money. I just like money.

Q: Did someone show you how?

Matthew: I paid for them to show me. I paid somebody a very large sum, $3,000. And I bought all the stuff.

As someone with extensive knowledge and experience making meth different ways, he had learned the various techniques from different people.

Matthew: It's different people, different, just when I want to learn it, I just find the person. There's always, when in addiction, there's always an addict lookin' for a dollar. So, I mean, you just find you a chemist and learn. It's not difficult.

For him, it was about learning how to make the type of product his customers would want to buy.

Matthew: Red phosphorus, ice. There's different things for different people. I'm not "everybody likes the same thing," and I knew that. And I was about the money.

Q: Were they different?

Matthew: Well they're all speed. [They all] keep you awake for days. One makes your body hurt more. That'd be the anhydrous. When you're coming down off it, it makes you real stiff. That's like wet. I've tried to smoke wet just a couple of times and all that is embalming fluid and jet fuel. And just different things. Makin' that ain't difficult.

He later applied his pseudocapitalistic approach to others wanting to learn. He discussed one such encounter; he was teaching others by participating in multiple cooks in a single location at one time.

Matthew: When I had these at this time is because I already had two going, and these gentlemen wanted to learn how. And I charged each one of them $5,000 to learn, to set with me. They were to not touch nothing, do as I say, when I say it, and how I say it. No ifs ands [or] buts. If you made one wrong move, you irritated me in any way, you was out and I kept your money. So that's why they were there. They were poppin' matches, poppin' pills, washin' matches. I had 'em . . . separating iodine crystals, things like that.

He went on to say, "Nobody's seen me make nothin' unless they paid." The only exception would be the stable runner who, in lieu of cash, agreed to exchange her services for a two-year period of time. It was a deal that would fall through when she eventually got caught.

Felix's entrance into manufacturing was almost solely financially driven. As a heavy dealer of cocaine, crack, and later methamphetamine, manufacturing was a means to an end; for him, it was all about profit. He talked about his initiation and the motivations behind it.

Felix: I didn't want to pay for it. Plain and simple, I didn't want to pay.

Q: Pay for it to sell?

Felix: Yeah. You get middled, like okay, selling drugs is all about money and it's all business, and any good business person understands that if you have to pay for your product from somewhere else, you are nothing but a middle man, it doesn't matter where you get it from, how cheap you're getting it, and you can't make near as much money as if you were just making the product yourself, so why not sit around somebody long enough until you know they're gonna throw off a cook and just, don't leave. Just keep hanging around and watch. You kinda watch surreptitiously at first and then you just straight out ask for somebody to teach you and then next thing you know, bam, you know how to do it.

He was different from the others. Felix was one of the only cooks interviewed who would climb the manufacturing hierarchy, eventually progressing to a point where he would only get others to manufacture for him.

Troy's participation with manufacturing started with acquiring pills for a friend who cooked. He describes how it changed over time.

Troy: They were making it, and what I'd do is I would go to [state] and buy these pills and stuff, and he'd give me like a certain percentage of dope from this.

Q: From the cook?

Troy: Yeah. And I was thinkin', "Well I mean if he could do it, why don't I do it," *and I could.* He was giving me a good deal or whatever but I'm thinkin', I'm just screwing myself really, and I asked him one day, I said, "Why don't you show me how to do that," and he showed me from start to finish and that's all it took, 'cause I've sit there and observed it, and he went from step one to everything, preparation and all that, and so I said, "Okay, I think I got it, let me watch you one more time," and that's all it took and then he'd give me a little bit of each little product, and I did it once, it come out right and then, hundreds of time over I did it.

As with each dimension, progression is not uncommon. Users became dealers. Dealers became manufacturers. Conner's pattern of progression was typical.

Conner: I got involved just because a friend of mine, I was using meth and dealing meth and I was buying it from him . . .

Q: You'd been doing that for a few years?

Conner: Yeah, for a few years and then I started buying this cooked crystal meth, from a local person, locally. And come to find out, he was makin' it right there in his backyard. Or, actually, a shed in the back of his house. And then so I got involved with that, and I started puttin' some money in on it, and he was makin' it for me and I was selling, I was the one selling it. I was kinda like the distributor of the manufacturing meth, and then I learned how the process was and then I started takin' over my own manufacturing.

Ray was the only male manufacturer who learned to cook from a female after she approached him looking for a place to make it herself.

Ray: She needed a place to cook . . . She offered to show me how if I would let her use the place, the building, the shop.

He would be limited by the emergence of new laws controlling pseudoephedrine.

Ray: My extent of manufacturing was never, it's probably an ounce at a time, never a real big cook. Enough to get money, to do another one and have a little left for myself. By the time I got into it, it started getting real hard. I mean they'd already started limiting the amount of pseudo that you could buy.

Before the enactment of precursor and chemical controls, getting everything needed to make meth had been easy. Troy explains why others were not needed at the time.

Troy: I didn't use nobody, I mean, I could go, before all those laws and stuff, I could go to where I'm from, to the town next over, 'cause I live in a very small community, but I could go to the next two towns over and they was, they're like twenty-two thousand people and five thousand people, they're ten to twenty miles away, and I could go get everything, round it up, everything, and just basic supplies that I needed, and I had the red [phosphorus] hookup and I would go to the pharmacy and get pills, I would drive to [state] and get pills too, and I could do all this stuff by myself and I could come home and prepare it, and 'bout twelve to fourteen hours later I could have everything done, you know what I mean, after preparation and then gettin' it started.

Katie learned to cook twice: first when she learned the red phosphorus method and later when learned how to shake and bake.

Katie: Well I actually got involved, for the first time, when I was about twenty-six. As I said earlier I had a buddy that used to cook it, he'd get so spun out of his mind and he'd call me. He's like, "Man come on, I need you to help me gas this stuff, help me put this stuff together. So I can get it made." So, 'bout twenty-six, and he finally went to prison after a couple years of doin' that and he got busted and went to prison.

She later learned the newer method of production from a different person.

Katie: My ex got me into shake and bake. She actually was a cook, and then she went to prison, and while I was in prison I met her. Okay, and we got out, we hooked up together and then . . . there was that period of time, before I got in trouble this last time, that I was cooking with her.

While learning to make methamphetamine is important, understanding how people learned is only part of the story. Learning why is next. As the following section demonstrates, it is a critical piece of the puzzle that is methamphetamine.

MOTIVES FOR MANUFACTURING

People make methamphetamine for many reasons. At the most basic level manufacturing brings them the most highly valued and desired commodities that exist in this world: money and methamphetamine. However, as people described their experiences, it became apparent that there was more. There is the seduction that goes along with being able to produce something you love, desire, and desperately crave; it can be irresistible to those willing to do anything for meth. Those who can make meth themselves avoid having to participate in the black market to acquire the drug; manufacturing is cost effective and results in a product that is purer and unadulterated with "cut." It can be a significant source of high profit for those who sell part or all of what they make.

Understanding the motivations that underlie manufacturing is important for comprehending this level of immersion. This is particularly true, as not everyone who uses meth ends up making it. This is something even more true today, given that it is more difficult to obtain necessary chemicals, and the penalties of detection are the highest they have ever been.

The following excerpts illustrate the strong and powerful seduction and attraction that accompanies manufacturing. Though secondary, it is a critical part of the explanation for why people become enmeshed. It is also one of the most revealing reasons why it later becomes so difficult to get out.

Methamphetamine. Money. Power. Control. These are reasons people manufacture and become entangled in the life. Their accounts elucidated the almost mystical attraction associated with the experience of making meth; it is a powerful draw to the life. The most revealing and insightful information came from those most heavily immersed. Zach provided one of the clearest and most simplistic explanations for why he started making meth.

Zach: That's where the methamphetamine was and that's where I wanted to be ... It was just, I think it was simple, it was just simple math. That's where the meth is, it's always there and that's the easiest way to do it.

Evan expounded on the ethereal aspects of manufacturing, while talking about why some people became cooks while others did not. He spoke with intensity.

Evan: It's the lure of easy money, the power. I think a lot of people do it to support their habit, at first. And then they think, "Well, if I just make a little bit," and then they see how much money comes from it, right away, and think, "Okay, well, I'm going to make a little more next time."

Q: So it's the money?

Evan: Yeah. It's the money, and everybody wants to be the guy holding the bag of dope.

Q: When you were dealing it were you buying it from others or making it yourself?

Evan: Well, I was friends with two other people that cooked it together, and if I wasn't able to get nothin', or to make it up, I could get some from them at a real good price . . . Yeah, but if you get it, most any methamphetamine around is made right here, and the thing about makin' it yourself or getting it from somebody else. If you make it yourself, you know it's 100 percent pure. You get it from somebody else it's probably 50 percent.

The profitability was just too high, and there are too many other things that money can buy.

Evan: It would probably cost you, if you spent a hundred dollars, you could probably make $2,500 out of that hundred dollars of materials, and you make it. It takes about six hours. You can't smell it outside the room you're doing it [in], and that's, it's just, [snaps] quick, quick, quick.

Q: Was money a big part of it?

Evan: Yeah. Yeah. Power. The money and the power, and then, feed my own habit.

Ray expanded on the benefits that came with making it himself.

Ray: Yeah, it was to keep it perpetuated. It was to keep the flow going, to get enough money to keep making it and then keep yourself some, so you won't have to pay for it.

For Ray, there were other benefits.

Ray: The money never was a draw for me. I didn't want to get my money that way, by manufacturing. Yes, mostly the access, plus quality. You always know what you're putting into your body when you make it yourself.

In an underground world where ingredients are unknowns and products adulterated, there seemed to be a benefit in knowing exactly what was being consumed, toxic chemicals and all.

Conner elaborated on why, prior to the implementation of legal controls, he and others made meth.

Conner: Well, actually, let's see. Back when it was relatively easy to get the chemicals, everybody was involved in manufacturing. They thought they was. That's why I'm tryin' to say, if they were tryin' to make a little eightball or whatever, they would come over and buy meth from me and think they could still go home and make it. Everybody was in when . . . pseudoephedrine was sold over the counter; to me, if you were using meth you were involved in manufacturing meth.

Q: Even if you weren't really successful at making it?

Conner: Right. Your goal was to try to make it.

Q: Because you could?

Conner: Well, you thought you could. If you were using it when the pseudoephedrine was sold over the counter, your goal [was] to eventually make your own meth.

He talked about the difference between him and those around him.

Conner: Well, for most people, you gotta understand something, most people didn't manufacture the way I did, so I would say most people they would just buy a few bottles of over-the-counter, and they wouldn't even try to make red phosphorus out of matchbooks, so they were really small amounts, but I was investing about $1,000 every time . . . And making tons of money.

As Conner was one of the only cooks to mention saving some of the illicit earnings, the money helped get him out of trouble later on.

Conner: Well, okay, like all the times I went to jail, that one time, the first time in '97, my bond was [over $100,000], okay, that's right at $10,000 cash to get out. Well, I buried my money, and I called my mom said, "Hey go," and she'd go [dig] up the money and she'd get me out of jail. I had the money to get out of jail, and then I had the money to hire an attorney and to fight my case. Well, most people, they're out there using the street's crack, I want to say crackheads or methamphetamine users, they're out there, all they're worried about is using, they're not worried about saving money or nothin' like this, and that's why I said I'm considered a methamphetamine manufacturer, and that's what I did is *I manufactured for money.*

It would also be the primary reason he kept making the drug after getting caught.

Conner: For a year and a half after my case I probably still was involved around methamphetamine, and manufactured. I paid most of my attorney fees with manufactured money, to be honest.

He continued to explain.

Conner: Okay, okay, okay, okay, okay, I'll tell you, I got the perfect story for you, okay. My wife I have now, we was just dating at the time, and I told her, I said, "Well I'm gonna go out here, and I'm gonna make meth." She was totally against me making the meth and all that stuff and I said, "Well I gotta do it for my money to pay my attorney fees," and I'd go out and make a bunch of meth, in the country. I'd come back and I'd sell it all and get a bunch of money and take the bunch of money to my attorney . . . and I'd leave it alone for like two weeks, 'cause I was scared I was gonna get another case. Then I'd go out and make it, about $10,000 worth of methamphetamine and then I'd come back to the city, and sell it all, then I'd kick back for a little while. You know what I'm saying? 'Cause I didn't want to, and I was jumpin' from place to place, basically. I was living at this place, or stayin' with this buddy, kinda hangin' out here, then I moved. I had my residence over here still.

While the money was good, in the end it was always about more than just the money. Ava's description of the surreal and seemingly indescribable attraction explained it best.

Ava: The cookin' just does somethin' to you. It turns you into like a mad scientist. That's the only way I can describe it from someone that doesn't understand it would understand . . . cooking is more addicting than doing it . . . that was my hardest thing in not wantin' to cook it.

Q: What makes that addictive?

Ava: Well, because, for example, what's your favorite thing or do you have something that you [like]?

Q: Let's use like candy or something like that.

Ava: Okay. Like what if you just, never had to buy candy? Anytime you wanted your favorite candy, if you could just make it and it just took you a few minutes to make it. I mean, that's the only way I can describe it, is to think of your most favorite things that maybe cost money and just imagine if you could just create it real quick. Whenever you wanted to. That's the easiest way I can describe it to people who have never done it, is you think of your most favorite thing and you can just make it appear, because it's just like, it's just like a science project.

Q: Well, we hear about the cooking being addictive because people are addicted to meth, not that the cooking itself is addictive.

Ava: Yeah, the cooking itself is, because you're making your own drug and you know that no matter what, if you don't have any money, there's always gonna' be dope fiends that want drugs. So they're always gonna buy pills for you. They're always gonna do this or always gonna buy you lithium batteries. They're gonna buy you this stuff. And all they want maybe is a quarter paper or half a gram, which is nothing.

For some, it was more about maintaining a personal supply than anything else. Patrick was among the few who cooked mainly to maintain a supply for himself and his close friends. In some ways, making it was safer than having to go get it. He spoke about why he started.

Patrick: Money. Plus . . . [exhales] convenience, money, and safety. When you're running back and forth to a dope house every two or three days, everybody knows what a dope house is. I'm out of the limelight. I'm out in the country with myself. When I make it I do it. It don't get sold. I'm out of the limelight.

He insisted that profit and distribution were *not* primary motivations: "I didn't sell it . . . It was for myself."

Q: You weren't trying to make money?

Patrick: No, I did not care about anybody gettin' hold of it. When I'm out, where'd I get my dope from? Just gotta make more, no, it was for me. I had a job. I did not need to make money illegally . . . I wanted to have the meth.

But even for him, the allure seemed to be as much about the process as it was about the drug.

Patrick: Yes it [manufacturing] is [addictive] . . . It's as fun to make it as it is to do . . . To watch . . . all you're doing is changin' one molecule, is all you're doin' . . . to watch liquid turn into powder is kind of a little . . . It's, it's neat . . . Plus when I get done I got somethin' to do. Yeah it's, it's addictive itself, it is. It's fun to make.

For Nicholas, manufacturing brought a sense of status and power otherwise unattainable in the life he lived.

Nicholas: I had been using and I saw the way that, looking back it's pretty goofy, but the way that the women would throw theirself at the guy that had it was a power thing, it was a respect thing, and I lacked that in high school, I was kinda the outsider, and when I cooked all of a sudden I had all these people who were twice my age, just looking at me like I was king, I would walk in the room and it would clear all the unessential people out, have a spot for me, all the women would be all over me, it was kinda like, you ever see the movie *Goodfellas?*

Q: Yeah, I love that movie.

Nicholas: Kinda like how he felt. All these people treated him like a respected adult.

Q: I can see how that could be seductive for a young kid.

Nicholas: Yes.

Making methamphetamine made him feel like a rock star.

Nicholas: Cooking is just as addictive as the methamphetamine, probably more so because you get there and it's . . . nobody really likes their boss but everybody's nice to their boss, it's kinda like that. You walk in the room and everybody's "Oh hey, how you been, how you been," and it's just, it's a power trip, here I am this, this teenager and these women are throwing theirself at me, and just, I felt like a rock star, I really did. I was to the point where if other people mess theirs up, they could call me and for half of what we get out, I'd fix it for you.

While multidimensional and complex, there are very real reasons they manufacture meth.

PATTERNS OF PRODUCTION

As with other dimensions, there is a great deal of diversity, or heterogeneity, in patterns of production. Differences exist within multiple dimensions, including duration, frequency, cook-related circumstances and situations, production processes utilized, and quantities produced. Variations are also present in the extent to which others participate in manufacturing. It is important to point out that there are possibly as many variations in manufacturing as there are production methods and manufacturers.

At the most basic level, there is the difference between a "hot cook" and a cold one. It is a distinction that lies in whether the production process utilizes an external heat source or not. Whereas hot cooks (i.e., red phosphorus method) require an external heat, cold ones (i.e., anhydrous ammonia method) do not. In the latter, heat is created through chemical reactions produced when specific ingredients are combined. Despite this difference, all methods of production are extremely volatile and dangerous.

These manufacturers provided a wealth of information on the different types of processes utilized.[2] Some of the most interesting information gained was not on specific recipes or processes but on variations in patterns of production and manufacturing styles. There were cooks who utilized helpers during the cooking process and those who did not. Depending on when and how manufacturing occurred, the amount of time and effort required to gather necessary chemicals and supplies varied. However, one thing was clear. Those who manufactured prior to the implementation of legislative restrictions and precursor controls had an easier time acquiring the necessary materials and chemicals than the ones who cooked later.

Because they were often manufacturing while living a life high on the drug, remembering how many times they actually made it was not always easy. Though Ava had an extensive history manufacturing, she responded to a question about the number of times she had cooked it with uncertainty.

Ava: I don't remember. Tons and tons. Yeah. I mean I'm sure there's been times I made it where I probably don't even remember because I've been so high.

Her manufacturing activities spanned over a decade. She made meth for years at a time both before and after incarceration. She talked about her pattern of manufacturing and how it changed after restrictions on pseudoephedrine were enacted.

Ava: Well, before the pill law came out, we'd cook pounds at a time. We'd always do it with a few people together because everybody wanted their cut so they're not gonna let one person just run off and do it . . . Yeah, when they made that pill law, it all changed. It was really hard to get stuff and you were just cooking maybe a little bit at a time.

The quantities she could produce depended on her abilities to access pseudo-ephedrine pills.

Ava: It'd depend. It just varies. I mean it really depended on how many, how many people you could get to buy pills, and say you had people buy pills for you, and you made some and your friend might have been cookin' some too. You would do the same thing for him. You would go buy pills.

Q: Were you involved in all parts of it then, everything from getting anhydrous, to buying the pills, to cooking it?

Ava: Yeah, I mean I've done it all.

Her role in the process would switch over time, depending on what the other cooks in her social network were doing. Manufacturing meth was a team effort.

Ava: The neighborhood I lived in, everybody cooked dope over there. We all did dope, we all cooked dope, we all grew up together.

While she primarily manufactured with a friend, the places they would cook changed from time to time. Her preference was for cooking out in the country rather than her home. She described the places where she had made the drug.

Ava: With my neighbor next door, that house was empty, been empty forever. Sometimes we'd even go in their backyard, which is so stupid 'cause that's just when you're really so ate up and far gone that you're an idiot.

Q: Were you actually sitting outside and making it?

Ava: Yeah, all in the woods, while the trees are talkin' to you.

She explained why making it in a motor vehicle was a good way to do it.

Ava: I mean you're drivin' down the highway, sittin' in the back seat, and you got your tank right here, and you got your jug on the floorboard, and you're just throwin' it off, and someone else is drivin'.

Q: Is that dangerous?

Ava: Yeah, because you can blow yourself up. Anytime you cook dope is dangerous, 'cause that anhydrous mixed with those lithium batteries, that is a dangerous explosion. I've caught a whole kitchen on fire before.

Though she herself had never been burned, she knew others who had. One friend in particular had a "whole back" that "is just burned." She talked about the dangers associated with making it in a car.

Ava: You're all paranoid. Everybody's paranoid. And they're like, "Roll the windows up, roll the windows down, roll the windows up. Roll 'em up," oh, believe me, you'll smell it if someone's cookin' it. And usually you go out in the country and drive and do it. I mean, if you're actually down the highway. I've went down the highway a lot of times but that's still dangerous, because highway patrol.

Q: What's the benefit of cooking it in the car?

Ava: It's just quick. You get it done. You can throw everything out of the window.

Q: Is it contaminating the car? It's got to be.

Ava: Well, yeah, it stinks. That anhydrous smells horrible. You can smell that miles away. It's horrible.

For her and others who cooked using the anhydrous method, acquiring anhydrous ammonia was an essential part of the process; it was a risky endeavor in and of itself. She described how she transported anhydrous and the risks of doing so.

Ava: In a propane tank. And then if it has a leak on it, you're drivin' down the streets stinkin'.

Q: So are people stealing tanks?

Ava: Well, now you have to get a propane tank like, I think five gallons. You gotta empty it out. And then you go up to the anhydrous tank, and usually you don't really do this in the daytime. We always did it at night, and I would hide under the tank and stay there. And then you just hook up your hoses to it. And you have to be really careful, because if you don't know what you're doin', it's like it's not boiling hot but anhydrous is cold boiling . . . And it will destroy your skin. I've seen people that's been burned all over and burned on their back, and you know if a farmer catches you, he's gonna try to shoot you.

Ava was not the only one who described manufacturing while driving in a motor vehicle. For a short period of time, Felix participated in mobile cooks.

Felix: I came up with the brilliant plan to do cooks while mobile . . . Rent a truck, do it in the back of a truck, drive around.

He continued:

Felix: You rent a [company] trailer, throw it on the back of a truck, and drive around. Just, seriously, just drive from there to [city] and back, and you can throw off a cook.

It was something not uncommon to him; he referred to seeing news stories of such mobile lab busts in the past. When asked why he rented a truck for the cook, he said: "Why would you do it in your own truck? . . . That's terrible." He recounted how he would go about getting the chemicals and supplies needed to make the drug as it became more difficult to do so.

Felix: The hardest part was getting the supplies. Especially in [state], like you need crazy crap like ephedrine and red phosphorus . . . Yeah this was right around the time they're really starting to crack down. About 2001 you see the big meth lab busts every-where and, especially in that region, down in the southeastern corner you have like around, there was a bunch of towns down there like [city], and [city], [city], [city] . . . So it was right around the time it got real dangerous to get stuff like red phosphorus and pure iodine, and it got a little difficult, but you just figure out a way to get it. I always steal it.

Q: Steal what?

Felix: The supplies. Because if you pay for 'em you're still getting middled. The whole point of doing it is to cut your costs to zero, and if your costs are zero, you're making all the profit and you don't even really have to cut it, and if you don't have to cut it, you bring in more clientele, because why? Because you're selling them pure stuff where somebody else is selling 'em stuff cut with God knows what. Because when you cut it, all's you're doing is matching colors, it doesn't matter what you cut with. Like I've seen people cut dope with lye, simple, because the colors matched, because you're never really sure what color it's gonna come out, I've seen it come out pink, I've seen it come out brown, I've seen it come out yellow, and then it's simply a matter of like, comparing vitamins and crap at the store, it's the same color, you crush it up, bam, there's your cut.

Q: Sounds like going for paint.

Felix: Yeah! It really gets to be that you have no idea. First of all you're messing with a substance that's got like, it was called a "cold cook," you'd use anhydrous ammonia and lithium. Seriously, anhydrous ammonia, if you breathe this crap in you could die, and this is stuff that people are banging into their arms, it's got Red Devil lye in it, red phosphorus I mean, this stuff is ridiculously bad. It's made of a whole bunch of crap that independently would kill you, and together somehow it makes this magical little thing that, woo-hoo, I feel great and it's ridiculous, but yeah the whole point is to cut your cost to nothing.

Q: So for you it was mostly about money?

Felix: Oh, all about money. Always.

He talked about how his participation with manufacturing shifted so he could increase his profits while minimizing the risks. He explained how he strategi-cally placed himself at the top of the hierarchy.

Felix: Not really working for me, they work for the cook. The cook works for me. I set up a buy, right, like say I know a dude in [city] that needs whatever, well for a really long time the good shit was comin' outta [city]. It was comin' outta [state] and being trucked across the country, but then right around 2001, 2002, you had huge busts going every-where, so it couldn't come this way anymore, but there's still a demand here, so what do you do? Smart money says reverse the flow, nobody's expecting that one, so you go back that way. Now you take the dude that was supplying this whole region and you tell him, "Hey man, I got you, and it's some good shit, here's a sample." You take a road trip, you go up there, you risk it, you take the sample, an eightball, something real small that you can hide really easily, you can swallow if you have to, and then you take it over there, "Here's what I got, man, you want some more, because I know you're stopped up, I know the pipe is not flowing on this side, but I can bring it back on a Greyhound bus, what do you say?" There you go, bam, I can charge whatever the hell I want. Why? Basic concept of supply and demand, if I have it, you need it, I can charge whatever the hell I want because it's not coming from anywhere else.

By this time, the meth he helped produce was not being cooked just to supply users in the state. Though not directly manufacturing himself, by his own admission he made the drug on a weekly basis for a four-year period of time. He described his strategy and how it worked.

Q: How many people are cooking it?

Felix: Three.

Q: I've always thought of the cook at the top but you're saying you're a level above the cook?

Felix: It depends on the person, see, again, drugs in general appeal to the weaker of the species. If you're taking it beyond recreational use, you have something that's not wired right and you need them, you need that dependency, you need something to latch on to, so all you do is exploit that weakness. Whether you're selling it to people for recreational use, whether you're trying to get people to do stuff for you, all you're doing is exploiting that weakness. Okay, yeah, if a cook was smart, he would make it himself, do it as little as possible, put it out on the street. But if I'm already that guy, I'm doing it as little as possible and putting it out on the street. Manufacturing methamphetamine, man, that could put me in prison for life, and that's one of the scariest things that I can imagine. Not simply because prison is scary but simply because my life has to mean more than being behind bars for the next thirty years or until I get shanked or gang raped in the shower, none of that appeals to me. So what do you do? You take that intelligence to the next step and you pay attention to the people. Who are you buying, who's buying from you the most. Alright, well let's take this dude out of the equation, alright: "Look, man, I'll take a pay cut here, instead of getting your $200 a week, you already know how to do this, how 'bout I make a deal with you, you cook it for me, I'll give you all your dope for free and then we put that out on the street." Honest, I don't know a not-cussing way to say this, you just fuck with their heads, you get this dude to think he's your partner and honestly he's a bitch. You get this dude, you get him strung out beyond belief, and you have this dude who is now your indentured servant. He's not a slave, 'cause you're paying him, but it's like, you wanna know where the idea came from?

It was an idea he would borrow from the days when coal miners were paid with scrip coins.

Felix: This is gonna sounds stupid: coal mines. Coal mines way back in the day before the coal industries really took off in America, you know that saying, "I owe my soul to the company store?" . . . Where that comes from is they used to pay their workers in scrip coins. Scrip coins were only good at the company store. So you were working for a place where they were providing your house but you still had to pay rent to them, and they were paying you in money that was only good with them, you'd get paid at the end of the week, you take your scrip coins, and "scrip" comes from the word scrap of paper I think, you pay them their rent in scrip coins and then you'd take the rest and you'd pay it in food and groceries, whatever. By the end of the week you were actually indebted to them. You couldn't quit because you owed them money and they were paying you in money that was only good there. You take the same concept and you apply it to drugs and you make shit-tons of money and you put in no effort whatsoever. You are turning complete profit because you exploit people's weaknesses.

His plan minimized risks for him, transferring them to the people he got to make his drugs. He elaborated on why his approach worked.

Felix: He's [manufacturer] looking at it as, he's stupid, okay, first of all he's taking all the risk, absolutely all the risk, alright, I touch it like four times maybe, he's taking all the risk for me. He, in his stupid warped little methed-out world, feels that he's my partner, and really I'm just feeding him, I'm just feeding his addiction, to use him until he's done.

Those in it for profit would take steps to maximize the amount of money they could make. Matthew did this by having multiple cooks processing simultaneously in a single location. In his estimate he had manufactured hundreds of times. He described the pattern of manufacturing.

Matthew: I never made under five ounces. Never did.
Q: What would be the most you ever made?
Matthew: Well, in one cooking, we had several cooks goin' on in this room, but we had enough stuff to make twenty-one pounds . . . I had me and my two helpers. Nobody comes in, nobody went out. I had like five electric skillets going, five labs going at one time in one room. And that one was done in a motel room.

His helpers were the people who paid him to learn the process. Others worked as assistants, or runners; they were charged with helping with other aspects of the cook as needed.

Matthew: A runner would be people that would go get me ingredients, like if I needed more iodine, or if I needed more rubbing alcohol to wash with, gloves, surgical gloves, filters, 'cause everything I do is filtered. I never gassed where I was at. More pickle jars, mason pickle jars. I did everything sterile, after I used everything once, it all got trashed, all that disposed of. I only used clean. I only used new.

When asked how often he cooked he said:

Matthew: As [little] as possible. Maybe once a month. You cook a big one. And then you take what you got, and you split it up. And you have your personal, then you sell what you're going to sell. Okay, when you go get the stuff to make another one, but you live on that money for a minute, and you do what you're gonna do. Then when you start comin' down, then you do another one. Never stay on it constantly. That's stupid . . . That will get you caught. Too much smell, too much time. You got to let your face be seen in the public. You can't just stay isolated . . . Anything after three or four days, motel managers start to get nervous and stuff. You gotta show your face.

On whether the motel managers knew what was going on in his room, he replied:

Matthew: Of course, of course. I'm sure, but a lot of times they were good friends. I paid very well money. I had a suite. I rented three rooms. I never slept in the room I cooked in. I rented a low-class room. And then I had a suite. And they asked, "What do you want three rooms for?" "I got friends comin' out of town, I want a suite, that's for them."

Q: How many years were you manufacturing?

Matthew: Probably nine–ten. I haven't had a legal job until now for about twelve years, other than drivin' that truck for about a year.

Ian cooked methamphetamine for twenty years. As an old-school cook, he preferred the now uncommon P2P method of production. When he first began manufacturing, there were few if any restrictions on the ingredients needed to make it. Even P2P could be purchased legally.

Ian: You could go to chemical places and buy P2P back then. I'm talkin' 'bout fifty-five gallon drums and stuff.

Q: So how much would you make at one time?

Ian: We used to make $80,000 to $100,000 worth at a time . . . On the streets eighty to a hundred, you're talkin' about $1,000 an ounce, so, seven, eight pounds, nine pounds, ten pounds.

Q: You were big-time right away.

Ian: Well I mean it's just, I didn't get there overnight, you know, but the truth is, you sit in for a couple times and you watch. It doesn't take a genius to cook methamphetamine.

As he described his method of production, he referenced the highly volatile and new shake-and-bake method of manufacturing occurring today.

Ian: What happens with these people today is they're under the influence and there's a new deal out now, they're makin' it in pop bottles and you can do it in a car, and you're gonna see a lotta bad stuff happen in the next few years in [the] city.

Though it used to take him three days to gather the glassware he needed, once he had everything it would only take twenty-four hours to have finished product. His $3,000 to $5,000 investment would net upwards of $80,000 in profit.

Ian: Well, a lot of it had to do with my situation, I was in rural Oklahoma and stuff. And it wasn't like today, I did things a certain way, I wasn't tryin' to save stuff. Today now, some of these dope cooks, they're all dope cooks, they think that they're real protective of their vials and their blah blah. Hell, I broke everything, got rid of everything.

Q: Did you use the actual stuff used in a chemist lab?

Ian: Sometimes yeah, I've had guys break in places and steal things for me. Shit like that . . . You can use whatever, and I've had things that you could never think of. My mom worked for [electric company], retired from there, they have the light bulb thing, and there would be things that they made us, like souvenirs with banks and stuff, some of it was too thick but it could be used in certain ways. It's just . . . I don't know, it's insanity. I think back about some of my life . . . [laughs]

Getting rid of the leftovers was simple in the backwoods of rural Oklahoma.

Ian: I'd break it. When I grew up in [city], [state], for many years there was a deal called The Slew, the swamp is what it is, and nobody had been across some of that territory since they built the railroad track through there, and the railroad track had been off for many many years, and I was, I'll go ahead and just be real with you guys, most sheriffs in most rural counties, they're six foot one . . . a white man who weighs 250–300 pounds, they're not gonna catch a guy like me. They're not, I'm gonna break brush, I'm not scared of the swamp, I'm not scared.

He elaborated on the role of others.

Ian: Two guys tops, two guys tops, two guys tops.

Q: Would that include people that would be buying the stuff, or would they . . .

Ian: Nah, only sometimes I would have other people involved in, ingredients and stuff . . . Yeah, but I, I want you to understand this, we'd even have what we call lab rats, I remember when the product was done, we let 'em try it out and make sure.

Q: Test it?

Ian: Yeah [laughs]. Yeah.

When asked whether his helpers changed over time, he said:

Ian: Yeah, well I mean, I mean I had friends die, but I kept things close to my vest. There's many times, ladies, I came back to [state], I wouldn't even try to let people know I was back, ya know. It'd be one or two guys that knew me.

Q: So a really small circle?

Ian: Yeah. Tried to be.

While the frequency of his manufacturing changed over time, he estimated that he had made meth a hundred or more times during the twenty-year period in which he cooked. As he described how things were back in the day, he hinted on how they have changed now.

Ian: I probably, see that's where things changed, sometimes only twice a year. I just wasn't really into trying to control the whole world, like I see some of these cats, think their ego and, I just wanted to do what I did . . . and I wasn't a blubbering idiot, I knew that if you bring heat down on you, and things really was a lot easier to get away with, like it's everywhere, and they make two to three ounces of methamphetamine in six hours.

During some of his breaks from manufacturing, he would move out of state and get the drug from his connections in the Mexican Mafia.

Natalie started manufacturing methamphetamine at age twenty-six using the red phosphorus method. She spoke about how she accessed the chemical at the time.

Natalie: Well, that was later, in the later years when we started using matches. I used to buy it [red phosphorus] right down here at the [store] . . . if you knew somebody in landscaping, because it's used in landscaping.

Q: What for?

Natalie: You know what, I have no idea. But I dated a guy that had a landscaping business, and I used his card and I would go get it and then later on, after the Oklahoma City bombing, because that was one of the main ingredients in the bombing, they quit selling it to everybody. They just put a major halt on it and so we started learning different ways. The flares for the road, we could use those matches.

On average, she admitted to manufacturing ten ounces of methamphetamine on a weekly basis; it would net her $10,000 a week. She talked about the difficulties she encountered acquiring chemicals after the bombing in 1995:

Natalie: After the Oklahoma City bombing, they quit selling the red phosphorus to just anybody. When you go into stores to get the acid, the muriatic acid, they write your name down, see, before I quit I was going into black pharmacies and they have Sudafed that they keep behind the counter. That's what they're using now. And you can only get two boxes a month so, a friend of mine would get me, my sister, several other people to go in and get this. And that's how they get quantities of it.

The frequency of her cooks varied depending on her access to the chemicals.

Natalie: Well, I was cooking, so I was getting unlimited, pretty much as much as I wanted. As much chemicals as I could get my hands on. You had these little stores where you used to get the pills, the ephedrine pills, and some of 'em back when I was cookin' would sell you boxes. If you found a good connection, which I did, they'd sell you big boxes and cases of 'em.

Q: Do you think they knew what it was for?

Natalie: Oh hell yeah. Yeah, they don't care . . . Oh yeah, you'd buy it by the case, just like anything else, you buy a quantity of it.

She described the different players as they related to her pattern of production.

Natalie: Two, two or three . . . Me and one other guy always did it. We always had somebody lookin' out . . . Somebody would look out and we would do the cooks. We'd always have somebody armed. Me and him would always leave the state. We left the state to do ours. We'd go to [city], [state], rent a cabin, and go up there and do it and drive back. It's about a three-hour drive.

They made the trip once a week. She explained why they would leave the state each time.

Natalie: Because they were bustin' everybody here for doing it. Down there, just no attention, no distractions. We were out in the middle of nowhere . . . I made it here at a motel one time and I was so paranoid I couldn't do that. I didn't do it again.
Q: You weren't worried about the transporting process?
Natalie: I never worried about anything . . . Yeah, we'd all come back together.
Q: Did the people or their role change over time?
Natalie: Well, we'd change. One would get busted or drift off into another crowd. We'd pick up somebody else.

Her description of the places where they would manufacture was chilling.

Natalie: Well, we'd [manufacture in] different cabins, I mean, pretty much the same area.
Q: And they didn't know?
Natalie: No. These were little vacation cabins down there for white rafting . . . No, we'd get out in the middle of nowhere . . . We'd do it in the cabins. We'd usually go to the top of the mountain and the cabins up there are like miles, you know, several yards away from anybody else.

They were the same places regular people go to "get away." On the basis of her estimate, she had cooked more than a hundred times with approximately ten other people over a period of years.

To get enough pills to make meth, Ray would either buy them from different locations or trade meth for pills. At his height he was making an ounce of meth each week using a process that took four hours from start to finish. He described the red phosphorus process he utilized as "pretty simple" and stated, "We had it down to a science." As one of the cooks who made the drug alone and with the assistance of others, having a place to manufacture the drug was critical; the frequency of his manufacturing decreased once he stopped making it at the auto shop where he used to live. The significance of having a set location was not lost upon the network of cooks in the area.

Ray: There was, there towards the end we stopped using the shop. I don't know why. Paranoia. We started using other people's houses around the city, ride to other people's houses. Sometimes them houses had kinda like an open swinging door effect, and there'd be a couple people sittin' there cookin' at the same time. Sometimes, we would help each other, sometimes not. Sometimes we wouldn't even talk to each other, just be in separate rooms doin' our own thing.

Manufacturing was a group activity. Ray described the different roles.

Ray: No, just kinda take up the slack, do what needs to be done. But everybody pretty much knows the role when it comes to cookin', what the steps are.

In his estimate, he had manufactured methamphetamine thirty to forty times during the three or four years he was making it. He expanded on the frequency with which it was being made at the time.

Ray: Once a week, but I don't know, maybe it was being cooked once a week, whether I was doing it or not. Okay, there was some times I would just sit there in the office and let them do it at the shop.

Q: Was there a network of cooks?

Ray: Yes, definitely. I mean, and what I heard the most, is the cooks that were running around doing all this at different houses, big cooks at one time that had been busted up . . . Yes, they were making larger quantities when you could still buy the ephedrine, the straight ephedrine, the white crosses. I was going to say that, taking that off the shelf and going to the pseudo, really put a damper in that, too.

Lucas was one of the few cooks who insisted on working completely alone when it came to the actual production of methamphetamine. His helpers only assisted with other parts.

Lucas: Never. I never let nobody see what I did.

Q: But they would bring the pseudoephedrine?

Lucas: Oh yeah. I had lots of people doin' that. They knew what was gonna end up with a product . . . That's it. Just the [pseudoephedrine]. That's how I learned to make my own [pseudoephedrine]. I got that from the Internet, thank you very much.

On the basis of his own account, he too cooked over one hundred times; he was making meth from the time he was sixteen until he turned thirty-eight. He would later describe cooking for the Mexican cartel.

These examples demonstrate the variations in patterns of production. More often than not, manufacturers operated as part of a loose network of people working in concert to do whatever it took to make the drug. They were activities coordinated for one common goal—to maintain a local supply of meth.

CONCLUSIONS

Understanding manufacturing is essential for comprehending the immersed life. Recognizing the motivations that underlie such activities and attractions is crucial for grasping the challenges inherent in responding.

A few things are clear. First, people may participate in manufacturing meth directly or indirectly, and they do so for very specific reasons. Not everyone involved directly produces the drug. There are people on the periphery who assist with different types of manufacturing-related activities. Second, people learn how to manufacture methamphetamine. Though recipes are available online and elsewhere, in general they learned from others they knew. Third, manufacturing is heterogeneous. There are possibly as many variations in patterns of production as there are people who make methamphetamine and ways to make it. This is a reality that complicates our ability to understand the problem and respond. There are reasons that people make methamphetamine and, as you now know, it is about much more than just using the drug.

As these stories demonstrate, social relationships and the broader environment within which these individuals lived play important roles in their eventual involvement in manufacturing. Those engaged in using and dealing methamphetamine are already, and increasingly, part of a drug subculture with others who cook. In communities and environmental contexts where others are manufacturing and where the chemicals and supplies are readily available, moving from dealing meth to manufacturing it is somewhat of a natural progression for those immersed in the lifestyle.

Though they are more difficult to obtain today, there were limited restrictions in place for chemicals such as red phosphorus and pseudoephedrine at the time. In the rural farming communities where many of them lived, obtaining anhydrous ammonia was as simple as going outside to the farm or co-op where anhydrous tanks are maintained, often out in the open and without locks. In the end, understanding manufacturing requires that we accept the fact that those seeking the drug and all that comes with it may choose to begin making it themselves. It is a progression from getting or buying what one wants to creating it oneself. In an environment where such activities are doable and already underway, learning to cook and becoming involved oneself, be it directly or indirectly, is what they did. They cooked because they wanted to and they could.

The fact that many of the activities described here occurred in rural settings should not come as a surprise. There is a long history of the clandestine production of intoxicants; the search for intoxicants that help people escape their realities and the ingenuity that accompanies making them oneself is as old as moonshine, especially in rural America. It is as Roman stated when asked why he thought some people manufactured methamphetamine while others didn't.

Roman: Lifestyle. The way they're brought up. What I found, too, it's like moonshine. Daddy made it, passed it down.

It was as old school as it gets.

CHAPTER 6

An Intoxicating Life

It was a glamorous life. You gonna have a rough time telling that story. When I speak to kids, depending on [who] I speak to, kids, adults, I speak to impact panels, I speak to judges, I speak to a lot of people and it's, it's a hard story to tell; it's in the wording. Because it is a glamorous life, it's a fun life. You know? But in the long run it's, it's trouble. I seen out of my graduating class, it was about sixty-five kids, there are less than twenty of us alive.

—Patrick

INTRODUCTION

The world of methamphetamine is intoxicating. It is filled with highs: meth, money, sex, power, and control. It is as good as it gets. It is, in reality, too good to be true. Use is not the only "addicting" factor. Rather, it is addicting because of what it provides. There is something enticing about the intoxicated life, more than just the drug.

The intoxicated life is an ongoing party in which meth provides everything you've ever wanted. It is seductive precisely because it offers what conventional reality does not. To understand how and why people become engrossed in the world of methamphetamine one must appreciate the attractions of the intoxicated life.

In this world, inebriation is normal and daily activities revolve around doing anything and everything to get drugs and stay high. Despite variations, one consistency remains—intense focus on maintaining the high and sustaining the life. The lifestyle is characterized by high levels of energy, endless partying, heightened sexuality, large amounts of cash, and feelings of importance, self-confidence, power, and control. Each dimension cumulatively contributes to the attractions of the lived experience.

In the beginning, life is better than ever—fun, exciting, and overly stimulating. Positive physical drug effects combine with sensual and psychological ones; it is the antithesis of everything that a normal existence offers.

One must understand the seductive aspects and grasp the manner in which networks facilitate the life. Users, dealers, and cooks interact with peers, acquaintances, and others to maintain access to meth and sustain the lifestyle. Users turn into dealers as they observe the benefits of selling the drug. Dealing provides two critical elements to maintain an intoxicating life: money and methamphetamine; there are few things worth more in this world. Dealers evolve into manufacturers as they come to appreciate their ability to create the one thing they and others desire. It is powerful. It is seductive. It is methamphetamine. It is valued more than anything else, and each level of involvement brings a new dimension of intoxication.

Immersion in methamphetamine requires an expanded definition of addiction. It is no longer just about getting high. Nor it is just about avoiding withdrawals. It is something more. It is relishing, desiring, craving, and enjoying everything. Risky, dangerous, and illicit activities bring new senses of intoxication. We call it addiction because we lack better words. But it is more than that. It is the illusion of having everything you ever wanted. By the time this occurs, they have become addicted to so much more than the drug. Ava best encapsulated the way her use of methamphetamine fit into her intoxicated life:

Ava: Well, when you're actually high, you don't worry about anything. I didn't. That was the whole reason of staying high, because it just, anything, any problems that you did have or things that you worried about, it just took it all away.

LIVING THE HIGH LIFE, A.K.A. ADDICTED TO MORE THAN THE DRUG

It has been argued that to truly comprehend why people do what they do, we must learn to understand the often neglected, but ever important "attractions within the lived experience of criminality".[1] Our abilities to truly appreciate the motivations that underlie behaviors depend on our willingness to see, admit, and accept that there are aspects to behaviors that make them sensually compelling and even attractive. It is one of the most significant challenges in attempting to understand methamphetamine. It is the difficulty inherent in telling this story the way that it needs to be told.

The intoxicated life is magnetic and attractive. There is a rush that comes with living as close to the edge as possible, with doing things that are forbidden or wrong. It can be enthralling. It becomes all-encompassing. There is a sense of power and control that comes with having the one thing you love more than anything else—in abundance, any time you want it. There is pleasure in seemingly endless supplies of drugs and money. There is seduction in being able to create, with your own hands, the very thing that seems to give you everything you ever wanted. It is enticing, even if it is not completely real.

Themes about what people liked about methamphetamine and loved about the life reverberated over and over again throughout the interviews like a broken record. At the end of the day, it was all really about the same thing— it was about the drug, the life, and how it made them feel. Their experiences were as overwhelming as their descriptions. We start with Olivia and her explanation of what she liked about meth.

Olivia: Honestly . . . there at the end it'd have to be the cook . . . It got you higher than the drug, yeah.

She elaborated.

Olivia: Just watchin' it, you know the bubbles comin' up, big ol' dots. Then when you gas it off, watchin' all that dope fall down.
Q: Is that as addictive or more addictive than the meth addiction?
Olivia: It's more addictive, because with that comes the high, the money, the, you know, everybody wants to be your friend . . . And you still got all the joy of getting high with it. So it's ten times more addictive than meth.

She spoke about the sense of power that came with possessing something everyone around her craved.

Olivia: It was a really small town. It was a really small drug world, and then at the end . . . I owned the world . . . Yeah . . . In that world, in that, in that setting, in that world, you do own it. You can get anything you want with that little bag. Anything.

It was a power over others. It was intoxicating. It was something that the man who had taught Natalie how to make meth warned her about when he reluctantly agreed to teach her what she was desperate to learn.

Natalie: We were really good friends. We'd been friends since we were in school and he told me, he said, "Natalie, I want you to know something before I ever do this," he said, "This is not a blessing, this is a curse." He said, "I will teach you if you want to know." He said, "I really don't want to."

She described the intoxication:

Natalie: That's an addiction all of its own ... That's an addiction all in its own, the cookin' ... You can sit there and watch it and watch it and it's exciting to watch it come out, it's exciting to know that you have some good shit.

Q: So, it's a power kinda thing?

Natalie: Yeah, oh yeah.

As she and the others would learn, money brings a whole other dimension of attraction. She recalled why she started selling the drug.

Natalie: The money, that's a whole new addiction ... The power, the money, the respect.

Q: How much were you making at the height?

Natalie: The most I ever made, let's see, within a period of a couple of months, I'd made over $90,000.

Q: Where did that money go?

Natalie: Partyin'. Just flaked off. Motel rooms ... It's a lot of money. I'd love to have it now. I wouldn't take it the way I got it before.

Matthew elaborated on the significant sums of money that could be quickly made in the world of methamphetamine. Unattainable to most, they were amounts that would be attractive to almost anyone. For him and many others, it was a significant seduction. It was something he mentioned while explaining his progression of use.

Matthew: My excuse wasn't about the high. I liked the money. 'Cause if I had money, I had power, and I liked to be in charge. I don't like bein' told what to do. I like tellin' people. And it was my own business and I found that I could make anywhere from $5,000 to $25,000 a day.

He was not alone. When he got busted, Conner had enough chemicals in his possession to produce sixty to seventy pounds of methamphetamine. At his height, he too was making $5,000 to $10,000 a day.

Troy spoke about why he could never go back to manufacturing again after incarceration. By his own account, he only used after he got out. He elaborated on the different levels of intoxication that accompany the diverse aspects of the life as he attempted to explain why he could never go back to making the drug again.

Troy: Yeah. Because I ain't messed with it, I won't ever go back there, that's a whole 'nother level, you know what I mean, the manufacturin' and all that.

He described what it was that made the cook so different.

Troy: I don't know, for me it's like, makin' it I was, I got more of a rush, I liked doing it, and it was just a complete, I don't know, it was like I was addicted to that almost more than doing it, you know what I mean . . . I guess it's just the complex or, I don't know, I guess it's because you think it just empowers you and it's the money and, just, all that, you know.

In addition to the high of the drug, the money, and accompanying power, there was the thrill that went along with doing something wrong and not getting caught. Lucas talked about the rush that came with not just making meth, but avoiding detection.

Lucas: Making it just made me get so high, you could stay awake for a week at a time. Just cook a batch, you don't have to touch it. All you have to do is cook it up, and the fumes and the fast and the rush from knowin' that you're doing something wrong. I mean just [groans].

Q: So the making it is also a kind of addiction?

Lucas: Oh yeah, it's the rush, 'cause you know what you're doing is wrong. You know at any second somebody could walk through that door, or walk through that area where you're at. So that's where I took my precautions. I always went to a river, to a lake, somewhere where I knew there wasn't gonna nobody be there. There was no chances of nobody pullin' up on me. And if they did, it went right in the water. They had no proof. Watch stuff. You gonna dive fourteen foot down in the water off the surface? No you're not, to figure out what am I doin' out there.

For him and others, meth becomes deeply enmeshed with other pleasures. He explains his motivations.

Lucas: Money, baby. Money. Money and sex.

Q: And to get it for yourself?

Lucas: Mostly for myself with the sex and the money. I mean I liked the drug. Right. It was all three. It was a combination. If you got dope, you got money. If you got money, you got pussy.

As a manufacturer who worked legitimately, he described how meth fit into his life.

Lucas: Methamphetamine is for a workaholic. Okay. I worked fourteen to twenty-one hours a day. I ran a hog farm and a mechanic shop. There's no time for farmers to sit down. When you got thirty-seven head of cattle and 240 pigs and then eight sheep and sixty-five chickens . . . It helped me be productive. It helped me keep going. I could do everything I needed to do. And it just basically just rolled on, rolled on, and rolled on.

As a self-described "working manufacturer," he described his strategy to maintain his weight and keep his meth use undetected. It was a diet that consisted of popcorn, hot peppers, cheese slices, and chocolate milk. It was critical for balancing both aspects of his life.

Lucas: [That's what] kept me alive. That's the only thing I could eat because the meth, you just have no taste, I mean, if you smoke a little bit of my dope, you're not gonna wanna even smell water. Your pupils are dilated, your sense of smell is highlighted, your touch is highlighted, you're gonna smell that water . . . You'll smell somebody's breath from across the room. You know what I mean. Nothin' tastes good. Popcorn, I forced myself to eat that, because I didn't want my family to know I was strung out. So I had to keep that level of sanity toward myself. And I was runnin' a business, plus racin' a race car, plus havin' a family, plus cookin' dope.

Those with legitimate jobs primarily worked in positions that aligned with the drug lifestyle. Roman explained how he managed to live two incompatible lives simultaneously. While he never manufactured meth, he had heavily dealt it for many years.

Roman: I was doing it during the job, because my job consists of moving around the city and stuff. Every job I've ever had fit in with my drug and drinkin'. Every job I've ever had. Luckily, I wonder if it wasn't by plan. But every job I've ever had and I've worked . . . It had to fit with my lifestyle. I couldn't be drug tested, couldn't be; if I did, I only had to take one in the beginning. Every job I've ever had fit in with my lifestyle.

Not everyone would be able to do this, and in the end, not even those who did could sustain it over time. More commonly, immersion was progressive. Eventually, drug-related activities and associations would take precedence over all else.

As a result of her heavy immersion, Ava experienced difficulties in maintaining a job; she would come to redefine what she thought of as her job while engaged with meth. Getting high and staying high eventually became her primary function.

Ava: You're always on a mission. Whether you're high or not high. And if you are high, you wanna continue to get high.

Lucy elaborated on the subtlety of the grip the lifestyle had on her. It was a topic that came up as she explained using meth to help her come down from the pain pills she used.

Lucy: This was horrible, and this made it feel a little bit better, and so when the pain medication was completely out of my system then I was actually able to get the high that meth gave you, you see what I'm saying, and when you've got other chemicals involved, or other substances, it changes the high, it changes the difference, but the lifestyle is addicting, very addicting.

Q: What specifically?

Lucy: The people, the money, I mean it's a life, you know. It's not just the drug, you do meth, you do the drug but you're doing the life too. You can't have one usually without the other, I've never known anybody to have one and not the other. Meth takes you so quickly there, and it's really kinda subtle, you kinda really don't see it coming and the, just the next thing you know, bam you're into it.

Dillon expanded on the positive aspects he experienced.

Dillon: It's harder to know now, because like I said all the cravings is gone, but if I remember right, for starters it was the rush, when you first did it. Because there was just like this, this kind of a rush, it's kinda weird euphoric, it's almost impossible to describe. And it's just a heavy euphoric feeling, and then from there, I guess it was a lot of the lifestyle, that kind of got addicting too. I learned that while I was in prison, that's why I quit doing [it], because I was hustling tobacco and coffee, and when I started realizing what I was doing, I was like okay, I'm gonna give up the hustles, and do things legitimate from here on out. Because that hustle turns into an addiction.

Q: So like the dealing and all that, was that part of lifestyle?

Dillon: Yeah. The wheelin', the dealin', the cookin', the power.

This sense of power and importance was a theme reiterated over and over again.

Dillon: Yeah, the money, and usually not so much the money, because the money comes and goes all the time, you never really stockpile anything, regardless of how much you're doing or whatever, you hear stories talkin' about people buried so much and all that, they're lying. Anytime they say they buried meth, they're lying [laughs]. Because you never stockpile it. 'Cause it rotates, and then it's like, it's the power more than anything. You're important all of a sudden, everybody needs you, they come to you for their drugs and all that, and it's just a feeling of power and importance, you're somebody.

Q: That must be hard to give up.

Dillon: It is. It really is. That is, it's the same thing with prison, that's what part of institutionalized is, not just 'cause the simple fact you don't want to pay bills and stuff anymore, but in prison, you can actually become somebody in a nobody world, and I mean you can tell all the lies you want, you can create your own little character almost, like World of Warcraft, and you can become a part of the Aryan Brotherhood, or the Crips and Bloods, or whatever, and you become somebody. You get out of prison and you're just one of another billion people.

There were benefits to living on the edge while high on methamphetamine. Vince, a fifty-six-year-old former dealer and cook, elaborated on what living the high life had been like for him. Other than the few times he had stopped, he used daily for twenty-five to thirty years.

Vince: I went to prison for five months, I didn't do none then. I done some when I got out, and I think I, for two years, it's in there somewhere, I slacked up and kinda quit, you know? But other than that, my daily mission was methamphetamine. Either goin', chasin', findin' it, goin' to the cooks and gettin' it from 'em. I dealt pounds, quarter pounds, half pounds of crank at a time. I had people I'd go get it, bring it home, weigh it up, separate it up in ounces, then I'd go take it to my people in ounces and whenever I got my money back and money for them, I partied. I'd go from house to house to house, you know doin' shots and doin' crank and then just bein' awake. I was actually, I think I was awake for thirty years, you know? And I, that's not possible but I'm sayin' whenever I would lay down it'd be like, you know, an hour later I'd be ping! My body got a little rest and I just . . . I had so much methamphetamine in me.

He further expanded on the "fun" of the manufacturing process and what specifically attracted him to it.

Vince: It's a rush . . . It's not physically addicting. It's just mentally addicting. 'Cause I can make dope. You know I can make what costs me lots of money. For little or nothing.

Vanessa focused in on the high that went along with doing things she knew were wrong and trying not to get caught.

Vanessa: There's a high in walking into a facility that, even when they put that law into effect that you had to show your ID. "Will I get caught this time? Or am I above my limit?" Because when you show your ID you are only allowed certain . . . "Well if I get to this store and I get to this other store who's not on their same system, can I get that done in time? And who will I be to the people that need these if I am?" I mean there's some mentality around it and that in and of itself could be completely out of dope, have not slept for three days, and be as high, as if you were, because of that adrenaline that goes along with that process.

Q: That's amazing.

Vanessa: It is. It really is. There's so much more to it, coming out of it than just "I don't want to use any more." I mean you're attached at the hip to so much of the process, that you literally have to sever every contact that you have in that life, and they don't want to let you go. You're an asset to them and if you're on this side, they can't use you and they can't benefit from you anymore.

Though he no longer liked anything about methamphetamine, even Jackson talked about the aspects he used to enjoy.

Jackson: The rush, the money, I guess everybody is different from me. Right now, even though I've been clean for eighteen months . . . I don't miss doing it, as much as I miss the rush of manufacturing it, and the money.

Q: Why is that?

Jackson: My opinion is because of the adrenaline rush, I mean you can't buy the main ingredients to do it with and you have to steal it, and it's just, you get a big big adrenaline rush off of it.

In his attempt to explain the attractions of methamphetamine, Wes alluded to similarities between life on meth and the attractions for those who compulsively gamble.

Wes: Well, I guess it goes back to the same thing as using. For me, when even just getting the pills or even when people come back with the materials, you know. At first, I went and got the materials myself. But that takes months to have enough to do anything with. It's appealing. It hits that same receptor. I guess the same question is why do some people play the stupid machines—the slot machines, and some people do tables? They get a different feel. The slot machine is an instant gratification thing and gambling addiction hits the same receptors in the brain as cocaine. So, you know, that's what worked for them and the tables work for other people. For me, when I manufactured, it kept me high. And that was my ultimate goal. I didn't give a damn about nobody else. As long as I can get mine for cheaper, then it's worth it, and I think if you know the process, why not? Others think it's too damn scary and they're not going to prison.

For Felix, too, it was about the rush.

Felix: The rush. A rush is . . . for me it was always, I don't know it's more of a psychological thing. Like I've always been the small guy, it wasn't until recently I became average, maybe when I was twenty-four or something. I was always a lot smaller than everybody, a lot skinnier than everybody, so I always had little-man syndrome and whenever I got wired, whether it be on acid or meth or coke or whatever, I could feel myself get bigger. You get this roar in your ears, everybody called it the train. It's just like standing real close to the train tracks, that roar that comes with it. You get that roar in your ears, I could just feel myself get stronger, I could just feel power surge through me and at that point I could've beat anybody's ass, I could've punched through a brick wall, I could've took off and flown, it was just that rush, it only lasted for like ten minutes or so and then after that we'd usually just sit around, I'm a genius at darts now because we'd just sit around all night and play darts, but that's what I liked about it, just that. That and I really enjoyed the fact that I could focus, you know my mind goes in nineteen different directions all the time and on that I could just focus on something so well that, I don't know, I kinda liked it.

Q: Is that tweaking?

Felix: Yeah. Most of the time you'll see people tweaking on like drawing a spiral on a piece of paper, or cleaning or something, but for me it was always just intense focus on whatever I wanted it to be.

For him, as with many others, there was a rush that went along with each dimension.

With each level of progression, the attraction grew. The rush that came from power over others and dealing drugs without getting caught were things he would expand upon later.

Though Allie herself never manufactured meth, she too became enthralled as a dealer who partnered with friends who made the drug. She described how her circumstances changed.

Allie: Gosh, it was just a whole different world, everything was alive, everything brightened up, you can do anything, you have power, you don't have to sleep, you can get anything done, like I said, I was working my three full-time jobs without any problem, taking care of my kid, plus goin' out and partying.

As a single mother, meth brought her excitement and added significant amounts of disposable cash to her otherwise minimal income. For her, it was as much about the money as it was about the meth.

Allie: A lot of people out there will use and spend their money, and go broke, I became addicted to the money along the way, along with the methamphetamine, I probably was one of the biggest sources in [city].

While she herself was not willing to take the risks associated with making the drug, her partnership with manufacturers would fund her fast-paced life.

Allie: I had people that would make it for me, um . . . plus I made more money. I could buy the chemicals and everything the people needed to make it, they would get their little share of it, plus I would have mine, and I would make so much more money, instead of blowing myself up, and not really having a place to manufacture it, with a kid around.

On how much she earned, she said:

Allie: Well, okay, what I started off with was probably sixteenths, sixteenth of an ounce, I would spend $100 to $125 on it, and I'd end up with maybe about $400 out of it, so I started off with that and then I moved up to eightballs, and then I went to ounces.

Allie discussed how the addiction to money was just as important as the addiction to methamphetamine.

Allie: It, it really is, when you get down, you got twenty dollars, and you're making six dollars an hour at a job, "Oh, I need some money quick." Within an hour I could have four or five hundred bucks in my hand.

Then there were the truckers. One cannot truly understand what it's like to live in this world without examining the experiences of the truckers in this study. Although references to truckers were made throughout the study, an even better picture of the high life that exists on the highways across the country came from the truckers who participated in the interviews. There were three. They spent decades driving semis from coast to coast, navigating their way through conventional society and the world of methamphetamine simultaneously. They used meth and eventually got into making it themselves. They had lived intoxicated lives for decades and came to tell their stories. They painted a penetrating picture of what it means to live the intoxicated life— driving cross-country, working hard, moving both legal and illegal product, and staying high.

They came because they had a story to tell. They had lived a trucker's life. It was compatible with the life they had created—the one that revolved around methamphetamine. Each had used for decades, starting in the early days of meth tabs, white crosses, and diet pills. They became heavy users of the drug and transported drugs across state lines as they hauled legal products as part of their conventional job. For them, methamphetamine had become part of their life; it fit into everything else they did. They each talked about the life they lived riding high on meth. And what a wild ride it was.

Bryant was the first trucker to participate in an interview. A former IV user himself, he described hauling pounds of methamphetamine across state lines while employed as a trucker. His participation in the distribution network was clearly higher up the chain. On the basis of the amounts of product he was moving, he was likely close to big-time producers of the drug. He spoke about the biggest risk he ever took while distributing methamphetamine.

Bryant: We, we would bring pounds after pounds of it from [state] through here. You're not only talking to a manufacturer, you're talking to a dope dealer.

Q: Is that part of the trucking stuff to be able to bring it in?

Bryant: No it was, you can do it in cars, I did it in trucks, but you know for the biggest part it was, the area from [names city] west, everybody knew me.

Q: You were transporting large quantities?

Bryant: Oh yeah, I mean thirty-seven pounds at one time through [state].

Q: I was going to say that's crazy, but that's . . .

Bryant: No, that's plain-ass stupid. Anyway that's stupid. Well, we went through a DOT [Department of Transportation] check with it. Yeah.

He described what intense sexual experiences were like when both he and his partner were high.

Bryant: I don't mean to embarrass you or anything, but the sex, when you get into shooting methamphetamine, you shoot it and you just instantly, the sex is just, [you] drove hard for hours, where if you smoke it, it took a gradual [time] to get up there, and the fun that was involved with this, you know, I mean if you had a guy and a girl that they both done a shot of dope at the same time, that sex appeal, that instant, whatever you want to call it, went for hours, and it stayed there just like the start, that, that part of my life is gone and I'm sure that part of my punishment is all the drugs I did, that part of it, is there's problems. That's part of the problems I got to live with, and I done it to myself. I'm sure there's a cure, there's whatever, hell I've got another high, I can probably go get a high and do it. But it's not worth it, you know, it's absolutely not worth it.

It would be a positive aspect that would end when he stopped using meth. For him, this was like a game; when he got away with manufacturing he was beating the cops.

Bryant: Anytime you put your hands in chemical. That chemical will soak in, okay. You will get high. You know you see ATF [Bureau of Alcohol, Tobacco, and Firearms] and drug enforcement officers go in and bust these labs and they're all wearing these suits. There's a reason why they wear them suits, because if they don't wear them suits and they get any of that on them or they inhale any of that, they're getting high. So, so one of the biggest things that we did, I didn't use gloves. I didn't use rubber gloves. My hands are, they're like, I would stick my hand down in the cook you know freeze 'em to death and some of the fingers I can still feel, but for the biggest part you know the enjoyment or the addiction of that was, is what we were doing . . . but yet who we were beating at doing it. You understand that? You know if I'm sitting there cooking and I know that the police is lookin' for me because I am cookin' and they can't find me, by God I'm beatin' 'em. That's addictive, that's that rush that I was telling you about.

Q: That rush.

Bryant: That rush, that's the addictive part of it. The money, the finances that come off of it, that's addictive. That can be addictive. The high that you get outta making that, because you know it's yours and it's not somebody else's, it's your product.

He spoke about what it was to live the high life and the amounts of money he made.

Bryant: Oh it's probably, yeah I'd say hundreds of thousands. I mean if you combined the money I spent, the money I made, if I just had it now I probably wouldn't be driving a [year] model car, I'd probably have two or three new cars. I went through two wives, a trucking business, I don't know, I moved more times than military people.

Q: Lots of money going in?

Bryant: Oh yeah, and I always drove shit, I mean junky cars, and pardon my language, but just junk, and I have now something that I'm very proud of. I own my own motorcycle and that's something I always wanted the whole time I was doing drugs and I couldn't never get my stuff together to do it . . . Big dealers, we'd meet in [city], I would bring my stuff, they'd bring theirs and we'd all mix it and split it, and we'd go in a casino, there was one night we all went in the casino, we had $30,000 among three of us, blowed every dime of it. We had to sell dope in the parking lot to get home.

As a former trucker who had lived the high life for decades, he would explain it most eloquently. The thrill lay not in just going to the edge, but in leaning over it to see what would happen.

Bryant: I did, I had lots of fun with it. I like to drive fast, I like to live on that edge, methamphetamines puts you over so much, leaning over, not just being on that edge but leaning out to the point of, you gonna come or you're gonna break or you're gonna go. Are you gonna fall to the ground, or are you gonna stand up? It's like bungee jumping, but every day. I've never bungee jumped, I have fears of helicopters, I mean of airplanes, I don't ride in airplanes. I don't like spiders, I will make an entrance, or an exit getting away from a spider. Yeah big burly guy like me scared of a little bitty, trust me I will, I'll run from it. My mom and dad laugh about it all the time, but you know we did. I had a lot of fun drivin' them trucks, there's nothin' like being, and I know this sounds bad on the legal side of it, but there's nothin' like having a hundred thousand pounds behind you, live animals such as cattle and going 120 miles an hour, 130 miles an hour and everything going by, sonic speeds you know. It was fun, I mean it's that edge, you fall into a curve and everything just has to be in sync and you just, and it's just an awesome, awesome feeling.

The second trucker was Patrick. By the time he graduated high school he was shooting up multiple times a day; at his height, he was using an eightball a day. Like many of the others, Patrick had built his life around meth. It had become the one thing he loved most in the world. He remembered the time when they were making meth down the block from where he stayed. In response to a question about whether the manufacturing had started in or out of state, he said:

Patrick: I never 'member there not being drugs.

He lived the intoxicated life in the truest sense of the concept. He described what it was like when methamphetamine took precedence over all else.

Patrick: I work all the time. I missed a lot of my kids growing up because [of] the work. Like I maybe went to one or two activities my children were involved in, in the twelve [years] they were in school, one or two activities apiece, out of twelve years, I neglected my children badly.
Q: Working all the time?
Patrick: I did not abuse my kids, I neglected my kids, which is . . . it's something I try hard now to make up for. I'm beat. You know, I, I, I do it back to my grandkids now.

His life on the road would help him maintain his intoxication. It was as he stated in the middle of his interview, "I had a dope path between [state] and [another state], young lady . . . Bought it." When asked if he worried about anything during the time he was using meth, he said:

Patrick: Not really. I didn't tweak. I didn't get schizy. I didn't, I was always, somewhere else. Nobody knew who I was. I ran forty-three states . . . Moving all the time. Nobody knew who I was, or what I was supposed to be like or anything. I did my job. I did it well. I didn't worry about much . . . You would have probably thought I was high when I wasn't high if you had known me. My use was so frequent. A lot of people I know didn't realize . . . Didn't realize I was high. You woulda thought I was high when I wasn't high because . . . I was always high. That was my normal state.

Though he had been clean for six years at the time of his interview, his eyes twinkled as he reminisced about old times. He still loved it, even today.

Patrick: That's why I'm here. If somebody can be, not put through what I went through . . . but that's hard to say because . . . I had a lot of fun doing drugs. I enjoyed it . . . I liked making 'em, I liked doin' 'em. I was a junkie. If you'd asked me seven years ago what I was, I'd a told ya I was a junkie. I had no intentions of changing, until I got older and it was just, I needed to. I got tired of going to jail.

The connections that fueled his intoxicated life were vast and wide. He had hauled meth for the Mafia in the early 1980s and maintained associations in all the states he traveled. Though he never really got into selling meth, he hauled it cross-country for years. Despite his description of the life as glamorous, his biggest regret was the thirty years he wasted.

The last trucker was Vince, by far the most soft-spoken of them all. His demeanor would be part of his motivation for use. Having used intravenously for decades, he looked like just another farmer. According to him, methamphetamine had significantly improved his life, boosting his self-esteem and confidence. Self-described as a fat, introverted adolescent, he repeatedly came back to a single statement about why he liked methamphetamine—because it "made me ten-foot tall and bulletproof." His use progressed significantly once he began injecting. His comments on the notion of addiction were thought-provoking.

Vince: Never paid no attention to [addiction]. I never really wanted to try heroin 'cause I'd seen some stuff about how people get so, but I'm thinkin' the mental addiction to the methamphetamine's almost worse.

Q: Is it a physical addiction as well?

Vince: Well . . . it ages ya . . . Whenever I did quit I went from like thirty or forty years old feelin' to like retirement-age old. Just [snaps] like that, man, my whole body hurt. I hurt all over and just 'cause all them organs and muscles and stuff that was . . .

His use had begun with forms of the drug such as white crosses and meth tabs. When taken in large-enough doses their effects mimicked those provided by the clandestinely produced versions of the drug he later used. He described what he enjoyed. Methamphetamine transformed him into all that he wanted to be.

Vince: It enhanced mine. It really did. It made me from being so insecure and negative and "Nobody loves me," the whole, whole nine yards, it made me . . . "I'm just as good as you if not better." You know?

He elaborated on the negative effects meth has on some people, saying:

Vince: I've seen people so tweakin' and freakin' and peekin' and thinkin' the meth man's after 'em, and our other buddy he always said he never seen that. That's bull, you know? But he read into it like I did. I seen it, but I, I always give myself one rule. Don't make any decision about anything important unless you realize you are messed up. You're high. I don't wanna say the F-word, you know what I mean?

Q: Don't make any decisions . . .

Vince: Always remember you're high. There's a difference between a normal state and a high state of mind and people do stupid things when they're high, you know? . . . To me it was like I didn't ever say nothin', everybody thought I was normal. My grandma, when I got out of prison I was actually straight, she had me mowin' the yard. We had a trailer park and two houses and it was all-day mowing the yard. I mowed the yard all day long, right? I got through. I went home, took a shower. I was tired. I really wanted to get high and I wasn't high at the time and she'd come over and say, "Well, can you go mow this one other patch?" And I said, "No, Grandma, I can't." "Why, you lazy idiot." I said, "Damn, Grandma, you like me better when I'm high?" "What?" Because if I'd been high I'd a said, "Sure, I'll go mow it . . ." I'd do any . . . I'd do anything for anybody. Right down here, old boy had electric shop. He had a semitrailer full of electrical like plug-ins and stuff, boxes of it was supplies. He didn't have nobody to unload it. Friend of mine just got off of it. "Hell, we'll unload it for you!" "Oooo, for unloading it he said he'll pay us." "Nah, he don't owe us nothin', that's alright."

Q: Just have all the energy to do whatever.

Vince: Yeah, didn't care. Didn't need money . . . Drivin' down a road seein' a guy with a flat, a flat tire. I don't think it was a Mercedes but it was a nice sports car. "You got problems?" "Yeah I . . . have a flat." "Well hell, jump in." He jumped in, I run down to the station I used to work at and got his flat fixed, took him back up, put it back on there. "Well, what I owe ya?" "You don't owe me nothing . . ." That's just the way I always was, it didn't mess with me like it did most the people I seen. I have no idea why, to this day right now if I had my choice I'd have a prescription of Desoxyns, which I think it's methamphetamine prescription pill and I'd take one a day. 'Cause it made me so happy and so positive, but I can't. You know? I mean it's not legal.

In many ways the truckers in this study are unique. Their engagement in dealing primarily consisted of "moving product," and when they cooked, they did it mostly for themselves rather than for money. Though they were among the most heavily involved in terms of length of time and extent of use, they too had become attracted to the intoxicated life just as the others. They were but one part of the network that built and sustained intoxicated lives.

WEBS OF NETWORKS

It takes many people to sustain the intoxicated life. It is a world built on networks upon networks. While not unique to meth, linkages are critical. They are comprised of multilayered webs of connections that tie users with distributors and distributors with manufacturers.

The networks linked to methamphetamine facilitate access to the drug and have sustained the supply of the drug across decades. Existing at parallel levels, the networks are interrelated yet distinct, operating at the ground level as well as much higher up. They ensure that the supply of methamphetamine does not go unabated for any extensive period of time and have succeeded in maintaining a supply that continues today.

Though limited information is available, evidence indicates that the networks associated with methamphetamine—the ones that assist with the movement of finished product from site of production to end user, as well as the ones that ensure and maintain a supply of precursor chemicals—are simultaneously vast and expansive and small and connected. They operate at multiple different levels and include diverse types of people.

A picture of the networks that exist within the world of methamphetamine emerged from the stories told. Connections between involved parties both near and far began to show themselves, as people talked about their lives and the movement of meth across space and time. They included connections sometimes known and other times not, and links between people they knew and those they did not. In the end they all shared one thing—they all seemed to work together in concert to maintain a supply of methamphetamine to simultaneously fill and create a demand. As the following discussion demonstrates, what goes on in Oklahoma is not limited to the state.

The topic of methamphetamine produced in California by motorcycle gangs first came up with Conner. He talked about where the methamphetamine came from when he began using. Long before he made it himself, Conner was getting methamphetamine being manufactured in and supplied from California through a connection in his network.

Conner: Well, the clandestine labs that when I first started using it was actually in, it wasn't really in motorcycle gangs, but it was kinda connected. They were, the motorcycle gangs were makin' it down there. They were givin' it to my friends up here, and then they would sell it to me.

It was one of the first indicators of the links that tie larger networks to smaller ones.

Conner: It's kinda a network thing, back then it was pretty much, not really, you wanna say, a motorcycle gang but it was all interconnected too, I mean, motorcycle gangs is what they say, I never really relatively got firsthand experience of that. I just know it came from the clandestine labs, from California. I think the first methamphetamine lab if you ask my experience was probably in California. Wasn't in Mexico, it's probably in California.

He was right. Years before meth was made in Oklahoma, it was produced out of state and imported; historical evidence indicates the first labs were in California.

Within the stories of methamphetamine there are many links between Oklahoma and other places, including California and Mexico. The drug flows described were not always unidirectional, especially as the production of meth increased across the state. There were drugs coming into the state and drugs that were moving out of it. And as is the case with many things, the movement of drugs was facilitated by individuals and their networks.

Briana was the only female drug runner to discuss her participation moving drugs across state lines. As the only study participant to admit to once assisting law enforcement build a case, she admitted to moving product through other states to her rural town. As a runner, she moved methamphetamine produced both by out-of-state manufacturers and members of the Mexican cartel.

Lucas was the only manufacturer to admit to manufacturing for the Mexican cartel. During the time he worked for them, he was cooking large quantities of meth for distribution. When his connection to the cartel died, so did his link to the group. It was something he talked about when describing how his involvement with meth changed over time.

Lucas: I was going back and forth from those three–four little counties, four little states, my surrounding states, and you know I don't want to sound like a kingpin, but by God I was getting rid of a lot of dope. They wanted me, you know. They wasn't going to get me 'cause I sold to the cartel, to the Mexican cartel. I cooked for the Mexican cartel and that's all I did. And when he [his contact] died, I quit. I quit selling to anybody. I was already hooked on the drug. I'm gonna cook it for myself. This is mine and forget all everybody else. That's what I did for ten years.

He claims to have been producing "five-gallon buckets' worth" of meth for the Mexican Mafia. It would be something he could only pull off with the assistance of others in his network. He explained how he would amass the boxes of pseudoephedrine required to make such quantities of the drug.

Lucas: Every prostitute, every tooter, every person you could ever think of . . . Yeah, I couldn't cook it fast enough when I started selling to the people in [state] and [state], when I was runnin' an ounce at a time.

Q: You weren't just limited to one state?

Lucas: No. Hell no, I didn't wanna be. I wanted to be the kingpin.

Q: What would you make off that five-gallon bucket?

Lucas: At one time, if I sold it all at once, and if I had the cash all at once, you're talkin' $200,000 to $750,000 dollars, easily. And that's sellin' it at a cheap price.

Q: And you couldn't make it fast enough?

Lucas: I couldn't make dope fast enough, no ma'am.

Though it was sometimes difficult to distinguish between exaggerations and fact, his description of how his situation began to spiral out of control, eventually forcing him to slow down, appeared credible.

Lucas: When I first started was once a month. Then it got to be like once every two weeks. And then it got to be where I'd have to do it every week. Then it got to the point where, son of a bitch, I gotta cook again tonight. You know what I mean. Every night. It come down to the point where I was cookin' and cookin' and cookin'. That's when I said, "Okay look, I'm done. I'm movin'." And I shut everybody off. I got out of town and moved to another town and then it got to the point where I just cooked once a month again. You know what I mean. You get it right. You start all over.

When describing how his connections changed over time, Ian mentioned ties to someone with a drug connection to casino owners from the West Coast.

Ian: Well, I mean, that was back in the '80s, yeah. Back then he [his dealer] was an associate of the road bikers. Now today it crosses all lines.

Q: Did you know if it was a local supply when you would buy it or get it from someone?

Ian: Yeah. It was local.

Q: Did you ever have any that came from out of state or out of the country?

Ian: Yes ma'am. Yes ma'am. Later on in my life I got in business with a guy who told me that it was comin' from the West Coast and the people that were behind it owned casinos.

Q: Would they ever have any that came from Mexico?

Ian: No. I sobered up before that . . . Yeah, that's a recent deal.

Dealers in other states packaged their product differently.

Ian: Well it depends, if you're buyin' an ounce, it might be in a sandwich-sized bag. I bought it, I'm going tell you, in [state], I bought it in straws. Like this, [shows straw] they seal one end and then they seal the other end.

Q: How did they seal it?

Ian: Lighter, and just use the heat up, then they take a little, cut a [thing] with a tip and dump, and they put it on paper and dump it in and seal the other end. Yeah. That's a Mexican Mafia deal.

For some, there seemed to be ways to tell where the product was coming from.

More locally, networks are comprised of the people who manufactured and distributed meth. As a dealer for many years, Allie would deal to many different networks of users including friends, their family members, truck drivers, and even members of the Ku Klux Klan. While her claim to have been "one of the biggest dealers in the state" is not possible to verify, her extensive participation in dealing for a period of years makes it highly likely that her networks were as wide as she claimed.

Vast networks are critical for successful dealing, particularly when it comes to the movement of large quantities of meth over extended periods of time. Like Allie, Roman only distributed locally produced methamphetamine and other drugs; he never made it himself. But even he was keenly aware that developing and maintaining ties to local producers was critical for success and stability. He described how he solidified mutually beneficial relationships with manufacturers.

Roman: But the thing was, I built up a credit with a lot of these guys, because I always paid them on time, if not before. I was constant. It wasn't just . . . They built up a trust. They liked my personality. They liked me. They said I was cool. And "we like you." Plus, "When you make enough money, you're paying our bills. And the more we make, the more you sell."

Though directly tied and engaged in ongoing interactions, Roman seemed to make a strong distinction between himself and the people in his network that were providing the meth he would sell.

Roman: No, they, actually, I would never hang out with them in a million years. They were the dirtiest, scummiest people in the world. No teeth, sores all over their face . . . Weirded out, sores on their arms, sunken-in faces, unwashed, their hair, though, just tryin' to fix themselves, sitting there, pulling up their hair, and just freaks. I mean just everything you see. And then you got their wives or girlfriends and then you got the room, the living room full of all of the meth groupies. You know what I'm saying, just sittin' there waitin' for a fix. Just sittin' there waitin', just give me a fix, just give me a fix.
Q: That's creepy.
Roman: And they're all like this. And their mouths are doin' that number. They've got white cotton balls built up here from bein' so dry. They're sittin' there . . . and their jaws are doin' this number.
Q: Just waiting?
Roman: Oh yeah. They're *feening*. They're feening, is what we called it. They're feening for that drug and they're feening for someone to offer it to them. But I always thought it was funny, I was always a giver. I loved to share my stuff. I had plenty of it. And they'd

think I was cool. You know, building a rapport, making new friends, maybe somebody that could help me out later. Because I wasn't cheesy on who I hung out with. You could be the scummiest person in the world and I would drink a bottle of whiskey with you.

His friends would play a crucial role in making the introductions that were absolutely necessary to facilitate such relationships.

Roman: Actually, my buddies would tell them, because I didn't know them. They'd say, "Hey, give me some." Because they would look at me like I was a cop. So my friends would say, "Man, yeah, he can turn some for you. He can turn it quick." Because I knew different people I had dealt with, some of them were kind of dirty, lower class, but I dealt with guys that had really good jobs, oil field, going to school to be doctors and stuff.

Q: Different groups?

Roman: Right. These are people I've known forever. Pharmaceutical salesmen, I mean anything, it didn't matter.

The links between the people one knows and the ones they don't prove to be essential when it comes to networks in the drug world. It was something Roman would elaborate on as he described how he would generate access to meth.

Roman: Trading, but mainly I'd go straight to the cook, and because I worked my way up. I started out with, I don't know, this guy would know this guy, my friend would work with this guy, say at a lumber yard, and this guy was a dork, but he'd befriended them because he knew that he wanted me to meet the cook or whatever, because he's an uncle or something. And once we got past him and got in there, then we realized we had good sense and we could make some money in this little bitty town with some cash in and a bunch of people that had, not like a rich town, but yet they're a little above average as far as incomes go. We could move that money.

Networks also operate at a level closest to those directly manufacturing methamphetamine. In addition to people like Allie and Roman, who function primarily to move finished product, there are other, loosely organized and ever-changing networks that help to facilitate local manufacturing and often even assist with the cook. It would be incorrect, or at the very least misleading, to say that the only people who are responsible for manufacturing methamphetamine are the ones who mix chemicals and "gas the cooks." Rather, as the following demonstrates, networks operate even at the lowest levels of clandestine production.

There was Allie, who never actually made methamphetamine, but financed and organized cooks and then sold the part of her "take" that she herself would not use. There was Felix, who simultaneously managed to escalate and de-escalate his level of involvement with local production by removing himself from the actual cooking process. Rather than cooking, himself, he gave others everything they needed, manipulating them to make it for him so that they absorbed most of the risk. There was Vanessa, who at the height of her addiction convinced herself that moving meth cooks into her house would be a good way to try and get back her children. And there were others.

There were always networks around the cooks: individuals on the periphery assisting those who manufactured in various ways. Some helped out before the cooks, while others helped during or after. They helped because there was something in it for them. Most typically, they wanted meth—and/or the money that came with it.

They helped in various ways. They did whatever was necessary, legally or illegally, to obtain anhydrous ammonia or the pseudoephedrine pills needed to make the drug. They gathered red phosphorus and muriatic acid. They provided funds to purchase all of the ingredients needed and even went as far as offering their homes as locations for the cook. They even assisted with some of the smallest parts of the manufacturing process like scraping matches or removing pills from the blister packs they came in. They helped because they could. They helped because they wanted to. There was always something in it for them.

Mia's situation serves as a good example of someone on the periphery of clandestine production. Though she initially replied "no" when asked if she had ever manufactured, her response would change after she was asked whether or not she knew anything about the topic. It was true, she had never manufactured methamphetamine. She was not a manufacturer, but she participated—in some ways almost as closely as one could without actually mixing the chemicals. In exchange for methamphetamine, she allowed others to make it at her house.

Mia: Yes . . . I allowed it to happen in my garage. I wasn't there, but I financed it . . . But I wasn't there like shakin' and stirrin' up, you know.
Q: So, a little bit further removed from manufacturing?
Mia: Yes. Yes . . . I think my charges says maintaining a dwelling, so that's how they legally [classified it].

Like many others, she was tied to local manufacturing. She talked about the extent of her activities.

Mia: Well, I would, I tried to organize it and give people money and send them out to buy the certain supplies. And then I'd hired a cook to come in and then he was going to assemble it, manufacture it. I just know you have iodine and I think, I don't know, salt, I don't remember, and red phosphorus and pseudoephedrine. And you gas it and you let it boil or somethin', simmer, I don't know.

Q: You knew people who were making it and you purposely got them to make it for you?

Mia: Yes. And then I would give them a cut of it and then I would have my own big supply. So that was my reasoning.

A more complete explanation would only emerge through her responses to key probing questions.

Q: Was [manufacturing] always in your house?

Mia: Yes, in the garage.

Q: And would you be there when they were making it?

Mia: A couple times I was.

Q: Would you go out and see it, or not?

Mia: No, I wouldn't. Well, I remember one time I went into the garage and it smells, really. No, actually I take that back. I think I was there one time when they gassed it. But it was just, the rule was nobody was there when it was happening.

Q: Do you just find someone you know that's cooking and say, "I'll pay you?"

Mia: Well, no. I mean, it was like in that community of people that know each other, and when I started going to the other side of town to buy it, I met all this other group of people and they knew somebody and became acquaintances.

She elaborated on her role in the process.

Mia: I financed it. Trying to organize people is just like *pffft*, because everybody's high. Three or four times that it actually did come to fruition, and I can remember one time when they had finished and there was all this squabbling about who was going to get what and then it got, you know just, but I'd say I just financed it. Then I, after it was done, I would sell it.

Her responses to what would follow next illuminated the motives for herself and others.

Mia: I'd say—of course not being back in there when it was finished so, no telling how much could have been made, I don't know—but I'd say like maybe a couple of ounces [from a $500 investment].

Q: How much would you keep and how much would you give away or sell?

Mia: That person I think would get like half of it, the person that cooked it . . . As payment. And then of course I would give the roommate some and then I would keep some.

Mia would use her portion of the cook for her own use and to sell to others— allowing her to continue the process of financing cooks. Fortunately or unfortunately for her, she would only be involved for a few months before being caught at the height of the clandestine manufacturing problem.

Wes also talked about the different ways he would get key ingredients to make meth. There were two main ways: get them yourself or have others get them for you.

Wes: You have to sign for the muriatic and the sulfuric, I think, if you get it from like a plumbing supply store. I knew a plumber, too . . . He got me muriatic all the time. The farmers give you the anhydrous, you give 'em some dope, or you steal it. There's easier places than others to steal anhydrous from . . . Local farm, small-time guys. One of the places is on Indian land.

Max reminisced about the time he and his friends went on a spree to get everything they needed to make meth. They got caught after stealing anhydrous ammonia during a sting operation.

Max: And then the second time, one of my buddies called me, went to go pick him up, we went and gathered all the pills and everything, and went and got all the stuff to do it, we're on our way home, and stopped to hit these, anhydrous tank that we'd been hittin' . . . Yeah, and cops were watching it . . . They were watching the tanks. They were dummy tanks . . . I mean they had stuff in 'em but . . .

Q: So they caught you guys trying to get it?

Max: Yeah. Well they caught us after we got it. We got it and we're driving down the road and they came up behind us.

For those who cooked, stealing anhydrous ammonia was a good way to get the chemicals they needed.

While Sam had never participated with manufacturing in any way, even he knew about the activities of those motivated to make it. He described how groups of people would go on out-of-state runs to get pills.

Sam: I knew that they had, like some of their buddies would run up to [state] and buy [a pseudoephedrine] package back then and they'd send ten or fifteen different people all over the place to buy it, all bring it back, that was the main ingredient of cooking it.

Ava explained why, as controls on precursor chemicals increased, the numbers of people it would take to pull off a cook increased by necessity. She and the others were acutely aware of the cat-and-mouse game between those who cooked and those seeking to eradicate it.

Ava: Oh, you spend tons of money 'cause you're always buying pills, buying batteries or you're giving people money to go do it because people on dope are broke. Even though you're makin' money, you're broke all the time. Yeah, because you're always, all the money you make you're givin' away to have people go buy you more pills, especially since they passed the pill law. You have to find more people because they can only get so many grams a month.

Q: So, you just get more people involved.

Ava: Yeah, so that's more dope you have to give away. I mean when they passed that law that really . . . it really pissed us off because . . . Yeah, and then when they started putting the red dye in the anhydrous, a lot of the farmers . . . Because when they put that dye in there, you can't use it.

An inadvertent and unintended consequence of increased restrictions and controls was that more people were participating in manufacturing-related activities. She went on to mention another participant in her game, he was an officer who worked on the other side of the law.

Ava: And there was, see, there was a certain person that was, he has a farm and he, he's with the police department, and he was selling anhydrous to help make it. He's in law enforcement.

Q: What was he getting out of it?

Ava: He was making deals with the big dope dealers to rat on the little people, so he was giving them anhydrous. I won't tell you his position in law enforcement because if I do, you'll know exactly who it is.

Q: Do you think there may be more law enforcement involved than we know about?

Ava: Oh, there is. This guy has his own farm and he takes the big dealers and sells them the anhydrous and then they snitch on the little people, the people that are cookin' for 'em, and he gets his bust and makes himself look really good.

She described how available anhydrous ammonia is in rural Oklahoma; unlike some of the others, she would only ever use locally produced meth.

Ava: I never actually, I don't think I ever done any that was from out of state that I know of. Yeah, because this part of the country, especially [names region] and there's so much farmland. Oklahoma was really big for it because there's a lot of anhydrous tanks. Little towns, like [city], for example, there's nothing. You can drive thirty miles to go to an ATM. They don't take checks at their little cafes. They don't take anything but cash. The only place, they have anhydrous tanks just lined up and so places like that, it's really big down there.

The networks she described were wide. Before the implementation of tighter controls, even legitimate store owners facilitated the manufacturing at the local level. Once again, they did so because there was something in it for them. She explained how the transactions worked.

Ava: It just depends on the dealer, but like I said, if you're cookin' it yourself, like me for example, people I would have buy pills for me, I would give them the pills, I don't know how much they are now, but they used to be I think like $7.22 . . . Yeah, for a box of ten. And so you have, you get you ten people to buy you ten boxes of pills, and you're givin''em a quarter paper, which is like .025 grams and you're getting a sixteenth off of one box, if you know what you're doing, so you're actually comin' up and you've got your own supply for yourself. You've got your own supply to sell and you've got enough to give them, to make them happy, because you're paying for the pills and you're giving them dope. And they're getting' twenty-five dollars' worth of dope.

Q: And that's probably before they make you sign everything.

Ava: Yeah, this is before all that happened and like a lot of times we'd have people go to [state] and get the [brand] and that was a lot better because that you could make pounds of dope from the guy that had that goin' on, the Asian man.

Q: Did he know what you were doing with it?

Ava: You know, I think he did, but I think at the same time he's thinkin' money, money, money, because you'd have to go to the back of his store. You couldn't just walk in the front. And he'd have to know you. I mean you'd have to go in there a few times and, you know, get acquainted with him.

In addition to assisting with the movement of finished product and the manufacturing of methamphetamine, network ties serve as indicators of methamphetamine sources and otherwise support the intoxicated life. Here, Jackson explains how his networks facilitated his access to the drug at his height, when he was shooting up three to four grams of meth per day.

Jackson: You know, you get introduced to so many friends, family, or acquaintances or whoever, and you'd always go back to them and get it. I mean, if they had it, then they know who to get it from.

Within small networks of users, those who have drugs or the money to get them always have a place to stay.

Lucas: I've always had a home. I've never been homeless. Knock on wood, thank God . . . If a person's got money for dope, he got a place to live. If he got dope, he got a buddy. You hear me. So, a lot of that's drawn-out subjects just tryin' to make you feel bad. That's bullshit in my aspect. So if you got dope, you got friends. It doesn't matter if it's an alcoholic. An alcoholic, if he's got alcohol, he's got a buddy to go sit in the garage with.

In the rural communities where methamphetamine problems flourish, there never seemed to be any shortage of the drug for those who craved it. Lucy talked about the prevalence of methamphetamine in her community. It was a key part of what she came to enjoy.

Lucy: Well I mean once you meet, then you meet another, another, and I mean there's a whole family out there of people who use meth, 'cause, you know, like I was talking about the pain pills, where you go through the withdrawals and you have to go seek them, you have to go get 'em, whether you're lying to doctors and going to emergency rooms to supplement when your prescription has run out and that sort of thing. Meth is everywhere, it's everywhere, once you meet one, nine times out of ten, it's not an isolation-type drug, it's not something that you usually go use by yourself, it's, it's a lifestyle, that kinda becomes your life.

Troy described it as a plague, especially in the days before the enactment of laws that eventually made it more difficult to manufacture.

Troy: Uh, I've just always knew the people, and . . . If I didn't have it, if I didn't make, then I just, I knew people, where I'm from there's just it's, it's, it's like a plague there, you know. Especially during the time when they was, when they were cookin' dope and stuff, and there wasn't so many laws, that they have now, it's like an epidemic, I mean it's just, everybody was doing it. I mean you couldn't go about, I guarantee you, one out of five houses that you come across, someone was making drugs in that home, you know, the area I was from.

Q: And when they passed the laws did it go down a little bit?

Troy: A lot, yeah . . . Yeah, it did go a lot, it really did. It's a good thing, too.

In small town America, methamphetamine manufacturing seemed to be a normal part of life.

Ava: Yeah, I mean in the neighborhood I lived in, everybody cooked dope over there. We all did dope, we all cooked dope, we all grew up together.

In the intoxicated life, networks shift. Those immersed in methamphetamine increase interactions with others similarly immersed while simultaneously decreasing links to those who are not. It is part of the change in networks that occurs as methamphetamine increasingly becomes the center of daily activities and social relationships. Zach was one of many who noted the impact his increasing immersion in methamphetamine had on his relationships.

Zach: It affected all my relationships with family and friends . . . Yeah, I mean I couldn't be around my family if I was dealing, so I wasn't there and they knew why I wasn't there, because they knew I was dealing and getting messed up on methamphetamine, and . . . Yeah they don't want to be, and I don't want to be, I didn't want to be around family whenever I was high, 'cause none of them were high. And they would know I was high and I just didn't want to do that. And as far as friends go, I mean I had some friends, and there was some friends that we known each other for years, and I wouldn't say our friendship was based on drugs, 'cause even if we didn't have any drugs we would still be friends, but I would say I liked you a lot more if you had drugs or if you had money to buy drugs.

Q: So it kind of enhanced the friendship?

Zach: Sure.

Q: Were they all involved in meth?

Zach: To one extent or another, a little bit.

And so it goes with intoxicated lives.

There is a duality in the way networks operate at the street level in the drug world. In a world where everything revolves around drugs, the networks that endure are those that link to meth. For those who are immersed, all others eventually go by the wayside. And in the reality of the world of methamphetamine, where things are not as they seem, even "friends" eventually show themselves for what they truly are—only customers.

CONCLUSIONS

The benefits that accompany living intoxicated lives abound. Using, dealing, and manufacturing each served to meet multiple needs. There are reasons people become enthralled with the drug and everything that goes along with it. At the center is the high from methamphetamine and other stimulating effects of the drug. However, there is much more to why people become and stay involved as long as they can. It is because the intoxicating life carries with it many of the things that people desire and crave. In addition to meth, there is sex, money, power, and control. These aspects attract people and seduce them into believing that they never want to leave.

The intoxicating world of methamphetamine is comprised of and sustained by diverse types of networks interacting at various levels. There are small, intimate networks primarily made up of close friends and family members, and larger networks that include social acquaintances and "friends of friends." Networks may consist of ties to externally connected persons associated with larger or more distant networks.

The networks that underlie the world of methamphetamine include users, dealers, and manufacturers. As critical links that connect users with dealers and manufacturers, collectively, they are networks focused on maintaining the supply of methamphetamine and the associated lifestyle. By ensuring a continual supply of methamphetamine, the networks simultaneously meet and create demand for the drug. They vary in terms of stability, organization, and operation. At the most basic level, networks are composed of various parties including peers, family members, and acquaintances. They include direct participation by members of and connections to subgroups including motorcycle gang members, truckers, and drug cartels. The interactions facilitated within these networks contribute to the excitement of the lifestyle, at least at first, as they are the direct link to the most desired commodity in this world.

Methamphetamine seems to provide its users with everything they ever wanted. It is true that this is something they come to believe. But it is equally true that the intoxicating life is fueled by methamphetamine. It only exists as it does when methamphetamine or other drugs are around. And just like everything else, it changes over time.

Though their accounts of the intoxicating lifestyle seemed seductive, the truth was much different. In reality, the world of methamphetamine transforms from intoxicating into dangerous, illicit, and risky. But by the time that one starts to see the world for all that it really is, it is often too late.

CHAPTER 7

A Risky Life

It's a very chaotic event. You're sitting there, and it never happens when you expect it. You're paranoid all the time, always lookin', waitin' for 'em. It will never happen. The moment you're like relaxin' for just a second, all of a sudden, it's just so hard to describe, just entire chaos breaks loose. You hear BLAM, and usually they'll, they'll knock and kick the door in at the same time. All of a sudden people are rushin' in, flashlights, guns, dark people, they're all dressed up in blue and black, snatchin' you up, throw you on the floor, stick a knee in your back and shotgun to your head, and they're screamin', lights out, I'm tellin' ya, from being a moment of peace to that, and after several times I remember having nightmares. I mean, yeah, it's like, being somewhere all of a sudden just [imitates gun sounds] . . . I think home invasion, I bet you, is a lot of the same.

—Dillon

INTRODUCTION

Risk is inherent in an immersed life. Dangers lurk deep within the shadowy corners of this world. Those involved are pursued—not just by users wanting the drug but also by the police. Drug raids represent just one of the dangers. Dillon experienced six. Costs and consequences increase with further immersion.

Each dimension carries numerous and diverse perils, threats, and hazards. The presence and possibility of risk, violence, and death are real and consequential. Over time, methamphetamine use transforms and becomes characterized by paranoia and hallucinations. Auditory and visual delusions make distinguishing between reality and drug-induced perceptions difficult. Likewise, dealing is dangerous due to the risks and uncertainty in the market within which the drug is bought, sold, and traded. The fact that those involved are often high themselves makes these transactions some of the riskiest of all. With no formal rules or legal controls, violence and retribution serve as regulators in the black market. Manufacturing is the most precarious and perilous aspect because of the highly toxic, volatile chemicals and processes utilized. Cooks become willing participants in an activity that can result in their own downfall. They simultaneously place others at risk. As the most hunted, they risk everything—families, freedom, and their lives—all for methamphetamine.

In the midst of meth-fueled binges, reality is indistinguishable from perception. As physical and mental fatigue set in a battle between the drug-induced effects and side-effects ensues. The unnatural high causes abnormal effects that eventually result in more sinister and deviant experiences.

It is at this point that the illusion of methamphetamine begins to reveal itself. Disillusionment ensues. The transformation from an exciting intoxicated life into an unsafe and perilous one is insidious. Money, sex, and drugs become risk, danger, and death. The new reality is not one where users can have everything they've ever wanted. Rather, it is an existence filled with paranoia, hallucinations, and hazards. It is the zone of illusion. Nothing is as it first seemed. It is the treacherous and uncertain place from which many never return.

BINGES: TWEAKING, PARANOIA, HALLUCINATIONS, AND SHADOW PEOPLE

Over time, once highly pleasurable experiences convert into ones characterized by distorted reality and altered perception. Binges and the lack of sleep take a toll on body and mind. It is not natural to be high or awake for hours and days on end. The consequences of deprivations are dire.

Prolonged periods of drug use clash with long-drawn-out periods of time without sleep. Staying awake for days and sometimes even weeks is not uncommon. Bryant expanded on the impact of lack of sleep on his well-being as he talked about the longest period of time he had stayed awake while high.

Bryant: In the trucks you always had partners, helpers, whatever you want to call 'em. So you didn't get much sleep, sometimes you had to take what we call "power rangers." Power rangers is, lay down and get you fifteen- [or] twenty-minute nap and when you wake up you're refreshed and you're ready to go. But as far as staying up, my God, I don't know, a week, two weeks, I mean it's hard, I mean it's hard for me to look back and tell you exactly how long, because I can't remember.

Q: But multiple days at a time is not unusual?

Bryant: Absolutely, no, no, no, and when you start skipping baths and showers and, you know, letting yourself run down and everything, you hope you have a partner that's gonna say, "Hey buddy, you're stinking," or "Your eyes are getting pretty rough," and my rescue or my area that I would run to at that point was [ex-wife] and she'd say, "You gotta get some rest, lay down," and I fought her to do it. We may go through three days of fistfighting. And I mean physical abuse too, and finally I'd feel so bad that I'll lay down and get a little bit of rest. Well when I laid down I may sleep for three or four days. Just 'cause you would wear yourself.

Q: And then get up and start again?

Bryant: Get up, first thing you do is do a shot of dope and go.

As Vince spoke about staying awake for extended periods of time, it became evident he was trying to understand what the sleep deprivation experiences he lived through actually looked like. When asked what the longest period he had stayed awake had been, he responded:

Vince: God I have no idea. Depends on what you consider . . . without an eight-hour stretch of sleep? Months.

Q: Months? Would you get like, nodding out a little bit here and there?

Vince: Every now and then. But usually when I'd nod out, I had so much methamphetamine in me, pretty soon when my body'd go to rest, ping! I'd wake right back up, yeah. Messes with your mind . . . Makes you see meth monsters. They'll stay if you look at 'em and you don't realize that you're messed up and you think, "Oh, whoa, that's real!" That ain't real.

Hallucinations were a very real part of the experience.

Zach reminisced about the activities he engaged in during a three-week period within which he claims to have not slept.

Zach: Oh just do a lot of speed and get out and about and, I don't know, hang out. You're out using drugs.

Q: Are you eating?

Zach: I would eat, I would force myself to eat occasionally after I was really into this, the drug speed culture, you realize that you needed to take care of yourself or you were going to get really crazy. So you needed to ingest some calories. I think the acidity level of your body gets up a lot whenever you do methamphetamine. So we would eat spoonfuls of Arm and Hammer baking soda to get it down and I think it would keep it a little more clairvoyant, not clairvoyant, a little more . . .

Q: Balanced?

Zach: Yes, yeah, and you wouldn't get as far out there.

Eating baking soda is not as strange as it got.

Conner and his friend had once "shook the moon" while high on methamphetamine. The incident occurred during the seventeen-day period he claimed
to have stayed awake "without battin' an eye."

Conner: Actually in the time I was up for seventeen days, you know, I was so weirded
out that me and my buddy of mine we had thought we had *shook the moon* . . . We found
these little concrete rocks, and listen to this, okay, my neighbor had just put a new sewer
line in his yard so he had busted up his driveway. But there's some concrete rocks left
over from that and we thought they were moon rocks. We convinced ourselves they
were moon rocks.

For him and his friend, they were moon rocks that night. Though it is not
possible to validate the unnaturally long periods of time people discussed
remaining awake, Ava insisted she stayed awake for approximately thirty-eight
days. When asked if she remembered the entire experience she responded:

Ava: No, I know I stayed up that long because I was in a competition with somebody
to see how long, so I was marking off on the calendar, but after that, I don't remember
all those days but I do know I've done some horrible things to people when I've been
up that long.

She would elaborate on the meaning of "horrible things" later.

While there are physical limitations to the number of days a person can
survive without sleep, such limitations become skewed by the ingestion of
large amounts of methamphetamine over periods of time. When asked about
his experiences, Dillon claimed to have gone without sleep for "thirty-three
days approximately." He spoke about what this meant and how his body
responded.

Dillon: I nod out and come back, and there was even a time where I walked in the store,
and I was walking back, and in a blink of an eye my body just shut down, and thirty
seconds, thirty minutes, I had no clue, I woke up, and I was like "whew," and I kept
walking thinking, "I hope a couple of [cops] don't stop me."

Q: So how long would you sleep then?

Dillon: It's always power naps. All the time, and then when I finally came down after
that, the thirty-three days, when that month was over I went to my mom's, and I went
into like a coma almost.

For Evan staying awake equated to getting "spun out."

Evan: Yeah, that's just getting high, it's *spun out.* They call it spun out. That's after you've
been awake for seven or eight days, you think you're talking clearly but its just comin'
out a bunch of gibberish. And you think, "What's a matter with you?," you know, when,
when someone's sittin' there, and they're just all twitchy and can't sit still and if you look

at my eyes you can see the brown, and then the pupil. Well, when using methamphetamine they're just all pupil. Your eyes dilate, to take in more.

These were the effects of heavy use. According to his recollections, he had stayed up for fifteen days one time. He talked about what would happen next.

Evan: When the normal people go without sleep very long, you get irritable. You get incoherent kind of, you're not real sure of everything. I always got real paranoid. Thinking, "Why'd you ask me that?," and I'd get up and look, I'm looking out the window to see if somebody's pulled up outside. I had miniblinds, and I had one slat fixed where I could stand back away from the window and look outside, as if anybody was going to come over or anything, but that's just peepin' out the window.

In the aftermath, he would wake up, shower, and go get more meth.

Tweaking and staying awake are part of the meth experience. Their experiences illuminate the relevance of tweaking, paranoia, hallucinations, and "shadow people." In the midst of such binges, there are some who do not eat or care for themselves (e.g., personal hygiene). Behaviors become increasingly strange and sketchy as the artificial high, lack of sleep, and paranoia collide. Users become tweakers.

Understanding tweaking is essential for comprehending what goes on during drug-fueled binges that last for days. Tweakers engage in unproductive activities for hours or days at a time as a way to pass time while high. It is separation from reality.

Dillon was not alone, in that he laughed when asked about tweaking. There was something funny about explaining it, as it was a question many had never been asked or had to answer before.

Dillon: Tweaking is things you do while you're high. It can be variation, it can be peeking out the windows, it's just whatever it is, remember I told you it, it makes you, makes you focus real hard, whatever it is you're focused on.
Q: Like the phones?
Dillon: Cell phones, yeah the phones, started takin' them apart, I was tweakin'. I also got into cryptology. For some reason my brain worked a lot, I was a big pencil-paper person, and I turned around, I'd like make encryptions and stuff, I'd make like three-stage encryptions, and I'm tellin' you, if somebody could turn around and make something that did the same effect, it could be used as a progressive thing.

The experience was complicated. Hallucinations intermingled with altered perceptions.

Dillon: It'd be such a touchy little line right there, because I'm telling you, you focus *so heavy* on whatever you're doing, that now I honestly believe that, methamphetamine also

... how can I say it without sounding crazy, I don't know what-all powers there are out there, okay, I never believed that nobody could control 'em, I believe that there are information grids and there're just all kinds of stuff around us going on that we're not aware of, that peeks its head out every so often. People getting miraculously healed, things that happen that have no explanation. I don't believe that people can control it, I don't, all these people who say, "Oh I can read your mind, I can do this and that," I don't believe them, I believe they're trying to make a hustle off of it. I believe this stuff exists, but we don't know what it is or ... control it at this point in our evolved life, and I believe that methamphetamine, maybe because the Indians do a long time ago, when you deprive yourself of sleep and water, that you weaken your body, strengthen your mind, or your spirit. They had something, you *see things* that most people don't. Not just hallucinations. But they're just, you're open to another realm almost.

Q: A different level of awareness?

Dillon: Yeah. Yeah, even though you're sleep deprived. It sounds *insane* but it really does kind of work that way.

In the confines of tweaking, there is no distinction between what is real and what is not.

Bryant referred to tweaking as *"maniac-ing."* He explained.

Bryant: Tweaking? Maniac-ing? ... Okay, we always called it "maniac shacks." We would take a maniac shack and inside this shack you may have, oh hell, truck parts, radios, tools, something that was broke, something that didn't look right. We could take this coffee creamer and we could think of a million things to do with it to turn it into something that was going to be positive in our lifestyle.

Q: So is it like focusing on things?

Bryant: Your recorder, something would be wrong with it and just by me sitting here looking at it and I would pick it up, and I'd start tearing it apart to fix it. And the end result is I'd have to go get a new one.

Things were not as they seemed.

Ava described what she did to pass time during the two days she stayed awake the first time she got high.

Ava: The very first time I ever did it I remember exactly what I did, and it's really stupid but I took this cassette tape and I completely unrolled it, and I rolled it back up over and over. It's funny now ...

The seemingly monotonous and repetitive activity was pleasurable while high.

Ava: Well, it was really fun when you're high ... but that's what I did the very first night. That is the very first thing I ever did. The first time I got high, that is what I did ... It's enjoyable, when you're high. It seems like, they call it tweakin'. Things that you would tweak on when you're sober.

Q: Like you get focused?

Ava: Yeah, on things you have to do to. Is going to be time consuming and maybe repetitive, get really tired of it when you're sober doing it, but when you're high, those things are fun. I mean it's just, it's just a great time to unroll a cassette tape.

In addition to finding activities to keep busy during tweaking experiences, there seemed to be a need to make sense of altered perceptions and hallucinogenic encounters. The term "shadow people" was first mentioned by Ray as he explained his need for psychiatric medications to deal with the severe psychosis he experienced.

Ray: Oh, at the height of the methamphetamine use, psychosis was horrible.

Q: Like what would you do?

Ray: It was just, hiding from people that weren't there, the voices, the . . .

Q: We've heard people say they look out the window all the time trying to look for people or . . .

Ray: Oh yeah. We used to, oh yeah. Me and my girlfriend, we had a joke about calling them *shadow people.* Yeah. You just catch the shadows, and you think it's a natural person.

He and his friends had created an unusual explanation for these hallucinations.

Ray: We even made up a little story about why there's shadow people . . . I had this theory that the parallel universe runs on a faster time. So when you speed up your body, you catch the remnants of what the people were doing in the parallel universe . . . I've got a lot of crazy theories.

Even in the midst of such craziness, there seemed to be a need to try and make sense of perceived realities. He alluded to the change in risks as he discussed what he worried about most.

Ray: In the beginning, I worried about being busted, yes. There, closer to the end, I was worried about *dying.* You get mixed up with the wrong people . . . It got bad. I won't lie to you.

Q: What does that mean, it got bad?

Ray: It just, the longer in it you are, the further down the chain you go. Some real dangerous people crossed my path.

While some people avoid risks, risk taking in and of itself is not necessarily uncommon or deviant. The excitement of risk taking was alluded to by Zach as he talked about his experiences tweaking.

Zach: You look out the window shades like five different times within five minutes.

Q: So you get paranoid?

Zach: Yeah, I think you hallucinate after a while, audio hallucinations and visual hallucinations after you stay up and not eat for a while. Deprive your body of water and sleep.

Q: What do you hear and see?

Zach: Shadows, and out of the corner I used to see movement.

When asked if such experiences were scary, he responded:

Zach: It was both scary and exciting. Some people, it was scary that they would believe that's what they saw and sometimes if you weren't sure, it was kind of exciting because you're like wow, I'm really tore up.

It was part of the experience. Such stories were not uncommon. Ian described a story about a man who had hallucinated to the point of thinking he could pass for a lamp in a window.

Ian: I'm gonna give you guys an example of some stuff. Like when they talk about the blinds they need to have here, well, people like to peek out the blinds 'cause they see shadows, you believe that there's tree people or the cops. My sponsor guy helped me go through the steps of Alcoholics Anonymous . . . He talks about peeking out the blinds through a straw. Now I have sponsored guys that were five-star chefs, I mean real successful guys, they cooked for the [names popular entertainers and music groups], and stuff, and talked about being in a hotel room down in [state] 'cause it was where they were from, and they were using and they thought their families were lookin' for 'em and stuff, and they didn't want to peek out the blinds so they took the lampshade, like most hotels have a little lamp by the bed, and they cut two eyeholes on it, put the lampshade on their head and raised the blinds and stand there. I'm tellin' ya this is a big black guy, it's not like people are gonna think he was a lamp. That's the insanity of, yeah. That's funny, though.

The difficulty distinguishing between perception and reality was unmistakable.

Ian: Ah, shit . . . I hear people say they stayed up for a month and stuff, I don't believe that's true. I think that as alcoholics and drug addicts we like to exaggerate, but I've stayed up well over a week before. I wouldn't even know what day it was.

The increasing chaos that defines methamphetamine-using experiences over time plays a key role in the shifts in perceptions that occur. Wes provides one of the clearest explanations of how his experience eventually changed.

Wes: That first two years after smoking it for such a long time, and constantly, when it progressed to an everyday thing, then I think that's when the visual hallucinations and audible hallucinations really came into play. Because I would smoke so much that even if I was looking at a blank wall, I would see words and numbers and stuff like that, and I got into the paranoia, watching out the miniblinds, and that's when I started feeling it wasn't fun no more. It didn't feel good. The next step after that was because the people that shot it, yeah, they were kinda crazy. They might say some weird stuff but at least they felt good. So the first time I tried it intravenously that's all I did. I didn't even smoke it anymore.

Ava expanded on this change and what she disliked about the drug now.

Ava: The worst part is the comedown, when you're comin' off of it. And the comedown is really horrible when you shoot it. Oh yeah, I've known people that have felt suicidal and a lot of times too, when you come down off of it, you really literally schiz out, like as far as hearing voices and things like that. It's really bad.

Q: The hallucinations?

Ava: Yeah, if you've been up for a long time, when you start comin' down, or even if you're still high on it, that is the worst thing because you wanna keep gettin' high but you're losin' it. And you really, really see these things.

Q: I've had people talk about the shadow people.

Ava: Yeah, I call 'em the tree people . . . Yeah, I swear I've talked to trees before. And they've talked back. I know that [when] I'm sober that that's not possible. But when you're high, I mean even when you're high you know it's not possible but it's real.

She highlighted the fact that people sometimes talk incomprehensibly while high on meth and the paranoia she experienced.

Ava: They're talking in circles . . . But see, when you're on meth you have a different language, too. People on meth talk in circles and when you're on it with them, you understand exactly what they're talking about. I mean I still understand them, I understand what they're talkin' about because I did it for so long, but it's because they're always paranoid about the police or somebody bein' a snitch, but yeah, people that have been up for a long time, they mumble. They don't make sense.

Q: Is it the meth that makes you hallucinate or is it the being up?

Ava: It's the being up. I don't think it's the meth. I think it's the lack of sleep.

Q: Do you become psychotic?

Ava: Some people do. I have a few times, I mean I would just usually get really paranoid and stay in and I would sit on my couch and stare at the TV, which would be watching them all outside my house. I also had a camera pointing at me. I had three TVs stacked on top of each other, filming.

Not being able to communicate clearly is part of the binging and tweaking experience, at least for some. Briana discussed what it meant to be "dope fucked."

Briana: There was another thing that is a side effect of meth use, that I don't know if anybody else [has] ever brought up, and that is mumbling . . . One of the dope houses that I used to go to, I would ask them because they'd have all these, okay, I am going to speak frankly, okay? Okay, they have a bunch of dope whores walking around, and they were all walking around mumbling, and I asked 'em, I said, "What are ya'll puttin' in the dope that's making these girls walk around mumbling?" Towards the end of my use I walked around mumbling too. And what it is, and once again, excuse my language, this is not how I talk today, but it is what they call dope fucked, and that is when they would give them a shot of dope waaaay too big, and towards the end of my use I guess just because I was using more, I got to the point that I walked around mumbling too.

For some, negative consequences included seemingly real physical effects.

Matthew, one of most skilled and knowledgeable manufacturers in the study, recalled a time he was pulling shards of "ice" from his skin as he attempted to explain the difference between ice and meth.

Matthew: It's the same effect, or basically the same effect. But it comes out in, see that scar, right there? That's ice. That's what ice causes. I was a mainliner. That is how I used. Anywhere in the black was my vein [shows tattoos]. Anywhere in the black, that's why I do my own tats. So I'd shoot it, okay. See all these scars on my body. You can't really see 'em no more. They were sores where I was pulling slivers out of my body. I've got 'em where they're healed up, and they're going away.

Q: That's got to be terrifying.

Matthew: But it just slithers. It looks like acne, heavy bumps, or these lotta people's gettin' cysts, and gettin' tumors. . . . It's coming out through your pores in your body. Yeah, it has to exit. It comes out through your urine, through your eyes. These slithers.

He explained what this looked like.

Matthew: It looks like a crystal. And it recrystallizes, and after you smoke it, you kill it, but if you shoot it, you don't. 'Cause you don't have to have heat to break it down. Just a little bit of water in a little spoon, burn it down, and you're there.

Real or not, his description fit with those of others. A number of people described ice as a fungus that grew in their bodies and extricated itself through their pores. Natalie reminisced about an infection that got so bad she could no longer wear pants or shorts.

Natalie: It's a bacterial infection. I cut myself open with a razor blade when I was in the bathtub and took it out . . . It looks like snot. I don't know exactly what it is. Yeah, the pus comes after the green stuff . . . Yeah, if somebody touches it, it hurts.

Q: Once you cut that out, then it healed up?

Natalie: It healed up. Well, it healed up as good as it could. I still have scars.

Q: Did you put anything on it or ever go to a doctor?

Natalie: Taped it up. No, hell no. I wasn't going to no doctor.

For her and others, negative health consequences and risks accompanied immersion. During the last ten years of her involvement, she lived dangerously.

With no stable residence to call home, she stayed anywhere she could, including tire shops and drug houses. She elaborated on how her life changed.

Natalie: I was never scared of living that way. That was just how I lived. Now, to me it's scary. But then it just . . .
Q: How did you get to that point?
Natalie: Using every day. I drove anybody and everybody away. I became completely unemployable. I couldn't hold a job. Then I got to where I was using so much that I couldn't pay my rent, I couldn't function, whatsoever. There are such things as functioning addicts. People who have jobs and keep jobs. But I was not one of them.

In reality, going without sleep, tweaking, paranoia, and hallucinations are what make this a dangerous drug. Such experiences increase personal volatility and uncertainty. Reality becomes indistinguishable from hallucinations. Perceptions and experiences are distorted as physical, biochemical, neurological, and psychological systems clash and become essentially dysfunctional. It is at least in part what makes the methamphetamine-using experience what it is. It is also part of the illusion that is methamphetamine. Yet changes in the direct effects and side-effects that accompany use are only part of what makes this world increasingly risky and dangerous over time.

METH, DESTRUCTION, VIOLENCE, AND DEATH

The world of methamphetamine is filled with hazards and uncertainty. There is desperation and danger in the underground world. Here, money buys methamphetamine and methamphetamine brings power; having either can place one's life in jeopardy. It is ironic that the most highly valued and desired things are the same ones that are so perilous. Vince described the dangers of dealing a drug that is desired by so many and exactly how much one life is worth against the power of methamphetamine.

Vince: Dealing is dangerous 'cause you can get in a bad situation real quick. Even bein' a good guy and honest and good-hearted, you still get in those spots that your life's hangin' from their thread. Homeboy told me, went over one time, he said, "Picture this: here's a cliff. You're hangin' from a rope right here. This meth addict has got ahold of the rope. There's a shot of dope right over here he can't quite reach. What do you think your life's worth? Zero. 'Cause he'll let go of that rope and go to that shot. You're a dead man."

Ian provided great insight into the potential for harm that exists, as he discussed the importance of "inches and seconds" as critical for separating life trajectories and outcomes. It was something he mentioned as he tried to explain how he would protect himself from detection.

Ian: I took precautions, I'd meet new people, and it's seconds and inches . . . seconds and inches, I'm no better, no smarter than anybody else. *Seconds and inches, it changed our lives,* and I know that many times I had people that I grew up, that I knew for twenty years show up with a new boyfriend, or cousins, but I stuck to the way [name] told me and, "How could I know you from twenty years and never met your cousin?" And I would, I would embarrass people, I'd say, "Dude, you know what, it really doesn't matter to me if you're a cop or not, it don't bother me, you know what, you leavin."

Q: What do you mean by seconds and inches, because I like that?

Ian: I believe them men that comes in my life, and that I've tried to help them find recovery, it's all the way from men that have taken other men's lives to what we call high-bottom alcoholics and drug addicts, I believe it's seconds and inches are the only things separating us, I'm not better and no worse than anybody, I don't know why I've never taken another man's life, and one of my buddies have, it's just seconds and inches.

In the risky world of methamphetamine, just as in conventional society, what separates one trajectory or outcome from another often comes down to just inches and seconds.

Vince remembered an encounter that led to a girl getting killed; he missed being in the room by thirty minutes. Though he himself did not participate in the violence, it was part of his world.

Vince: It is [violent] to a lot of people. It's not to me . . . I seen a lot of violence . . . Yeah. Walk into a house and some guy's standin' there tweakin' or whatever with a gun pointed, had three or four people sittin' on a couch, you know? "What are you doin', man?" "Oh one of these guys stole all my dope." And I said, "Okay, I'll let you get on with it." "Don't leave, Vince." And I said, "Nope, this is y'all's problem. You gotta figure it out. I'm gone."

Q: So you saw a lot but you weren't really involved?

Vince: And one guy when I first started he was, same way. He got off too good and he come 'round crazy-eyes wantin' to hurt somebody or . . . was in a motel room one time and 'bout thirty minutes after I left some girl got killed . . . I'd a seen that on the news and they showed the room number and I went, "Woo! I was just there!" I never had a lot of trouble with the tough guys, 'cause I had good dope. If you ran a place and you're cheatin' 'em, lyin' to 'em, they're gonna cut your throat.

He briefly explained how he avoided such violence.

Vince: I did good straight upstanding business. Some of the meanest bikers in [city], when they seen me it was all smiles, "How you doin'? Come to my house."

Bryant described a close encounter with law enforcement. He had been making meth in the back of his truck.

Bryant: When you're to the peak of that high, nothin' mattered. An officer stopped me at the [number] mile marker, I was so high I had [a] meth cook going on in the back of the pickup, she never smelled it, she never saw it, the wind was blowing just right I guess. She walked up, she took my driver's license, my hand's on a pistol right beside my seat, she took my driver's license, she walked back to the car, she come right back up there, she said "Mister, I'm sorry, here's your license, go." I'm going, alright, they're setting up a sting operation on me, that's the first thing that popped into my mind. What did I do, I went three or four miles down the road, I gassed what I was doing, I got my product and left, hell, you know. So there's no fear, there's none.

The situation could have played out very differently had the cook been detected—inches and seconds. Lucas elaborated on the violence inherent in the lifestyle.

Lucas: I'd beat the brains off somebody owed me money . . . 'Cause they used my dope, instead of payin' for it. That's my money.

Q: Is there a lot of violence around?

Lucas: There can be. There can be if you front the dope to the wrong person. Nine times out of ten that person is cut off. I grew up in a small town. So if you owed me twenty bucks, John knew about it, Larry knew about it, Joe knew about it, and everybody said, "No, man, you owe Lucas. You better get that money to ol' boy right there." So it just didn't happen much.

The large amounts of money that can be made from methamphetamine distribution and production are part of the attraction; they also can be, for some, part of the illusion. The sums of money discussed by those who dealt and made the drug were significant. They were amounts much higher than any normal person could earn in a week, month, or sometimes even a year. The money was fast; it powered the high life they lived. However, in the end, even the money doesn't last forever. It rarely does. It is yet another one of the aspects of the life that are difficult to maintain in the world of methamphetamine. As Felix explains, *fast money goes fast.*

Felix: When I lived in [state], I was making like stupid amounts of money. Like $30,000 a week, and maybe three people dealt with me.

It was money that would be spent frivolously on whatever he wanted.

Felix: Fast money goes fast, though, like seriously I have . . . like, I have nothing to show for that. Absolutely nothing.

As one of the most successful dealers in the study, he was an anomaly in that he was the only one who had taken his manufacturing activities to a different level. He didn't make the drug primarily to fulfill a personal high and fund the accompanying lifestyle; he manipulated "junkie cooks" to make it for him, thereby making them take most of the risks. He had made significant amounts of money during his time on the streets.

Felix: Selling drugs? I don't know, probably close to a couple million . . . The bitch about it, though, is you get to a point where you're making that much money, but as soon as you do, heat comes down fast. As soon as that much weight is being pushed out on the street, heat comes down fast. That's when you start noticing black sedans parked everywhere and you start, you stay off the drug yourself, so that you know you're not in like some drug-induced paranoia, but you see that start to come down, and then you immediately have to slack off. Because the best way to keep yourself out of trouble when the heat comes down, ninja vanish. Just that whole like, poof, gone in a cloud of smoke, everything stops, just because when you keep trying to force your way through, that's when you get caught . . . It's called a ninja vanish, just bam! *Gone.*

Wes described the extreme lengths he had taken to avoid detection with large amounts of amphetamines in his possession. The incident occurred one day when he was pulled over; he was high at the time. He elaborated on the would-be arrest that would eventually turn into a trip to the emergency room.

Wes: Amphetamines. What happened was he pulled me over for probably DUI, probably thought I was drunk because I was kinda all over everywhere. When I would carry large amounts of amphetamines on me, I would have a gallon jug of water, and I wouldn't carry them in separate bags because then you can get intent to distribute, and all this other stuff, so when he pulled me over, I knew I was in trouble, I put the amphetamines into that water, kinda shook it up and started drinking it. I had probably two or three eightballs on me at that time. As I was drinking it, he was knocking on the window, telling me he was about to break the window, and he was going to take me out. But he had the ability to recognize that something was wrong. They didn't test that water, I don't think, because what they got me on was possession, and it was the leftover residue from what was in the bag. Possession at that time was possession of CDS [controlled dangerous substance], possession of paraphernalia, and driving under the influence of methamphetamine.

Chaos ensued. It was what his life had become.

Wes: Early part of [year] is when everything kinda came to a head for me. Like I said, I went to the hospital. I didn't go to jail from there. I recognized these tickets, and I'm like, "What happened?" After I ingested all that, and I don't know how much I took, but ten days later I woke up in the hospital and realized what was going on. They had me chained to the bed and stuff, but they released me from the hospital to my ex-wife. From there, I used in the parking lot. I didn't even get out of the parking lot of the hospital 'cause I felt like crap and what better to make it right than the stuff that almost killed you. I think those were the three charges there.

There had been other events that eventually led to encounters with the police. One would start with a visit to his ex-wife's trailer, where methamphetamine was allegedly being manufactured while his children were present. He had been met at the door by a guy with a gun who threatened to kill him and his children if he didn't leave. The events ended with hallucinations that led to an illegal entry at a "friend's" house that occurred right after he shot up in the car.

Wes: I walked up to the front door of this friend of mine's house, and knocked on the door, and they said, "Come in." At least that's what I heard. To this day, I don't know if it was just an audible hallucination. If that's what I heard, or did they really say it. I don't know. So I walked into the door, and as I walked into their house, they walked out of the house and called the cops, which the cops showed up instantly almost, because they were right behind me. The cops met me at the front door. Actually a friend of mine met me at the front door and said the cops are on their way. I went back to the truck, ate what I had. I didn't want to get in trouble again for possession, ate what I had, ate the methamphetamine, now at that time it was the ice kind and I ate that and I just waited. Because I knew that the [police] were behind me to begin with and I knew that it was just a matter of time. So, they arrested me and when they arrested me, I was already peaking and being at that real high point. I sat down in the back of the police car and I remember asking, and that's kinda one of the strange things about amphetamines, I remember everything that I said, you know when I overdosed twice, I don't remember, there's bits and pieces there, but even when I was high, even extremely high, I still remember what I did, what I said, the things that were immoral to me before I started using that I did, so, anyway, I asked the cop, "Where are we going?" Like we were going to get some ice cream or something. He said, "Well, you're going to jail," which again was a blessing in disguise, and I spent six months in the county jail.

The chaos and confusion precipitated a paranoid-fueled suicide attempt in jail. He described his charges and what happened next.

Wes: Charged with burglary and I think it's second degree, where you just cross over the threshold of somebody's house without being asked. Yeah, I think it's second. And then I was charged with possession, CDS again, methamphetamine, possession of paraphernalia, and while I was in the jail, I was kinda freaking out, I thought they were trying to kill me. I thought they were friends of my ex-wife. All the paranoia set in. So they locked me in this pastel-colored room with a paper gown at about forty degrees. And I was in there for almost a month or so, and at that point, through the middle of that, I tried to slice my wrists and I tore up a blanket and ended up braiding it, and this was all just after a lot of [hallucinations] in between all of that, fighting with the cops, and things like that, when I braided up my blanket, I made a noose, of course, and tried to kill myself then, but there was no place to hang myself, so I couldn't, I mean which was also another blessing. So I got another charge that was malicious injury to city property.

While he himself states that there was "no rational thought," decisions were being made. They were decisions skewed in the direction of preserving his drug lifestyle. His explanation of why he didn't just throw his drugs out of the car instead of consuming them shed light on the significance of participating in such activities in a small town.

Wes: No, they would find it. They would find it, and the thing is, is that town knew me. They knew who I was, they knew that I knew a lot of other people that manufactured. However, most oftentimes I wouldn't manufacture it to sell. I would manufacture just to use. And if I sold in the process, then it was just extra money.

In the heights of paranoia, excessive risk becomes the norm.

As Lucas recalled the time he stayed awake for thirty-seven days straight, it was apparent that he came close to the edge.

Lucas: Thirty-seven days. And it about killed me. I mean . . . I mean I was up for thirty-seven days straight . . . I made this batch and we smoked all night long that night. Everybody came over. I was sellin' and smokin' and smokin' and smokin' and smokin' and smokin' . . . Thirty-one days later, I was still awake. I tell my wife. She was my girlfriend at the time. I said, "Look, there is a red light." I was tweakin' out the window as you say. Just peekin' out the window. I couldn't go to sleep for nothin'. I was scared. I was drinkin' milk tryin' to come down, but I couldn't come down. And my buddy come over and he says, "Dude, you need to go to bed. You're freakin' out. You're gonna die." And that made me worse. Because I had the paranoid state goin' too. People were watchin' me. People were lookin' in the windows. And I was in on a second-story building. I seen lights in these windows across the block. It was in this real big high building that was over there. There was a little bitty camera light starin' at us.

He describes the confusion that ensued.

Lucas: It was all hallucinogenic because after seventy-two hours, your mind will hallucinate on anything, even just regular coffee. If you just stayed awake for seventy-two hours, your mind is going to hallucinate. You're going to see fog in the air. You're gonna see something, shadow people. There's something. And so I kept telling the wife, I said, "They're comin'. They're comin'. They're gonna bust us!"

His paranoid mindset led him to flush nearly all of his drugs down the toilet.

Lucas: I flushed everything that had to do with any kind of drug, except for marijuana. I had three quarter ounces of marijuana weighed up in a tray and it was beside my bed in this little nightstand. I wasn't carin' about no weed. What's weed? Weed ain't nothing.

Only this time his paranoid thoughts were real. The police arrived shortly thereafter.

Lucas: We wasn't asleep like five minutes and I saw these lights in there and I said, "Oh my god, here they are." It was the police. It was DEA, come in lookin' for stolen guns. I didn't have nothin' to do with no stolen guns. I never messed with a gun in my whole life and I never will mess with a gun. And I still to this day will not touch a gun. You hear me? So I'm like "Yeah, search the house." I say, "You sign a paper saying you're lookin' for stolen guns. And you can search this house," because I didn't know what I had left layin' around. But everything I knew of with the methamphetamine was already gone, in the trash, out of the way. He finds the three quarter ounces of marijuana and finds all my money. He said, "What's all this money?" I said, "This is my savins." He said, "Why don't you use a bank?" I said, "Why should I use a bank? Is there some law sayin' I can't not use the bank? That's my money. Get your hands off my money." Well, he tried takin' my money. I called my attorney. The attorney came in and said, "You can't touch that money. There's $38,000 cash there. He's got three quarter ounces of weed. What in the hell is going on here?" So needless to say my lawyer, thank God, saved my money. Which was, it was dope money but they didn't know it was. They was still tryin' to take it. Because there was three quarter ounces of weed layin' there. Three seven-gram baggies of marijuana, which when they took us into the police station the next day to interrogate us to find out where these stolen guns were, because somebody told 'em they traded me a stolen gun for this methamphetamine. So they wanted the meth. So they're asking my wife all this stuff, and they're asking her, "Is he a user or a dealer?" She said, "He's a user. He's been usin' me for ten years." So that really made 'em mad. So then one thing led to another and we walked out of the police station. But I still got to kept my money. And they couldn't charge me with the marijuana, because they stated they were lookin' for guns. So then we moved that night, when we come home from the police station it was five o'clock. By eight o'clock that night, we already [had] everything out of the house in a U-Haul and down the road.

The dangers are not restricted to those that come from the police. The world itself is violent. It can become deadly. In a world where violence becomes a necessary part of everyday existence, there are many who get hurt and others who die. Death was a common topic. Sometimes deaths were due to drug overdoses. Like others, Ava spoke about her friends who had overdosed and died.

Ava: I've had three. This is my third one. [Name] and his wife, they just had their second baby on Easter Sunday and their baby got taken because she had been doing Oxycontins, weed, and I don't know what else was in her system, but she went to jail like a week after the baby was born. I think her and him got in a fight and the night she went to jail he was taking Oxycontins and drinking gin like he always does. I mean, just not trying to overdose. And he suffocated on his own vomit. And now before that, a few years ago, when I quit back in [year], and I guess it was [year] I think I quit, but I had a friend die then. And that's what made me quit that time.

Death can be an outcome of the violence linked to the drug lifestyle. Felix described an encounter where somebody had been shot but lived. Having come from a rough urban city, he arrived to a violent world in a small rural town.

Felix: It was absolutely terrifying, it's just this little rinky-dink country town, but seriously. I was playing a poker game one time, we were just sitting around playing poker in an apartment and this dude walked in and everybody was like, "Hey, what's up?," and he pulled out a .25 and shot somebody in the head. Why? Because that dude ripped him off on a sixteenth of meth. And then somehow the guy didn't die. It was really weird. The bullet went in and then around and out, and somebody called the cops, and dude went and hid in the bed and pretended to be asleep, and then after the cops left they were hugging and he was like, "It's okay, I understand," and I was just like, "Guy shot you in the head, are you serious?"

Q: He didn't have to go to the hospital?

Felix: I mean we tried to get him to go to the hospital, but he was spun, he didn't care. But there's violence all over. All over attached to it, people will kill for that, people will, quite literally, die for it. I've known of people who go kill for a bump. "I will give you an eightball if you rub this dude out" . . . You see it with meth and crack.

Zach talked about the negative consequences for others he had known.

Zach: I had some friends that had died and got locked up for a long time, and I had just got out from getting locked up for a long time, and I knew I couldn't stop and so I wanted to stop. I didn't want to die like that. That was pretty much it. I did not want to die.

Q: So, is it true what they say: you stop, die, or go to jail?

Zach: Yeah, pretty much.

Q: You had friends that had died from meth use?

Zach: Meth use or been murdered or just that whole lifestyle.

He described the violent methamphetamine subculture.

Zach: I think a lot of it's the drugs. I mean the people I hung out with and did drugs with and manufactured and bought drugs with, we would stay up for weeks at a time and things would get really crazy. And so we wouldn't eat that much and we were all dangerous and as opposed to, I guess, I assume a heroin junkie, they're actually sleeping, and they may be just as dangerous, but you get deprived of sleep for a while and you become pretty irrational . . . I mean we would carry guns and . . . Yeah, it was a violent . . . subculture.

Q: Like fights and things?

Zach: Yeah. And people tend to get mean the less they sleep and the higher they get. We'd get mean.

He elaborated on the violence.

Zach: Physical violence . . . Physical. Eventually it got to where weapons would be involved. I've had somebody come after me with a hammer, and we've shot at people and had people shoot at us and . . .

Q: What causes that? Is that the illicit market or is just being high on meth?

Zach: I think it's both. I think the longer you stay up it's a lot easier to get more violent . . . That, and I mean the subculture is violent anyways. And the more you get into it, the more violence is an option, and so I think people on stimulants, whether it's cocaine or meth, I think it's more violent.

He spoke about some of the facilitators of violence in the drug world.

Zach: Came close to getting caught a lot, I've been shot at and shot at people.

Q: Were you ever hit?

Zach: No, I've never been shot. Or stabbed or anything like that.

Q: Was that all because someone didn't pay, or what is it?

Zach: Someone didn't pay or, or they felt that it was cut too much or things like that . . . Yeah, it's a violent market. I mean that.

Being coldhearted and mean were essential to survival in the world of methamphetamine. It explained much of the reason Zach manufactured after being released from prison. He combined knowledge learned while incarcerated with that obtained from a high-school friend. He talked about the partnership they developed and what he brought to the table with him, a willingness to do what was needed to protect himself and his friend making the drug.

Zach: I think he had it down more, I brought, I think I brought . . . I don't wanna glamorize it. I was . . . I was meaner, and everyone knew I was in prison before, and so that carried some weight for him. And I think he, he, capitalized on that. Saw an opportunity, and I'm not, no one's a victim, I'm just saying from my perspective I can understand how that would work, you know. 'Cause he didn't need my help in manufacturing it, he knew how to . . . he needed somebody who was willing to pull a gun on somebody, or somebody who was willing to jump up and do something.

And that was something Zach was willing to do.

One of the men who had taught Felix how to cook eventually died making the drug.

Felix: It was this weird nasty way that I didn't really like, it combined both, it was really, really dangerous and the dude that taught me blew himself up.

Q: He died cooking meth?

Felix: He died in an explosion in his house. He was like eighty years old, and he had like the most country name in the whole world, but thirty years prior he had been diagnosed with terminal lung cancer, and they'd given him three months to live and he was like, "Well screw it, I'm just gonna keep doing what I do" and "I'm not gonna change, I'm not gonna do chemo, I'm not gonna [do] any of that, I'm just gonna keep smoking cigarettes, keep drinking." Dude lived for thirty more years, right, and finally died because he blew up a meth lab in his kitchen.

Q: That's crazy.

Felix: Yeah. Yeah. His son was gone too, his son was just off. I was sitting there with him one time and he was like, "Hey man, you wanna see how to get real tore up?," and I was like, "I guess," and he's like, "You take a shot of vodka and then a shot of lighter fluid and you just keep doing it," and I was like, "Dude you can just . . ."

Q: A shot of lighter fluid?

Felix: Yeah, I was like, "You can just drink vodka or whatever," and then he like lit a cigarette, I was like, "Are you serious?" That guy was crazy, he's dead too ... He OD'd [over-dosed] on meth.

When it came to surviving in the drug world he once lived in, Felix preferred violence over death.

Felix: They dealt with other people, I didn't care what they did as long as I got kept out of it. I personally don't like guns, I just think it's a terrible way to die, just in an instant your life is done, it has to mean more than that, and I don't like guns at all, I don't mind fighting, and I was very violent. I guess I've been on my own since I was twelve. I've been taking martial arts forever, I'm a trained fighter, I understand how to not only win but completely incapacitate you, and if I have to break your arm, break your leg, whatever, well then so be it. You only have to do it once.

Q: But that probably helped you?

Felix: Yeah, you only have to do it once, to set an example, people leave you alone. You brutally beat the shit out of somebody and everybody kinda leaves you alone.

He discussed the steps he took to protect himself from these dangers.

Felix: I don't know, pay attention to your surroundings ... Yeah. Pay attention to your surroundings. Watch the people that randomly show up, watch where they're coming from, watch who's dealing 'em, always, always have a gun on you ... Always, always be ready to fight. You always carry at least one gun, whether you're willing to use it or not. I used to carry a razor blade in my mouth and always had a knife ... Always keep a razor in your mouth.

He elaborated on the purpose of the razor. When asked if it cut his mouth he responded:

Felix: Not if you cheek it right, you take the sharp part of the blade and you put it up there and then if you need to spit it out you just let it fall on your tongue and spit it out and bam, you got a weapon.

Q: What, if anything, did you worry about when you were dealing?

Felix: Getting killed, going to jail.

He would survive despite attempts by others to take his life.

Emme's experiences changed as she became increasingly immersed. Her life evolved into one characterized by violence and danger. The potential for violence was aggravated by the production of fake dope that she and her boyfriend made and sold when money got tight. She described the violence she witnessed.

Emme: I've seen him be violent with other people . . . People he would sell his fake dope to. People would come back and want their money. And then they'd put a gun to him or whatever, and he'd beat the livin' tar shit out of 'em.

There were dangers that existed in dealings with others as well as those closest to her. She recalled the two times her ex-husband tried to kill her.

Emme: My ex-husband, I've seen him to where he wanted so much more. He's sittin' there tryin' to get whatever he can off that bowl. To me that's a junkie. "Go to bed. Who cares? Get some more later. It's like it's not going to be there. Who cares? Go to bed." He needs a big reality dose, he tried to kill me twice.

Q: This was while you guys were using?

Emme: Well, we had got off of it, he was kind of off of it. When we got back from [state], when we were arrested in [state], we went a couple months without doing it, and we were with this friend of his, and he became one of my best friends, he's now dead. And he was a pillhead, he wasn't a meth user, but he was like my angel at that time. I was talking shit, and I'm very big about that. I'm [a] very opinionated, expressive person. And I had walked away, and he [ex-husband] came behind me, picked me up and snapped my back, and threw me on the ground and he covered my mouth. I couldn't feel my legs. I couldn't scream, I couldn't breathe, and his eyes were black and he wasn't high. And this friend heard, because we lived in the top part and he lived down here. He heard something. He ran up, knocked on that door and ended thrusting the door. If it wasn't for him, I probably would have been dead. Did I stay? Yes.

Q: And then what was the second time?

Emme: The second time, he was high. He was gone. This is the worst he'd ever been. He'd probably been up for weeks, days, months, I don't know. He held me hostage in my own living room. It was like he was two different people. It was, it was indescribable. I made my mother come get my kid and my dog, but I stayed. How stupid is that, right? I shoulda have left then, but I didn't. He accused me of sleeping with the guy that was the heroin addict, because he would come home in other people's clothes. It was amazing. And this guy's boxers were upstairs because he came home in 'em, and so he accused me of sleeping with him because his boxers were upstairs. I was like, "Are you kidding me? Are you serious?"

Q: He probably didn't remember?

Emme: He didn't. And he would just go off on me, and he had a knife to my throat and, and then he would fall asleep in the chair, because he was so high, and then he'd wake up and he'd see me crying a little bit and he'd go, "What's wrong? Are you okay? Are you okay? What did I do, what did I do?"

Q: How long did he hold you hostage?

Emme: About four hours. I didn't want to leave him. I've cleaned his shit, cleaned his puke. I've fed him, I've bathed him when he's been on it, because he wasn't capable of doing it for how long he's been on it. I think at the time the guy that he was running with, I think he was putting heroin in it, because he would have the symptoms, come down off it, you don't act like that. I don't care who you are, unless you're shootin' it. That was my only explanation.

Q: Do you think he knew he was taking heroin?

Emme: No, I don't think so. I think [dealer] was trying to make him more addicted. One time he came home and I was at my mother's house. He called my parents at three o'clock in the morning and I ended up running back to him. And I went in the house, and he stood there, "Where the fuck you been?" He just went splat right on the floor. I carried him upstairs. I fed him. I bathed him. I cleaned him. I put him to bed. I laid beside him to make sure, I was scared if he regurgitated or puked, that he would die. So I made sure he rolled on his side and he had got, rolled on top of me and he cried, and he said he can't do this anymore. Well, what do you do when somebody does that? How do you walk out on somebody like that? What do you do? And I didn't know what to do. Our lives were pretty messed up. He's a good person, but he's messed up. And he's the love of my life. I don't care what anybody says. He's the only person that under-stood me. He's the only person that gets me. He knows me to a T. Nobody else will ever, the guy I'm with now, he doesn't know me at all. We've been together three years. How ironic is that? [Ex-husband] treated me horribly, but a lot of it was dope. It wasn't him, it was the dope.

One of Emme's biggest fears was being killed for selling fake dope. To sell methamphetamine that has been diluted or "cut" is one thing; to sell com-pletely fake dope is another.

Emme: I was afraid of being killed, 'cause I sold a lot of it myself. And I even know how to make fake dope . . . You need money, you need money, you'll do what you can. That rent's got to be paid, you're gonna do what the hell you can. You know, I would sell a lot of fake dope for a good amount, $200 or $300.

Emme seemed to have figured out a way to trick users into thinking her fake dope was real meth (i.e., by adding codeine pills or "some other shit in it"). As she became more immersed, her involvement in crimes to fund her drug life-style progressed. She eventually started shoplifting and committing other retail theft-related crimes to get money to support her drug use and life. She had to be high to pull her crimes off; being high is often part of what it takes to engage in such risky activities.

Emme: The only way I . . . ever, ever would know how to do something like that, I had to be high. I had to be high. There's no way I would have done it consciously. No way. I would take it back to [store]. I knew that you had to have a cutoff. You'd get a [store] card. You'd have so many things in there, fifty dollars, you'd have somebody come in there and look at it, then you get questioned. You want cash right there, it had to be less than ten dollars. Take a gift card, you go buy a phone or whatever, get a gift receipt, take it back, get your money . . . I did that a lot. One day, he had his bail at six hundred bucks. It took me twelve hours, but I did it.

Q: You got $600 in a day.

Emme: [Yes]. I've taken stuff from stores and taken it back to [store] all over the place from [town] to [town] to [town].

Q: And they never caught on?

Emme: Nope. Nope. Thank God. I was never caught. I'll never do it again. A lot of those stores I won't even go in them now. I stay away from them. I won't even go in them.

The things she did impacted her even now.

At her height, Vanessa was using *"all day, every day, nonstop."* Though her use had been functional for decades, it proved to be unsustainable in the end. She eventually struggled to maintain her conventional life as things began to spiral out of control.

Vanessa: When I look back, it went with, how devastating, I felt in this, in that time period in my life, so with my first marriage, when it hit a low I started using really, really hard. So probably I was about twenty-one after I'd had my first kid, and I was back from [state], we was in [state], and used hard. Just used as hard as hard could get, with drinking and marijuana all together. Meth, drinking, marijuana, always together. Used hard-hard-hard-hard. Then got pregnant. Stopped. Have the baby, drinkin' starts again. Marijuana starts again. Meth, here it is, let's do it again. Got so sick, and at the end of the '90s got so sick I probably weighed about eighty-nine, ninety pounds.

She had to go to great lengths to escape detection. At the height of her use the county drug task force moved in across the street to practice their enforcement-related activities.

Vanessa: I had a three-bedroom here in [city] when I had first moved here, and fell back hard into my addiction, was losing the home, and the drug enforcement task force for this county moved in across the street from me ... Right, and used the house as a experiment house to do mock break-ins.

She held mock garage sales to move drugs.

Vanessa: As I am using my house as what I called a crack house, because all I was doing was runnin' drugs out of it. I was moving, using a mock garage sale as a traffic cover ... Yeah, yeah, with them using their house as a mock bust house right across the street from me ... What is that? [laughs] See, addicts are brilliant people. We are brilliant. You want to take me out of addiction, I can be an engineer, the things that we can do ... Mock garage sales.

Q: So what if somebody showed up?

Vanessa: I mean I had everything out there. Everything was priced ... I was moving, so there were things that were happening that were legitimate ...

Q: And they had no clue?

Vanessa: Never knew.

Q: My goodness.

Vanessa: And that's another thing about with my addiction, I was very, oh I don't know, I don't want to say militarized but "don't be a jerk in my house," and we used to call 'em window ninjas. If you come in my house, and you get high, you'd better stay away from the window . . . "Don't be looking out the window. I'm not going to open it to the community, but I don't need you up there doing that. You can leave" . . . I was very smart.

On the violence that was present, she said:

Vanessa: Well, with me and my partner, whoever that was at the time, whether it was my husbands or my partner, like one instance, we had been up, and it was just a bad moment, I think that we either were waitin' on some dope, or we had some dope and neither one of us would share, but to the point where he was chokin' me out, upside down in the car and I actually broke his finger gettin' him off of me, so I was just as violent. I split my first ex's eye wide open, and he didn't even know I was using, and he just came at me the wrong way so I just laid him out, which that doesn't make any sense to anybody, I'm [a] very gentle spirit now, but then . . .

Q: Is that enhanced by the methamphetamine?

Vanessa: Absolutely. You're a, oh *you're a powerhouse.* There's no pain, the adrenaline is so high, it doesn't matter. And driving down the road one time I've got two pounds of meth, and probably four pounds of marijuana in the car . . . And we come up this hill, we are on the highway and two Highway Patrols have a road stop, and I pull right up on 'em, "What's up?," never blinked an eye, just arrogant.

Q: You are kidding?

Vanessa: No. One time I went through this town, and my car had a issue with its headlight to where it would juggle and it would come loose, I got pulled over. I'm sittin' there, I've got three ounces of dope in my bra, paraphernalia in my side cart, and then marijuana, and I had to push-start it to get it to going, so he pulled me over and I turned it off and I said, "Okay." I got out of the car, I said, "Now you have to help me push-start my car, because I can't get it going, because you pulled me over." Arrogant.

Q: When those things happened, you weren't afraid?

Vanessa: No . . . If I was going I was going. If I was going down I was going down.

Her confidence, or cockiness, increased over time.

Vanessa: Well you get so cocky, twenty-three years of drug use and then I finally get arrested. The more that you get away with it, the cockier you get.

Q: The more confident you become.

Vanessa: Absolutely, and it's ridiculous.

Q: So when the stop happened, they basically talked to you and let you go?

Vanessa: Yeah, well they said, "Your headlight's out," and I was like, "Oh," so I got out and I fixed it and I said, "Yeah, I'm having some issues, now will you please push-start my car so I can go?" And I'm a female, now that don't work with males, it would be a totally different.

Q: It was probably to your advantage to be hiding it as a female versus a male?

Vanessa: And I can guarantee you that, if you look online, with women, they all have a codependent. And this is from my personal experiences, and every woman, plop, right in your lap, "You can hide it." And we take it, you know, we just, there's just that codependency and then, lack of self-esteem and, "Yeah, we'll take it for ya ... We'll take the charge, take the drug, take the charge, whatever." Just like with those pounds, he's like, "Here," I'm like, "Okay."

Dillon expanded on the chaos.

Dillon: Yeah, I ran out of choices. The best cliché is that you make your best choices when you're out of choices. And things like that, I ran out of options. I stayed at the halfway house, it was like a sober halfway house thing, 'cause I went to a detox center first, I remember I had two dollars in my pocket, I was walkin' the streets and was walkin', nowhere to go, kinda paranoid, not knowin' what's goin', not from drugs 'cause I hadn't used in a couple days, and I was just paranoid because there was so many people lookin', lookin' for me, and I went to a mutual old friend of mine, and I went by there to rest for a second, and she was like, "Well, I'm on my way to work and you can't stay here," and she's like, "Where do you want me to drop you off at?" I'm like, "Over there I guess," I mean, one spot's no better than the other, and so she dropped me off over on [street] and [street], south side, and I was walkin' and it started raining. And I was like, I don't know what to do now, then I remembered that detox center, and I took one of my two dollars and went to the bus station. Took the bus to the referral center, and I stayed there for like seven days, and they got me into the halfway house.

Life had become transient towards the end.

Dillon: I was constantly unstable, I was in motels a lot, my car, I'd sleep in my car ...

Q: Were you homeless or would you say were just kind of transient?

Dillon: Transient slash homeless. It was like I said, I was sellin' all the drugs for motel rooms and stuff like that, and you never really wanted to stay anywhere, because if you stood somewhere for very long, paranoia and the heat [police] and all that would come along, and we would take over people's leases, if somebody had an apartment, they're movin', and they have like a month or two left, we'd take over, and we'd basically squat there until the sheriffs were comin', and then we'd bail out.

Q: So you just kind of went wherever?

Dillon: Yeah. Whatever's available and whatever you could afford.

Risks and danger came from many sides; when asked about what he worried about most, he said:

Dillon: Getting caught, and getting set up, because there's such treachery involved in the methamphetamine world, that you're always worried about somebody setting you up, settin' you up for some kind of some deprived thing or something.

Q: Backstabbing or doing something behind your back or something?

Dillon: Yeah. *Hot shot* is what they call a lot of 'em . . . They take something that would probably kill you, and put it in your drugs, or in your needle to get rid of you, because you either done too many people wrong or you're taking too much money from them.

Q: So you had that in the back of your mind all the time?

Dillon: Yeah, and most of it was paranoia, 'cause, I don't know if it ever happened to anybody, but that's always somethin', for some reason it's always talked about, and somebody always knows somebody, but I personally have never known it actually happening to anybody.

He spoke of the risks that went along with the sharing of needles among users of the drug.

Dillon: Hepatitis, AIDS, all that, yeah, matter [of] fact a lot of the group that I was messin' around with did, and when I went to jail, when I went to prison, one of the first thing they do is test you for all that stuff, and I was waiting for the results and I was *sweatin' bullets.* I was worried to death 'cause I almost knew, 'cause that's another thing, you know, people who shoot up, some of 'em are honest, and some of 'em will try to say, "Oh no, I never shared," they're lying. No junkie can sit there and say they never shared a needle, and you don't care, somewhere in your head you'll say, "Okay, I'm gonna wash it with water several times," and all that, but it comes down to you're gonna use that needle.

To avoid having his manufacturing-related supplies discovered, Troy had taken things as far as attempting to burn down his own house. He failed and was charged with second-degree arson and endeavoring to manufacture methamphetamine.

Troy: They tried me with first-degree arson, if I would've had a lawyer I probably could of beat it, and I should of got me a good lawyer but I didn't, but they couldn't really charge me. They lowered the first degree to second degree, which made it from a violent to a nonviolent. So that's why I took that, but really if I had a good lawyer I could have beat that, because my home at the time, it didn't have insurance on it, and so it wasn't like I was trying to burn it for money or something like that, I was just trying to burn it *to burn the evidence.*

Q: How far did it burn?

Troy: It didn't even burn, none of it did. But I did all this in front of the cops and they seen it, they kind of witnessed it, so.

The chemicals in his possession at the time leave little doubt that he was manufacturing.

Troy: But when I got busted I had like, a couple products that I had hid out in my shop, I had half [a] pound of red phosphorus and like four hundred grams of iodine crystals . . . And I had I think about 170 grams of ephedrine, and that was enough to bust me, with a endeavorin' meth, but they didn't catch me. Why I got endeavoring to manufacture is because they didn't catch me like in the process of making it.

For him, there was a difference between being caught with products to cook with versus in the process of actually making it. The latter had never occurred. This time the police had been tipped off after somebody in the drug world had snitched.

Troy: Somebody snitched on me . . . I kind of got leery of them, and I didn't sell no drugs to 'em, but they was kinda comin' around and I think they was tryin' to set me up with guns and stuff, I noticed.

Q: So they were trying to set you up?

Troy: Yeah, just the person that did that to me was like actin' real weird and I kinda had a feeling, I said, "Something ain't right," 'cause I can pick up on stuff like that, and plus they was like tryin' to set me up with these guns, these assault rifles and stuff, and I was thinkin' "that's weird" and she was tryin', the last time she come over, I don't know if this is 'cause they wanted to get me a bigger sentence or something, but I was already a felon at that time and I was thinkin' I don't need no guns or anything like that.

Q: So you didn't keep guns?

Troy: She's trying to give me a cut-off shotgun. What is it? A sawed-off shotgun. And I was thinkin' "man something ain't right." She's wantin' to buy some, and just kind of relentless with it, but I guess she kinda knew most of my business at the time or what was going on. I was just too involved with all this stuff and I didn't play my cards right, I wasn't smart at all about it and they come in on me.

He explained what happened next.

Troy: They told me, when they got there, they read me the warrant and everything, and that they got me out of the house, me and my wife, and they said, "Y'all can leave but y'all can't be around when we go search this house, you're not arrested right now, you can leave, but if we do find something then we are gonna put a warrant out for you . . . There's gonna be a warrant out for your arrest." I'm thinkin', man, I got some . . . it was on the search warrant, I had it in my shop, and I had some in my house too, and so I just went out to the shop and got some gas, I act like I left, and while they're all lookin' and stuff, I started like dousing my house with gas and stuff and I lit it, and they seen me and then they ran and tackled me.

It is a risky game, one of life and death. The stakes are high and the risks tangible. For some the consequences are long-lasting; for others they are permanent.

So why are people willing to go to such lengths and accept such risks? The answer lies in part with the love of methamphetamine; it is something many of them speak of even now, even after losing it all. Another part of the answer lies with the excitement and thrill that comes from doing things that are forbidden and living life on the edge. Those in a world where violence and retribution are commonplace have to be willing to engage in certain risky activities themselves to stay safe and secure. As is often true, the higher the risks the greater the rewards.

CONCLUSIONS

Risk and danger are ever present in the methamphetamine world. Dangers accompany each aspect of the life and present themselves from those in one's immediate social network as well as those on the outside. In the illicit world there are some risks that can be controlled or minimized and others that cannot. It is not possible to eliminate all risks.

Those who become immersed eventually break the illusion and begin to see reality. Over time, use spirals out of control and truth becomes indistinguishable from hallucination. Informal and illegitimate rules govern the underground black market within which meth is bought, sold, traded, and made. It is a world where violence, retribution, danger, and death become known truths of everyday life.

The rewards of using, dealing, and making the drug seemingly outweigh negative consequences and risks, at least for awhile. Over time, the costs of involvement shift, as perils become unavoidable. As people become further immersed, things transform. Eventually the lines that separate right from wrong and good from bad are crossed.

As the intoxicating life becomes a risky one, the truth, the reality, and the costs begin to reveal themselves as they really are. What started out as fun and exciting inevitably turns into something much more. Things are set in motion to become even worse when people arrive at a point of willingness to do anything to maintain and sustain the lifestyle they are leading. Just as in real life, it is darkest just before the dawn. The truth of the tragedy is that the world of methamphetamine is perilous and precarious. There is an ominous truth to living life so close to the edge. Everything changes when, like galaxies or planets spiraling through the universe, the lives of those immersed in methamphetamine spiral into darkness.

CHAPTER 8

A Dark Life

There's a price to be paid and I absolutely traded my soul for meth and I believe I lived on the edge of evil for a long time.

—Ian

INTRODUCTION

As human beings we carry all that we do within us. Only we know of the darkest places we have ever been to and the truths of the ethical and moral boundaries we have crossed in our own lives. It is rare to speak of such things aloud, much less tell them to a complete stranger. As the adults spoke, it was evident that they were conscious that by even speaking these realities, they were once again bringing into existence the most hidden facets of their own beings. The risks of even *admitting* to such things were high, even now. The risks were not those related to being detected and punished for what had been done, but the risks of acknowledging the truth of this dimension of their lives. But they did it anyway. For this, I will always be appreciative.

Be forewarned that the stories presented here are among the most gut wrenching and haunting of all. They will likely settle in your mind in a way that makes forgetting them difficult. These are the specific parts of the interviews and the lives they conveyed that were the most difficult to accept. They are among the most challenging to comprehend. Even now, these stories seem incompatible with the faces of those who spoke them. The stories reveal some of the obscurest edges of humanity and shine light on the depths of danger, destruction, and despair that exist deep within this world. The darkness that exists within each of us comes alive in the world of methamphetamine.

It is critical to understand that darkness is not just related to clandestine manufacturing. Rather, it relates to each dimension—to each aspect. It exists within users who find themselves doing anything to get methamphetamine or the money to buy it. It exists within dealers who relish the deleterious power they hold over the bodies, lives, and souls of those who desperately crave the drug, and the lengths they are willing to go to maintain some semblance of order and justice in the underground world. It exists within those who manufacture the drug in clandestine laboratories. They are the cooks, the ones who create the very thing that they know, perhaps more than anyone else, has the potential to destroy the lives that come into contact with it. They are the cooks who carelessly and frivolously put innocent lives at risk of peril. It is reality; it is a force that must be confronted, recognized, and acknowledged. It is real. It is hard-core. It is darkness. It is methamphetamine.

RISKING ALL TO STAY HIGH

Those who become immersed do whatever they have to do to get high and stay high. At his lowest point Dillon had isolated everyone, including the dealers who had been supporting his habit. He described a time he went without using. While this was not by choice, he made a point of clarifying that it was not due to him being incarcerated at the time.

Dillon: I went like six to nine months, I'm not exactly [sure] how long. And that was because I got to the stage where nobody would mess with me. My family hated me, drug dealers were lookin' for me, I was hated by everybody. Nobody would even let me in their home or nothin'. 'Cause I would steal, lie, cheat, whatever it took to get the drug.

When asked about what he disliked about meth his response was clear and concise.

Dillon: I think meth is treachery, deceit, and . . . paranoia.

After years of heavy but secret and seemingly functional use, Vanessa's life became unmanageable and out of control. Her husband, a veteran, eventually became involved too. Within three months of using, he started manufacturing. Vanessa reflected on her divorce and how her own desire to maintain access overrode any concern she had for her husband. She kept him cooking to maintain her pure supply of the drug.

Vanessa: So we're going through this divorce and we got the kids, maintaining two households, 'cause we have a business, I mean we have a very, very, profitable business [we're] running together. So I'm tryin' to keep him at bay, and keep him cookin' the dope that I get for free.

Q: And you're running the business simultaneously?

Vanessa: I'm running the business, taking care of the children, and keepin' him cookin' dope inadvertently. I'm *manipulatin' him*, he doesn't know it 'cause I know I'm gettin' the pure dope, he's not even aware that I'm even takin' the dope that he's makin', that was my first experience with that, and the life, his life just changed so dramatically, and watching from the outside in, what they would start doin'. They started stealing, because at that time it wasn't necessarily ephedrine-based dope, they were still using, oh my goodness I can't remember.

Q: Was it P2P?

Vanessa: The cattle fertilizer that they eventually put, I think it was still phosphorus, but maybe not red.

Q: This was the '90s?

Vanessa: This was in the late '90s, yeah. But this is . . . rural, and this is just learning, so. That was just, I was in awe. I was in awe of what was actually happening. 'Cause for a minute it was hidden from me until I was, wow, this is what's really happening.

Q: That he was cooking it?

Vanessa: Yeah, because it was everywhere, I mean not like everywhere but it was just, there was so much of it and finally he, yeah, he actually showed up on my doorstep one day and he had the acid that they use splashed on his face so he had acid burns all over his face and I was like, "What's goin' on?" I took him in, took care of him, and he's like, "Here's what I'm doin', and I've been up for seven days now," and I'm like, "Wow, wow, okay, I don't know how to handle this, but give me your dope" [laughs]. So sick.

It is the sick and tragic reality of what eventually happens when methamphetamine becomes the most important thing in one's world. In this reality, people find themselves doing things that under any other circumstances would be deemed unacceptable.

Putting oneself and one's addiction before the health and well-being of loved ones was a common theme. Vanessa expounded on her thought processes the time she believed moving manufacturers into her home would help her get her children back. It would be nonsensical anywhere outside this altered world.

Vanessa: This was my thinking at that time . . . I tell this story because I was, I actually told it in group in my program and my counselor was so astounded by the fact that I said it. I said, *my mentality was* that if I could *move the meth cooks*, and *cook meth in my house, that I would get my kids back.* Which makes *absolutely no sense*, but I was convinced that that was the solution to my life at that point. Because my kids were not in my life . . . I actually ended up homeless for a while and I said, "Dad, take the kids, I can't take care of 'em."

In her experience, this had been different from the other drugs she used.

Vanessa: But [I] ended up fallin' in my addiction even further, so I didn't come back out of it, it's so deceiving, the addiction is, and then that type of drug is not enough to harm you on a daily basis to the point where you have [to] detox, or you are feeling any physical ailments immediately from not havin' it, but enough to not let you go. So you function daily, you may function daily, or weekly to the point where it's not defined that you're even sick, because, and I've looked at other uses like with heroin, I mean you literally, immediately, you've got a monkey on your back, you're hurtin'. When I used cocaine, I don't want nothing else to do with it, 'cause as soon it was gone, I hurt, I physically hurt. Marijuana, if I had smoked it, I'm all good, but if I didn't have it for like a couple days I got really, really irritable, really testy and just like, "What's going on?" Same thing with the pills, but with meth it was just like you went to sleep. So it was really deceptive, and by the time you woke back up it was already there again so you just did it. So I don't know if people would make a choice. I know I didn't and I wouldn't have at that time . . . as much as I wanted to. It's so conniving that it can convince me that I was okay in my own life, that I could continue to use. That's why I used for twenty-three years, and maintained a business, raised my children, no one ever knew, and *I used,* I used, I mean *I used.* I went to college. I maintained an A average . . . Nobody knew.

The fact that she had successfully hidden her use from those she lived with surprises her even now.

Vanessa: My kids, they never knew. My eldest, he'll talk and he'll be like, "Well, you know," and God bless him, he just did a conference and there was some questions about the conference and they were askin', "Well, what happened during this time period in your mom's life," and his statement was, "Well, she wasn't doin' it at that time," and it was one of my highest-using points. He said, "I knew like marijuana maybe but she wasn't using meth at that time."

At her lowest point, she began doing anything, things she never imagined, even becoming what she self-described as "slave labor."

Vanessa: I know at one point I was spending $225 a week just for personal use. This was during one stint, that was even before this last time, which was more selling, and unfortunately in my situation it was almost like slave labor, they were, they had to have me in a position where *I did what they said, for the dope.*

She estimated that during the course of her twenty-three years of heavy use, she has spent $40,000 to $50,000 on the drug. Given the extent of her use, the estimate could be low.

During her deepest periods of use, Ava showed a willingness to inflict harm on others. As she talked about how she changed as a result of sleep deprivation, she recalled the time she asked her friends beat up an ex-boyfriend she dated for six years. The event occurred during the time she had mentioned staying awake for thirty-eight days straight.

Ava: I had a [friend], he was a dope cook. He was cooking dope for some people that I had known a long time, and he had stole a lot of dope from them, and they didn't know it was him that did it. I told them, because I had known these people way longer than I had known him, and they all jumped and beat him up really, really bad. I mean he was in the hospital and it was all because of me. And I had helped them . . . Yeah, I mean I helped them, you know, beat him up and it just it makes you feel horrible afterwards 'cause I mean why would you . . . I'm not violent.

In her experience, meth had been unique as well.

Ava: Oh, every bad quality you have that you would keep inside of you, like your violence or anything that you tell yourself, okay, I just need to calm down and relax. When you're on meth everything comes out that's bad . . . meth just makes it, everyone will call it the devil's drug, anybody on meth, because it is.

Q: It's different than all the other drugs?

Ava: It is. It's so addicting and it just grabs you so fast and it's a demon. It is a demon, because it makes you that way. It makes you evil. It makes you, it's horrible. It is the worst. I mean if they could do away with any drug in the world, it would have to be that one because I've done 'em all and that is the worst. It's horrible.

Ava placed her own grandfather at risk multiple times. She contaminated the house he let her live in by manufacturing meth in it, and had once left an anhydrous ammonia tank in the back of his truck for two weeks.

Ava: I mean my grandpa rode around with a tank of anhydrous for like two weeks and he had no idea, while I went to jail. And I called my mom and I was like, "Mom, you gotta get that propane tank out of grandpa's truck," I said, "and go do something with it." And I said, "Go have one of my friends, the guy who came and cleaned the house out, and," I said, "he wants what's in there. Tell him to come over and get it because I don't want you riding with it and grandpa has no idea," 'cause my grandpa went and picked it up from my garage and puts it in his car and is just riding around with this anhydrous, had no idea. So I had someone go over there and get it.

Demonstrating a willingness to put others in harm's way is not surprising given meth users' willingness to harm themselves. Mia discussed her own personal moral failures as she talked about the impact of her use.

Mia: Oh, well, morally, I mean I slept with people, I mean, I wasn't . . . I wasn't married. I didn't believe in premarital sex.

In addition to placing herself at risk, she exposed her child to risks as well.

Mia: Those people that would come over when I'd have her on every other weekend. And then my relationship with her, I was not emotionally there. I wasn't emotionally supportive. I couldn't emotionally connect.

Q: So it impacted every part of your life?

Mia: Oh yes, yes, in a negative, negative way. It's like you lose your soul. And I was just so, I just remember. There's a saying that sin will take you farther than you wanted to go and deeper than you wanted to go and longer than you wanted to, and I mean I am just so blessed that God had mercy on me and spared me.

Methamphetamine clearly impacted her and altered her unwritten rules of behavior. She changed all that she was and was not willing to do, for the drug.

Conner expanded on what he viewed as the "real crimes" associated with this lifestyle. He adamantly supported the need to tell the truth about it and the fact that people can and do get out. For him and others, this was a critical part of the story; it would be the main reason he agreed to participate in the interview in the first place.

Conner: Though it's only 10 to 15 percent of people that get out, *there is an out.*

Q: And that doesn't get told very much?

Conner: It needs to be told, and that's why I really am here, is I just want people to know that's out there using it, there is an out, and most of the time, I've never really met anybody that's got off methamphetamine without the help of the Lord, though. It really is the hardest, it's worse than crack . . . I don't know what it is, but it's an epidemic and I think it's Satan's tool to destroy our nation, and it's working, actually. It is destroying so many people's lives. And people always say, "Well, methamphetamine, it is not really bothering you that Joe's out here using," it but it's a crime to himself, is what it is.

Q: And that doesn't get talked about very much, either.

Conner: It's a crime to himself because, *it destroys everything about you,* I mean it really does, you know. I introduced [my brother] to it. He started messing with it, using a little bit and then he caught him a case where, for conspiracy to sell methamphetamine, where he'd went over to somebody's house, sold them meth, there was an undercover cop in the back room. They come out, they arrested him. He's on five years' probation for it now. He's cleaned up from it. He don't use methamphetamine at all anymore, either.

Conner would forever have to live with the fact that he was the one who introduced his brother to the drug.

Wes similarly acknowledged the impact on his own morality as he spoke about what he disliked about the drug.

Wes: Well, the weight loss. I looked like I was sick. When I looked in the mirror, it reminded me of my mom, because my mom has the sunken cheeks and stuff. I didn't like when I would get really high, I couldn't shoot up, so I'd have multiple injection sites and I guess the things that happened in my life, losing my kids, losing my family, gosh, the people I was around, the violations of my own morals that I was raised with.

His statements about the gun he kept in his house at the time were insightful.

Wes: I had a gun in my house. It was a .22, and I had it just for protection, because people knew that when Wes got done manufacturing, then there's going to be a lot at his house, not to mention all the chemicals needed to manufacture. And so people would break into my house to steal the chemicals or to steal my dope. And that's what I'm protecting. I'm not protecting my family. I'm protecting the dope. So the dope was more important than anything. There was the time I said about going to my ex-wife's house and a guy pulling a gun on me. How he would kill me and my kids if I left with 'em. I became a recluse after that. But when people would break into my house, I'd get violent, because that's my stuff plus my kids are there. You just don't, dude. If you need somethin' just tell me. Give me a call, or knock on the door or somethin', but you don't go through my windows.

Wes placed himself at risk to evade detection, taking personal risks over legal ones. Time and again, he placed his own well-being and life in jeopardy, and he had done it all for meth. He talked about the lack of concern for others when discussing the disposal of the toxic waste products left over after making the drug himself.

Wes: What happens at that point, and that's what people are dumping in the streets or in the sewers or somethin' or the frickin' side of the road. That's the leftover stuff.
Q: The waste. Is that toxic?
Wes: Oh yeah, very toxic, it's all of what you've done.
Q: Will it still explode?
Wes: I don't know. I never was around. So I'd drop that stuff off somewhere in the country.

While he seemed conscious of the environmental hazards that existed, he lacked concern about the effects of laboratory disposal and potential contamination. He took things one step further, giving leftovers from a cook to others who wanted the drug; this took selling to a new low. When asked if he disposed of the residual materials outside, he stated:

Wes: Yeah, and I didn't know; I wasn't aware of the damage that it can do to the ecosystem and the environment. Or you can try to sell it to somebody who's an IV user, that'll try to re-gas it. What they will end up with is the junk, and now they're shooting all that, the pseudoephedrine the pills have, there's just a lot of other chemicals that they're gonna end up shooting, which is not the amphetamines, but yeah, it's bad stuff.

He rarely thought about the impact of all that he was doing. Everything came second to the quest for the drug. He described what he worried about when dealing and making the drug.

Wes: The consequences of getting locked up. I never thought what I was doing to other people's families or anything like that until after the fact, which is also a motivator to not manufacture and to not sell. I sold to teenagers and stuff like that. Like my ex-wife's brother was fourteen when we got together, and he'd smoke weed and stuff, but when he knew that we were doin' meth and he started actually bein' home with us smokin' and he'd spent the night for weeks and stuff and we'd get high straight through. When I started shooting up, he asked me about it, and I wouldn't say I regret anything, but it was one of the things that was hard to deal with, but I gave him his first shot of dope. And now he's off frickin' I don't know where. I guess some of the thoughts were, "What am I doin' to that person?" Not necessarily what am I doin' to everybody else around that person, because I viewed me using as affecting me only. At the end of my addiction, I could care less whether you knew I was high or not. As a matter of fact, I'd tell you. I didn't give a damn who you were, the police, whatever, because I was hurting myself.

Putting others in harm's way is one thing, purposely getting them addicted is another. Lucas reminisced about a multiday-long binge during which he partied with people he didn't know in a new town. It was a party with a purpose: to get rid of the meth he had just produced and to get a new group of people hooked.

Lucas: I made this batch. And we smoked all night long that night. You know what I mean. Everybody come over. I was sellin' and smokin' and smokin' and smokin' and smokin' and smokin'. Everybody was sharin' because it was new to that town. I moved from where I lived at to another town. And I was introducin' it to these people in the bar. And it just got to the point where we smoked a whole ounce that night with people, sellin' it. People I didn't even know. I was just gettin' rid of it to . . . Just to get my money, just to get that town hooked more or less. Get the monkeys on their back. Just to be a little prick but yet to get my money back so I didn't have to go travelin' with the methamphetamine. It just come right across the street to me from the bar. I was so high . . .

His manipulation of others continued as he talked about one of the two females he had ever known to cook meth. He described a time he challenged a cook on the quality of her finished product versus his.

Lucas: She was old red cook . . . I think her dope sucked, if you ask me. I told her, "You take that junk home, don't bring it back to my house." She said, "I'm the best." "You ain't the best at nothin', bitch." That's the way I told her. I said, "Here, you try that and take that home with you. Put ten cents of that in your arm and see what you think." She come back the next day, still like, "You got any more of that?" "Nope. I got that from [state]. I don't even know where it comes from. I don't get it no more." 'Cause she was a bitch.

The power that came with the ability to give people the drugs they desperately wanted and the control that comes with giving it to them or withholding it from them seemed natural; it was power that accompanied having the very thing others so desperately wanted.

TAKING IT TO THE EDGE: LOSING SOUL AND DOING EVIL

There are levels of harm and danger within the world of methamphetamine. The blackness that permeates the world becomes brightest at the point at which all soul is lost. It is here, at this point, that all bets are off. This is where the most evil actions are committed—to those immersed in the lifestyle and those around them.

The most tragic and heartbreaking realities occur when completely innocent lives are placed at risk for meth. Natalie's story illuminates the complete power that immersion can have on a person. The fact that she delved headfirst into the world was unsurprising given that she had to learn to survive from a very young age. The abuse she had suffered as a child taught her that she had to be tough to make it.

Natalie: I was abused when I was a child. I was sexually abused when I was a child and therefore, in my mindset as a child, I got really aggressive. It wasn't towards women; it was towards men, and I would not intentionally, but I would pick men and I would fight with them. Well, it was to show them that I could take care of myself. I did a lot of treatment work on that and then I came to find out my aggression towards men and the abusive relationships that I've put myself in . . . stemmed from that.

Violence and abuse were normal parts of her existence from childhood. There had been no consequences for the sexual abuse she suffered as a child or for the rape she endured at age sixteen. She survived a suicide attempt at nineteen. Her several missing and broken teeth served as souvenirs of the chaos and violence she experienced. Natalie had gone straight from an abusive and chaotic life into one she would help to create, only hers would be worse. She admitted using and cooking meth during two of the three pregnancies she carried to term. She spoke about how everything eventually spiraled out of control due to her addiction.

Natalie: In my case it took me a lot longer than it does a lot of other people to hit bottom, but I still had my, my morals and my standards were somewhat in place at that time. And my addiction wasn't stronger than those at that time.

Q: When you were younger?

Natalie: Right, when I first started using, yeah. As I got older my morals depleted and, not my beliefs depleted because I always believed and I always knew that using drugs was a bad thing, but I always, I don't know. I don't even know how to put that. How would I put that? My addiction was stronger than any belief I had or any moral issue that I had, and as bad as I felt and as much as I wanted to quit, I couldn't quit.

While she had stopped during her first pregnancy, she continued to use, albeit less frequently, during the second. Having found out she was pregnant at three months, she didn't tell anyone until she started showing, six months into the pregnancy. With her third and final pregnancy, she continued using the entire time and carried the baby to full term with no medical care. She elaborated on what went through her mind during the times she was using and pregnant.

Natalie: I just wanted to keep gettin' high. I wanted to keep gettin' high. Somethin' in my mind, our disease tells us we can control it, and it's okay.

Q: Did you know anything about the potential risks?

Natalie: No. I figured, and this is so sick, I figured as long as I could feel him movin', then he was all right. Because sometimes when I'd use, I'd get sick. And throw up, you know, and I would think okay, I need to stop. And I figured he'll let me know. That's sick thinking.

The extreme danger she had put her unborn child in is difficult to comprehend even now.

Natalie: Oh, we took precautions about getting caught, but we never worried about getting robbed or nothin'. That didn't come till later. I got robbed twice at gunpoint when I was eight months pregnant with him. It was all within a matter of two weeks.

Q: What did you do?

Natalie: Cussed 'em out. Really, I was to the point at that time I just didn't give a shit. It pissed me off worse than it scared me.

Natalie compromised everything that was important, including herself and her unborn child. She compromised everything for methamphetamine.

Natalie: At the end of my use, I was using $300 a day, about a quarter ounce.

Q: That's a lot of money.

Natalie: Yeah. I never really got into the money part other than making the money, I never really spent a lot of money. *I sold my soul more than anything* . . . I mean I compromised everything I ever believed in. Taking care of the children, taking care of yourself, your family . . . for me to be eight–nine months pregnant using dope, I had turned into everything I hated.

The tragedy of her situation revealed itself when she explained her thoughts on what she believed needed to be done to deal with the problem. The stark reality of where she would be had she not tested positive when she had given birth to third son, who was now twenty months old, was unforgettable.

Natalie: We have to educate our kids. And parents have to start being parents. They're starting so early now having kids, most of the first-time offenders that have kids, we don't break the cycle, we have to take care of our children. Had I not tested positive, and had I kept him, I would be living in a dope house with him right now.

Q: Do they test everybody?

Natalie: No. Now they test pretty much everybody, but not everybody. I was obvious. I never had a day's prenatal care. I never did anything to protect my child.

She regained custody after successfully completing treatment, but this child would be the only one she would keep. The realities she had created were permanent. She explained the impact it had on her relationship with her now-nineteen-year-old firstborn son.

Natalie: My nineteen-year-old, he loves me and he forgives me but I don't know how, honestly. I was never there for him. I've never been there for anybody but me. I wasn't even there for me. My parents, I just quit lettin' my parents love me years ago.

Matthew similarly lost sight of everything that mattered as a result of his addiction and immersion. His was a no-holds-barred path of destruction and devastation.

Matthew: It didn't matter. It didn't matter. I sat in front of a probation officer and did a shot before I went in and seen her one day. I go in and my eyes are goin' [crazy]. I've bought it, I've made it, I've sold it, I've shot it, I've gave it away. I see a homeless person on the side of the road, look like they were hungry. They tell me, "I'm hungry" or whatever. I'm like, "Well, you want to smoke? I can get rid of your hunger pains." And I've sat in the truck and smoked right there in front of the mission, sat there and smoked in front of it in my truck. It didn't matter.

Having crossed the line of righteousness long ago, there were no longer any rules with regard to who he was willing to take with him as he went. He understood the seriousness of all that he had done.

Matthew: It destroyed a lot of relationships that I'm having to work real hard at to get back. My parents didn't trust me. My sister didn't trust me. Friends that I used to have. Me and my wife was fightin' all the time. Or me and my fiancé was fightin' all the time. Me and my wife, we was gonna work stuff out and she almost OD'd and had to go a nut ward. She started usin' it because I was usin' it, because she wanted [to] just fit in. And it was just a bad ordeal. I destroyed a lot of lives, and God forgive me for that.

He claimed to have once sold a house he owned for the drug.

Matthew: I owned a house once and I sold it for meth ... Moved to a motel. They said, "Man, I'll give you $58,000 for your house." 'Cause I was gonna sell it and buy another house, but I was wantin' sixty-five for it. He said, "I'll give you fifty-eight for it." Well, I had all good great plans, but like thirty-five thousand of that fifty-eight went to dope.

Matthew's willingness to put other peoples' lives at risk to evade detection was disconcerting. He had taken things to the edge of madness, claiming to have gone as far as rigging his vehicle with a detonator; the plan: blow up the car if it were ever at risk of being searched or stolen. He elaborated on the scheme as he talked about the safeguards he employed.

Matthew: I do use security cameras and I also carry the .357 revolver, fourteen-inch barrel, Smith and Wesson, at all times. I slept with it. I also had a remote detonator on my car where if it was searched or stolen.
Q: What would that do then?
Matthew: Blow up. Yeah. It would blow up underneath the driver's seat . . . It was built into the cushion of the seat. It was only dynamite hooked to a detonator . . . Detonator can't explode unless I detonate it, and I had to activate it. I only activated it when I got out of the car and was going to be inside for several hours.

He alluded to the risks inherent in coming clean about the destructive and criminal things one does. He made it clear that some things would have to remain unspoken forever.

Matthew: It took my family away. It took lives away. It took a lot of time that I missed out with my son. It hurt me in a lot of unhealthy ways. It just, I mean everything. I lost cars, lost relationships. I've seen lives lost about it. I've done things that I can't really talk about that I wish that I had never done, that I can only ask God, between me and him, can I ask for forgiveness, because the . . . That's one of the steps, you know, make amends, to where you can make amends, but there's some things you just can't make an amends to . . . to anyone but God, because . . . I'll give you an example. In AA, there was a guy that got sober. He was sober for twenty years or somethin'. Thirty years back, forty years back, maybe longer than that, he committed a rape in his addiction. Well, thirty or forty, fifty years later, when he got sober, he went to this woman. He never got caught. He went to this woman to apologize and she flipped out on him and locked him up. That amends shouldn't have been made but between him and God.

As bad as all that had been described was, in reality things may have actually been worse. Sometimes it is better to not know.

Lucy expanded on the life she once lived; here again, the contradictions between all that it offered and all that it took were apparent.

Lucy: I mean a lot of these people, gosh, are running around, getting busted with meth labs in cars, got three kids in the backseat and they just, I'm telling you, that is Satan in his purest form, methamphetamines, ice, and I've done a lot of time with drugs and dope and on the street and in the game, I have, but meth took me down a road that, I mean it scared me. It scared me, I've lived a hardened life, I've had a rough road and there's nothin' that you couldn't put in front of me that I have[n't] done or seen or heard about or experienced in some way, and methamphetamines being the number one on

the list as far as being the most tempting, the most satisfying, there's a life, there's tons
of money in it, you lose your family because you've burned all those bridges, you lose
your kids because of the choices that you make, but meth makes it, it's weird. It supple-
ments anything and that's why I believe it's evil. It is evil, it is evil. The people that are
doing it are evil, I mean they have no morals, no values, everything that they were, it's
gone. I mean meth just takes over, or it ruins your look, it ruins your mentality, it ruins
your emotional, I mean everything, you become so completely detached from reality
and as long as you're doing the dope, you don't care. You don't care, and that's the sick
thing about methamphetamines, it's so sick, I think it's an epidemic.

The illusion was a real part of her story. She spoke about the conflict between
what she now thought about her prior experiences and the way she perceived
them at the time.

Lucy: You don't care! You don't care . . . I liked the dope, I like methamphetamines, I
don't like the people, I don't like what it brings to you, I don't like what it makes you
become . . . *You lose you* doing dope, it's never what you figured you'd be. As a matter of
fact it was really crazy, 'cause a friend of mine that I went to middle school with, haven't
talked her in fifteen years, for the first time I kinda had to get on the phone and talk
about me and what I've done with my life in fifteen years, and I never imagined that I
would become who I am, and I never imagined, just because I wasn't raised that way. I
mean my grandparents were really involved in my life, they were Southern Baptists, and
I had kids that I loved and cared about and respected, I cared and I loved myself and
respected myself in a way, but you get involved in dope and I mean all that shit goes to
hell in a handbasket, I mean just bam, gone. You don't even know who you are, you don't
even know who you are. You lose everything, you don't care about love or commitment
or honesty or respect, anything that makes a person decent or right, it's all out the
window. As a matter of fact it's the complete opposite, it's all about the dishonesty and
who you can beat and how you can lie and how you can steal and who's car you can steal,
it's [an] all-out mission to get high. No matter what. It doesn't matter if you're risking
your kids, you're cookin' dope in the house, and they don't care, they just don't care. It's
all about the dope, that's how powerful it is, that's the high.

The dangers that went along with the drug-fueled binges she had lived
through seemed to humble her now. She talked about her own experiences
going without sleep for days and the dangers interacting with others similarly
sleep deprived.

Lucy: Those people have been up for two and three weeks at a time. Those people
would make me freak out, they would make me more nervous, that in itself. God, you
can tell when someone's been up for weeks, you can tell, you can tell . . . It's very scary,
it's not scary while you're in it, because you're in it, but on the other side of it, looking
down on it, it's very scary. So scary I will never go back. It's not my desire to be high. I
love speed, I love speed, but what outweighs that is the effects of it, what you go through
because of it, you lose. When you're a woman and you can't provide yourself monthly
products . . . it humbles you, it's humbled me, just because I've been there, I've been

there and I understand it, it's very humbling. Just that something, one something can take so much from you, you lose. Girl after girl after girl sleeping with this man for dope or that man, it was all about whatever they had to do to get high. At all costs, at all costs.

Daphne also went to low levels in exchange for meth. Even before becoming a heavy user of the drug she would sneak out to bars and have sex in exchange for it. She recalled her early experiences with the drug.

Daphne: That was just periodically in the four years prior to [year]. I would wait till my husband passed out drunk, and my kids would be asleep, and I could go to the bar that was only a block away and drink some beers and shoot some pool, and then somebody finally would come up later and it was generally a man, and he would say, "Hey you wanna go do some crank?" And I said, "Okay," and then I hate to admit, but I would have affairs with them.

Q: In exchange for crank?

Daphne: Not really in exchange for it, because . . . 'cause we were actually friends, they didn't expect that, but once you do that type of drug, once I did that type of drug, then all inhibitions were gone. Crank or meth.

She talked about the levels she would go to, once her use began to spiral out of control.

Daphne: Sleep with people, or try really anything, you were just on top of the world, if somebody said, "Hey, let's go kick a door in and steal all these people's stuff," which I wouldn't, I said "Sounds like fun," but I still, thank God, had that deep down, what I was raised with, morals, it wouldn't let me do stuff like that. Now when I lived in [state] until I was extradited out of there, I did so many things I never thought I would in my life, but, and I was definitely heavy in my meth use right then.

Q: Can you expand on that, or as much as you feel comfortable?

Daphne: I associated with a large bike group, Hells Angels . . . I did things, group-type, threesomes, things like that I never thought I would, I was in lesbian relationships and I actually questioned my own gender, my sexual orientation because, 'cause that was okay, I liked that, I was with, actually she was my girlfriend instantly when I was with her for the first time, just those two years of my life were just hell.

Q: So probably is a lot facilitated by the drug?

Daphne: Oh yes, yeah, yeah. She was a dealer and I couldn't afford the drug, so, "Yeah, let's try this, I'll try anything once," everything was okay to do and easy to do.

Sleeping with those who deal the drug is one way to maintain access to it; stealing from those around you is another. She elaborated on some of the attractions.

Daphne: To have [cash] in that world, that high-pressure world, that was very addicting, not as much as the meth high, but you've got people coming to you, someone came to me once and said they had a black leather jacket, a Harley jacket, I wanted one really bad, and people would come to us all the time and say, "Hey, I've got this, and I've got that," and said things like, "Hey, I've got this jewelry box," you could look at that and you could tell that that is great-grandma's, you could just tell. The pretty old little rhinestone things that probably don't amount, there might've been a diamond or two in there somewhere, and look at that and go, God, there were times that I'd say, "Take that back to your granny's, and here's a twenty sack, and don't come back to me with somebody else's stuff." But then there were times I would say, "Oh well, that's pretty cool, I like this box."

Promiscuity and the exchange of sex for drugs is not unique to methamphetamine. The heightened sexual stimulation that is viewed as positive in the beginning becomes transformed into one of the most troubling types of exchanges of all—the trading of one's body for meth.

Katie's final relapse would be the worst one she experienced. Her description of the situation and the lengths she went to maintain access to the drug was unnerving.

Katie: I waited a year. I got involved with someone. She had actually been clean, and we were dating, and I can't really blame her. I'm not gonna say it was her fault I relapsed because I, I've learned that relapse starts in our minds. We know we are going to relapse before we ever relapse. But she made a comment one night after we had left the club, "I sure wish we could get high," and I was like, "Are you serious?" and she's like, "Yeah," and so I went to my old dope man, and that was the worst mistake I'd ever made in my life . . . Because that was my biggest, biggest and worst, relapse . . . I lost everything. Everything. My son. Parental rights. My family. My home. My life. My freedom. My mind. You name it, I lost it.

By her own account, she had taken losing it all to a whole new height. In her attempt to maintain the high life, she found herself hiding under beds and lying in wait to prey on those who could involuntarily fund her now unsustainable drug habit.

Katie: I was literally, between her and me doing what I was doing and she was doing, together we were spending anywhere from $1,500 to $2,000 almost every day on drugs. Whether it'd be crack, cocaine, or methamphetamines . . . She was prostitutin' and connin' old men out of money and stuff like that, and I was robbin' 'em. I was robbing them while she was having sex with 'em . . . I was underneath the bed robbing them, taking their credit cards, taking their money.

She had clearly crossed a line; it was the line of willingness to do anything for meth. As she answered a question about whether or not she had hit rock bottom it became clear that she had reached a new low.

Katie: I think I'd went straight to hell. I think I passed rock bottom. I know there was times I hit rock bottom, but I literally think my life had went straight to hell. I was in *so much darkness* that I was in *living hell.*

Having been to nine rehabs in thirty years, she describes hell as she lived it.

Katie: I don't think it's where you put a person that's going to help. It has to be a state of mind . . . You have to want that. And I say that lightly because there are people out there that want it, but they don't want it bad enough. And I mean, for me . . . I'd hit rock bottom, but I didn't stop. But when I hit hell I stopped. And you'll know what hell is. When you lose your mind, and you've lost everything else, including your mind, you're in hell, you've got two choices. Give it up, or pretty much die, because you're already dead, I mean you might be walking, but you're dead, you have no emotions, no feelings, your body shuts down. Feelings? What are them? You're so out of your mind you don't know what a feeling is. Your kid, and I say this from experience, my son, he told me one time, he said, "Mom," he said, "Please just quit doing drugs and go to heaven with me." And I'm like, ssssh, "Yeah I will son, someday." What part of that wouldn't move a normal person? And I just blew him off like he was nuts. He's six, seven years old, "Mom, go to heaven with me," I'm like, "I will, baby." Just laughing at him, "You're so cute," I was so high that day, I remember that.

Having spent a life filled with hatred for her mother and self-destruction, she was keenly aware of the lines she would cross.

Katie: I became one evil person. Very evil. Sadistic. Evil.

Her experiences and memories of them continued to haunt her today.

Katie: It stands out in my mind, 'cause it's a part of me that hurts, it hurts me to sit back, and now that I'm in recovery, God allows all these little things to come to me so I can repent for 'em, that's my theory. All these things that pop up into my head when I'm watching TV, and it's God's way of telling me, "Hey, Katie, time to repent for that," so I do, I quickly repent.

It is important to note that not everyone who uses meth goes to the lengths mentioned here. Some had clear limitations on what they were and were not willing to do for the drug. However, for these adults, this was the exception rather than the norm. This was something Jessica struggled to understand as she talked about her use and the choices she made.

Jessica: I know one other reason why people stay using it, it doesn't make you feel bad, I mean no matter how long you use it. It's been fifteen years for me and it's always a good feeling. I mean it releases all that dopamine and it makes you feel good, and I don't understand the people that lose everything for it, they just go the other way, I don't quite get that. You start stealing from each other and robbing people and all that. I've never quite understood that part of it, but then again people who don't do it don't understand my part of it. So I can't say that they would be that way. I think you have some things in you automatically that makes you . . . I could never rob anybody. But I think maybe that some people that do that, they've always had things in them and it doesn't seem to bother them, and people who sell their bodies for it, and stuff like that, it's just something they can do. I could never do that, so maybe that's why I've stayed the way that I am.

More commonly, individuals struggled with their choices and the impacts of these on themselves, their lives, and their loved ones. Danger, risk, and death are very real parts of the world. They were aspects detailed with clarity and insight by those who had experienced them firsthand. For many, methamphetamine takes control over their lives, leaving them with two incompatible realities. It seemingly gives them everything they wanted while taking all that they had. It was a contradiction by any definition of the word.

Evan: It's sexy. It is. It's something, there's a power that goes along with having a bagful of crank. Everybody wants to be your friends. Girls will do anything to get it. I don't want to go into that, but girls will do anything to get it. Everybody wants to be the guy that's holding the bag . . . It's very dangerous to be holdin' the bag, too.

Q: Wow. How so?

Evan: Well, one of my best friends, not one of my best friends, but a guy that I went to elementary school with was a regular guy, and he had an ounce of crank. And a jar full of quarters. And he was hanging around with some people, they were smoking a joint, and one of these people was a couple years younger and he was always saying how he would kill anybody. He didn't care. He would, "I'll do [it]," everybody thought he was full of it. And they were sitting in a little circle smoking a joint, and he just took that gun out and shot my friend in the head and killed him.

Q: Was he on meth, too?

Evan: Well, he shot him, so he [took] his ounce of crank and his change, and then he did it at somebody else's house, and dragged his body to the garage, and wrapped it up in trash bags, and put in the trunk of his car and took it out to [an] area where they were building houses in [city] and set it on fire, and my buddy didn't deserve that.

Q: And that's why you say you don't want to be the one holding the bag?

Evan: Sure. Someone would cut your throat over an eighth of an ounce. A quarter of an ounce. That's, that's enough to keep somebody on for weeks, very dangerous. So usually if you're going to sell any or make any or something, you usually have some kind of a weapon, a firearm of some sort. And you can't just bluff around about it, either, I think you really have to back up what you say or nobody will believe what you're saying.

Q: Is that more of a risk to you than the police?

Evan: You're not afraid so much of the police. The odds of [the] police finding out, finding you, while you're manufacturing methamphetamine are a thousand to one, unless somebody doesn't like you or you've sold some bad, some low-quality [meth] to somebody and they call and say, "Hey, listen, so and so is makin' it." Yeah, you fear the other, people, not the, not the police.

He described why becoming malicious oneself is critical to survival.

Evan: Most times, let's say nine out of ten cases, to be involved in the manufacture, the sale, the use, of methamphetamine, you've gotta be pretty mean. You gotta be mean in the head, mean. You gotta be able to talk mean, to threaten somebody, "If this happens, then I'll tear your heart out, and I'll cut your throat, if this happens." And you gotta kinda mean it. And more importantly, the people you're dealing with and everything have to believe that you mean it. Because if you show any weakness or anything, you will get hurt, or overrun ... or killed. A lot of people have disappeared, and anybody who knows them probably knows what happened to them. But I also think it would be very hard to overdose on methamphetamine.

His ongoing struggle between his love of methamphetamine and the price of the lifestyle was unmistakable. He spoke with an urgency of life and death, almost seeming, in the very moment he was speaking, to be battling the conflict within.

Evan: I couldn't, I can't, I can't do it. I can't be around it. And I know I'm not going to be around it, because I got tired of my life being a living hell, because it seems like all the time you're lookin' for it, lookin' for it, lookin' for it, then you find it, then you get it and do it, and then you're lookin' for it again and again and again, and it just, I've done *some really bad things to get it*, stolen, I've stole vehicles, I stole an RV trailer, it's *a miracle I'm not in prison.*

Like many others, he had taken methamphetamine and everything that had come with it back to his home and family with him. He expanded on the violence his use of the drug had brought out—it was hurting those you love in the most real and immediate way possible.

Evan: I was married, at first, married with a child, then let's see, I had an apartment by myself when I started using it again, and then, after that, pretty much with my second wife, her and I together. My first wife and I used it together. Then I shot myself, and stopped. Then my second wife and I were clean and sober, and we started using it together, living together and everything, and I got wild, and beat her up, and went to jail, and stopped, and then when I went to college I had an apartment by myself.

His awareness of the link between methamphetamine, violence, and the risks that went along with immersion was enlightening. He described the interrelationship.

Evan: It's just a different life, of violence and methamphetamine. It kinda almost goes hand in hand ... It's very ... low class. Methamphetamine is for poor people, I think. Methamphetamine is a poor-people drug, and the reason I say that is because this much methamphetamine would get you high for thirty-five or forty hours. That much cocaine would get you high for two hours. You get a lot of bang for your buck, and it's really, really bad for you. Your teeth, your skin, your, it, it doesn't just speed how [you're] feeling and everything, it speeds up everything, and it speeds you right up to your death. I mean, you'll die early if you keep using methamphetamine. Everything speeds up, everything.

He expanded on the violence.

Evan: When you get high on it, there's just a feeling like I can almost do anything. I feel stronger, and faster, and I feel like tougher, and maybe I know what's going on a little more than you do . . . I'm thinking, I don't know, it makes me more volatile, it makes a lot of people more quick to do something violent, and erupt or something, do something bad and then get away. I've seen some people get really hurt.

Even he would refrain from speaking certain truths.

Q: Were you involved in any other violence when you were on it . . . If you don't want to talk about it, that's okay.

Evan: Oh, alright, can I not answer it?

Q: Sure, absolutely.

Evan: Okay, thank you . . . Okay. I don't really, that might implicate other people. I don't want to talk about their business. This is just me . . . Just me. I, I've never, I have never committed murder, or certainly not. Am I innocent of murder? Of course. Of course I am.

Bryant also talked about the permeating violence. Enforcers are a vital part of this violent world.

Bryant: How much violence do you want? . . . Well, I partaked with men in [city] who was in with the biker gang. One of my biggest things was, I don't know if you understand the term enforcer, I would run around with their enforcer. If somebody owed them money, drugs, whatever, we would beat the shit out of 'em, take it, whatever it took to get. We would take their kids' toys, it didn't matter. And I mean that's sad to say now, but there's no, no level of not doin' whatever it took. Many guys we beat the hell out of.

Q: So is it a violent world?

Bryant: It is a violent world, very violent. When I got out, [friend's] dead now, but I went and seen [friend] and I told him I was getting out, all the way around and he says, "We don't let people out of this very often," but he says, "You've showed us enough in all the years that you've been with us," he said, "We're letting you out" . . . I'd run into 'em at the courthouse or in a bond deal, 'cause I've still got a three-year probation deal through [city], conditional bonds up there, that I sit and I see these guys from time to time and it's like old friends meeting. There's a respect there, I quit, don't push it on me, if you push it on me then we're gonna have issues.

Getting and keeping respect is critical for survival in the world.

Bryant: They could have made it very difficult, but with one of their own, saying he's out, they have to listen to the upper chain. If one of your elders tells you, "Leave 'em alone," you leave 'em alone. One of the things I can never do, I can't never go back up to [city] or that area and run into somebody and let it ever get back to the higher chains that I'm wanting to get back in, okay. Because if you do that and there's lawyers involved in this outfit, if you go back up there and you do this, then your life is wiped out. One thing I do not want to do, jeopardize my family, what I'm building now, because everybody has got to do what they got to do, and it's nothing personal, if I go back up there and I run into "Steve" and I say, "Okay, Steve, let's cut a deal, give me some dope," I'm gonna go back and start selling. Well, I've disrespected them, and one of the biggest things, one of the key things in methamphetamine is respect. You have to have respect.

The violence that had become an integral part of his existence inevitably spilled over into his personal life and home. He explained why this was the case.

Bryant: You do it so, so much that that's all you know. I would never play with kids, I didn't want kids around me at the time. When I walked in a room, I took over that room. I didn't give a damn if everybody was watching me, I wanted everyone to watch what I was doing . . . I mean that's just the type of person I was, very coldhearted, very coldhearted.

Ian was living proof that things got even more ominous the deeper one got. Having delved headfirst into using, dealing, and manufacturing, he found himself part of a dangerous dance with those who were supposed to be on the right side of the law; it was corruption at its worst.

Ian: 'Cause . . . my active addiction went so long, the truth is, when I was in [state] I always tried to have a rural place. That couldn't be seen from the road, there was one way in and one way out, I did all kinda crazy shit . . . But the truth is, in the middle of this deal I'm payin' the cops $4,500 every forty-five days. But it doesn't really matter about that, the truth is if you can come to a bigger problem, and the cops are being investigated, they're not gonna go to prison for Ian. I realized all that, that's why I left [state] one time, is *I couldn't tell the good guys from the bad guys*, and I left.

The stakes of this and the risks involved are real by any measure. It is the blackest of places. It is a place where the good guys cannot be separated from the bad ones. When asked about what he had worried about most, he responded:

Ian: I worried about the police different times, especially [the] deeper I got into it, I don't, yeah, I was worried about the police 'cause I knew the truth about a lot of things going on there, and a guy that I was involved in the production of methamphetamine, he believed we could do whatever we wanted no matter what, the meth, and that wasn't the truth and he's dead today, they shot him. So, I'm not sayin' I was right, but I wasn't wrong either.

Q: Did you ever worry about getting robbed?

Ian: I been robbed but I always brought retribution down on people that robbed me. 'Cause, and I'm not proud of this, ladies, but I want you to understand when I'm in the methamphetamine deal, I'm a madman and I try to make more people afraid of me than the police.

His willingness to engage in anything necessary to maintain the life was a requirement. The lengths he admitted going to seemed to know few bounds. He expanded on the violence.

Ian: All kinds of stuff. I've hit guys with baseball bats ... Here's the deal: I took pride that I sold a lot of methamphetamine, and if you came to where I was selling methamphetamine and tried to get into my market or whatever, I fronted methamphetamine, now what I'm telling you is people who come to your house and are drug addicts and alcoholics or even sober are real bad about makin' promises they can't keep, and then I had to spend time ...go lookin' for 'em. When you get 'em cornered, "Well, Ian, I didn't have the money," "Well how come you didn't come by and tell me that? You came by when you didn't have money and wanted drugs," and I would get angry. They knew when I found them they were in trouble. I've taken people's cars, I've made them cry in front of their kids ...

Violence was an integral part of existence in this world. He described the impact of meth on rural communities today.

Ian: The truth is, I'm grateful that certain things never were involved, 'cause see, I started seeing the fabric of white Middle West America get torn apart, they start throwing mommas in jail and takin' their kids from 'em and stuff, and for many many years, the literature I try to live my life by talks about a loneliness that two people know about, and I know about that loneliness because I isolated myself from other people, now everybody wanted to act like they were my best friend, everybody thought it was great to be me, but the truth is, it wasn't. There's a price to be paid for living that lifestyle, and I was more than willing to pay it. It was nobody's fault, I was more than willing. 'Cause once again that "Just Say No," when I'm in my disease, alcohol and drugs do not take no for an answer. I was way past that.

He spoke of the illusion, the part he played, and why it required him being mean.

Ian: Well, drugs took a toll on our life, and we'd move, and we were gonna do better, and my family was always willing to do their part, I would go somewhere and they'd prop me up, and I think I meant it when I said I was gonna do better, I don't think I was lying to my family, I look back on it, man, how stupid. Because the truth is, I wasn't willing to let the drugs go. The problem [wasn't] Oklahoma or the people in [name] County or whatever, and the truth is, wherever I go I take the problem with me, 'cause the problem's me.

Q: You probably didn't look anything like you do right now.

Ian: No. I was mean, too. I was mean, and you know I been wonderin' for years 'cause, "Ian, you're mean, you're mean," and I didn't even see it. I thought, well, if you had to deal with the stuff I had to deal with you'd be mean too.

Meth took precedence over all else. Drugs were more important than hospital visits to his ailing mother. Ian was steadfast in clarifying that he had not "lost" anything to meth; rather, he had traded it all instead. The points came up during his reflection on when and why he got out.

Ian: I can tell you ladies this, many times I had consequences, and the truth is, for a guy like me ... you'll hear alcoholics and drug addicts say they lost this, they lost that,

I lost my family, I lost my freedom . . . I didn't lose anything, *I traded it.* I traded it, and when I was saying a lot of people say a lot of things, sounds to me like they misplaced it, and I don't want there to be any missed numbers about what I did. I know exactly where my freedom went and where my family went. I'm not proud of that, and that's the truth I believe about it. If I don't remember truth about me, my disease, I'm doomed to repeat that, and I paid a high price for recovery, and I think if you're like me there's a small window of opportunity. The greatest gift I was ever given, guys, was August 27 of 2005, God give me the gift of desperation.

His eventual pathway out of the world was indeed a gift, but it had come at a high price.

Roman and Felix were brutally honest, and by their own accounts were among the worst in terms of what they were willing to do to sustain their livelihoods. Their honesty was as illuminating as it was chilling. Roman was a self-described manipulator; he would give people methamphetamine, all the while making them think that they were the ones who were in control. He was conscious of what he had done and all that he was capable of doing.

Roman: I was the manipulator. You know what I mean. I made people think that they were in control. I made them think they were workin' me.

Q: That's scary.

Roman: Because that's just it. You have to be dedicated to this thing. It's a disease, but you've gotta . . . We always used to make the joke, me and one of my friends, and say, if you're gonna lie, you gotta own that lie. You gotta believe in yourself, and like I said, I'm capable of really being a bad person. I'm changing my life.

There were numerous serious and deadly experiences. Roman had once been stabbed by a man now serving a life sentence for killing someone. He had once witnessed someone getting shot at for smart-mouthing a manufacturer making the drug; the bullet just missed the man's head. He even recounted a time when someone got murdered for not paying a debt.

Roman: I don't know, I mean I really don't know. I just know it was a freezer baggie about that thick. The most I ever saw I guess was just these huge big old rocks that looked like the inside of a Butterfinger candy bar.

Q: And that was that strong stuff?

Roman: That was that really strong stuff, and they made that and murdered somebody before. He was a cook and he owed a meth dealer, or meth guy. He owed a lot of money, or he was gonna kill him, so he said, "I want you to kill this person that owes me money," so he drove a motorcycle, it was a female, and he drove a motorcycle dressed in black with a black helmet, you couldn't see him, pulled up next to her window at a stop sign and shot her with a child in the car.

Q: What was that for?

Roman: Owing money to a dealer, and he had to do it to try and save his life, and he went to prison for that.

Felix acknowledged the hard-core reality of all that he had done with some of the most powerful and yet disturbing words that would be spoken during the course of the interviews. It was about the seductive darkness he had left behind. He described the seduction and destruction inherent in producing something with the potential to destroy not just lives, but generations.

Felix: I found the money addictive, the cook, it's interesting because each cook is like creating a child. It's kinda like the anti-life, and it's kinda deep, but . . . it's essentially like creating a child, that is, it's like creating the Antichrist. You're creating this thing that will bring you all the money you want, that'll bring you all the good feelings that you want, but at the same time, it's just creating a path of destruction that will be felt for generations, and it's very, very empowering. I was never addicted to drugs, but I was totally addicted to selling 'em. That was my addiction, my addiction was the sale, like it wasn't so much the cook, but the cook kinda had this spiritual thing attached to it, you were creating this thing that could just be felt for generations. If you did it right, I mean its impact, its mark would be left on families for generations to come. You get one person addicted, addiction is hereditary, you get one person addicted, odds are their kids are gonna get addicted, and their kids are gonna get addicted, and you're creating this impact, it's the butterfly effect. This one thing you're doing is so deep that it's gonna affect everybody it touches for years and years, possibly generations to come.

Though he had been out for years, the excitement he seemed to feel was evident as he spoke:

Felix: It's very seductive . . . The, the power that comes from, okay, I'm sure you can tell just by talking to me, as far as selling drugs goes, I know my shit. Okay . . . And that in and of itself is so fucking seductive. Just that rush knowing that I own this city, it's mine . . . Not only do I own this city, I own the people. Because if I get you strung out on my product, I hold your life in my hands, I hold your happiness in my hands, I hold your fears, your anxieties, all of it, why? Because I can just sit and fuck with you, you are my puppet. Say I get you strung out right, say I give you a couple free bumps; most people, that's all it takes and they're yours. You own that person, you own their soul, because, say you're having the worst day in the world, I can come by and make it all go away. Say you piss me off, I can make your life a living hell and all I have to do is sit back and laugh, that is so fucking addicting, the power that comes with that and the rush that comes with knowing that I floated two keys of coke in the parking lot of the police station, that's just a rush that you can't get from drugs, that's probably why I never got addicted to drugs, because the rush I got from selling 'em, far exceeded anything that they did for me.

His negative attraction to the life he had once lived seemed to be about much more than just the drug.

Felix: I mean, like I said, I like to watch people and I like to see, this is terrible, absolutely terrible story, but just to give you an example, we used to do crackhead boxing.

Q: Boxing?

Felix: You know crackheads always ground together. You take out a rock, "Hey man, you want this? Yeah. You want that?" Throw it on the ground. "Get it!" Watch them beat shit out of each other and while they're doing [that], pick it up, put it back in your pocket, "Oh, I guess ya'll must of smashed it." I've just gotten two people, with minimal effort on my part, I control these people so much that at a minimal effort I've gotten them to beat the crap out of each other, and now I have them both on their knees, begging me. *Ultimate, fucking, power.* That's what comes from selling drugs, that what comes from being at that status, is you have ultimate control over somebody's, it's more than their life, it's more than their emotions, you control their fucking soul. And I can squash it, I can piss on it, I can do whatever I want, it's mine. That is so addicting, that power that comes with that is so addicting that it, it just, it was the hardest thing I've ever had to stop doing.

His response to a question about what had been the greatest disappointment captured the brutal reality of it all.

Felix: That I destroyed that many people, that it makes me feel bad that I have that much darkness in me, where I took that much pleasure in someone else's destruction. That whole puppet-master thing I was talking about, that's not normal . . . it's part of human nature, we are animals, and animals are all capable of this cruelty, but the fact that I'm able to tap into that cruelty, and that I got that much pleasure of that cruelty, that bothers me. I've always known that I'm more in touch with the primal side of human nature, and I know that I'm capable of doing things that a lot of people shouldn't be capable of. Not only am I capable of it, but I take pride in it, I take pleasure in it, and that's my biggest regret, that I took that much pleasure in the destruction of people, that just, whole families, ruined by my desire for money. I mean what kind of piece of shit does that make me?

Just like several of the others, he had transitioned from a life of chaos, violence, destruction, and death into one that he would create. It would be survival at any cost, except death. The dangers he had experienced from the very beginning prepared him to respond to the worst. He did what he had to do to survive. When asked if anyone had ever attempted to kill him, he responded, "Yeah." When asked how he would deal with that, he stated, "You try to survive, and then later you take care of it." While he didn't ever elucidate exactly what "taking care of it" meant, he alluded to the fact that he had participated in much more serious incidents than any described during the course of the interview.

Felix: I've done things that . . . I've done things that I'd never say out loud, you know, and I don't regret any of 'em. You do what you have to do to survive. I grew up in a fucking war zone, so I mean you either learn to fight or you die, and I refuse to be one of the weak. Not only did I make it out, not only did I survive it, I'm doing something better, and if I can use that to teach people, then fine, maybe I can teach a few people not to be weak. Because that's really all I see it as, is you're weak. You are too fucking weak to survive.

There are things that occur in the world of methamphetamine that are sometimes too terrible to speak of.

CONCLUSIONS

The world of methamphetamine is filled with risk, danger, destruction, and death. It is an illicit world that exists outside of social rules and mores. It is a place where blackness permeates. The only way to survive is to meet darkness with darkness.

The essence of darkness is doing what one has to do to maintain and sustain one's life. It is doing all that is needed to survive a world of danger; it is a world populated by others who are similarly desperate to maintain their lives. In this world, methamphetamine is life. The rules and laws that govern conventional society no longer apply. Calling the police is not an option in the world of methamphetamine.

These adults clearly took steps that led them to the deepest levels of immersion. Yet this is not the place they were ever setting out to visit; it was not an outcome planned in advance. This is difficult to comprehend, even now. Only after a period of time did the true darkness emerge and show itself for all that it is. It was only after a period of time that they came to know the depths of the darkness that resided within them.

Each dimension carried its own type of darkness. It existed in users who found themselves willing to do anything to get meth or the money to buy it. This included engaging in illicit and deviant sexual activities, committing crimes, and stealing from those around them. They lied, cheated, and stole— becoming someone different along the way. The darkness existed within those who dealt the drug and those who made it. They would come to learn the best ways to recruit new consumers and maintain stable customers. There is profit to be made in the world of methamphetamine; for them, it becomes profit at any cost. There are layers upon layers of darkness.

Retribution and revenge prove to be absolute necessities in this risky and dangerous world. They are critical elements of survival. One must transform into the type of person willing to do anything necessary to get what one wants and survive. So they did just that.

Survival in the world of methamphetamine is, at some level, dependent on fear and danger. People must fear those who deal and make the drug more than anything else. They must know the high price to be paid for crossing the lines of expectation and the informal rules that govern this illicit and underground world. There is a price for not paying debts, for engaging in unacceptable behaviors, and for turning others in to the police. Street justice prevails in the world of methamphetamine. Responses to wrongdoers are certain and severe, serving as rejoinders to wrongdoings and warnings to others.

Contradictions abound. The stories presented here did not match the people who told them. The people who participated in this study were not bad people. They did bad things. It is a critical and yet subtle differentiation. As the saying goes, *you don't have to be bad to do bad.* History is replete with examples of people, sometimes even highly powerful and respectable ones, who cross lines of ethics and morality for the greater gods of profit and power. Only here, the god is methamphetamine.

To the extent that these individuals acknowledged what they had done, they should be commended. Not because of *what* they had done, but because they were willing to tell the truth so that we could learn. Each took responsibility for some of the worst things they had ever done; perhaps not in the legal sense, but in the sense of speaking the truth about the darkest events in their lives, at least to the extent that they could. We must respect and appreciate the difficulties and challenges inherent in telling others of our own moral, ethical, and legal failures. For most, these truths remain forever hidden.

Those who become desperate for methamphetamine find that they have crossed all lines of morality. These adults escaped and lived to tell their stories. Their transition out of the world of methamphetamine was, and for many continues to be, a shaky one. Their participation in this study is but one step toward righting the wrongs of their lives and bringing purpose to their experiences. We have learned from their stories of the darkness of methamphetamine. They illuminated these truths so that we might understand. And now we know.

CHAPTER 9

Life after Meth

Living straight is one of the most fucking wretchedly disturbingly hard things, because it sucks so bad, you go to work all day every day, make chump change. Working at that group home, right, I get punched in the face, I have all this crazy stuff going on for what essentially, after taxes, amounts to less than a hundred dollars a day. I can go make a hundred dollars in ten minutes; every once in a while I'll get so hard up for cash that I'll start thinking, dude, I can go get a quarter pound of weed, I can flip this, do that, bam, and I'd just be set. But that's where my addiction came in, the sale, not even just the sell but the whole plan, the whole scheme, all of it, knowing that [I'm] sitting back with minimal effort, reached kingpin status, that I was untouchable.

—Felix

INTRODUCTION

Life after methamphetamine is the antithesis of the immersed life. At the time of their interviews, each participant had left the lifestyle. Their motives and methods of getting out and getting clean varied. Some were forced out by accompanying inevitable negative consequences. Others stopped for different reasons, including traumatic experiences, life reevaluations, and concerns for personal health or family. For many, the years of living the high life had caught up with them. A number were facing, or had faced, criminal sentences of seven years to life for meth-related crimes. As many learned, getting help within the context of a punitive criminal justice system is easier said than done.

Decision making is a significant aspect of desistance from methamphetamine. This is true even when a voluntary decision to desist does not precede the initiation of the process. Some quit because they have to. The risks and consequences of not doing so become too high. While making a personal decision to exit the life does not have to be part of the initial process, it becomes critical at the end.

Desistance typically followed instigating events and corresponding changes in life circumstances. The shift in events sets in motion a process that facilitates eventual attempts to exit. For many, this comes after an encounter with the criminal justice system. Those facing serious charges of years or even decades in prison are forced to reevaluate their life. However, arrests, convictions, and incarcerations do not always instigate change. Rather, they are more likely to do so when such facilitating events trigger a reevaluation of choices, options, and ultimately behaviors. For some, this occurs following a single encounter with the legal system, while for others, multiple contacts and periods of incarceration precede the initiation of the desistance process.

The lengths of time they had desisted ranged from one month to fourteen years. The majority had not used, dealt, or manufactured for years. In the end, they got out while they still could. However, the reality was that stopping use and other related activities was only the beginning. Numerous challenges littered the roads they walked during their transitions to life after meth. Gone were the days of long-lasting drug-induced highs, fast money, and potent senses of power and control. In every sense, this is a real transition from one life to another, and such transitions can be difficult.

For many, this would be their first time living as an adult without meth. Relearning and taking the steps needed to gain, or regain, a solid foothold in conventional society are essential. The possibility of being lured back to their former drug lifestyles will always remain, especially in their weakest of moments. Memories of the seductive aspects of their former lives will be ever-present. This is a transition that proves to be among the most trying of endeavors. It is the reality of life after meth.

With few exceptions, they reemerged as broken people with fractured lives that must be pieced back together—to the extent that it is possible to do so. Such journeys are delicate and unstable. More commonly than not, stigmatized, demonized, and criminally labeled, they are expected to successfully navigate, often alone, a life they were never quite able to gain a solid grounding in in the first place.

Life after meth is particularly challenging for those lacking the resources, skills, support, or knowledge to "make it." The journey becomes even more problematic when identities are forever tied to nonremovable labels containing words like *methamphetamine* and *manufacturing*. There will always be some who are able to get the essential support and assistance they need to succeed, who, despite all they ever did, manage to avoid the application of stigmatizing labels. Yet there are, and will always be, more who never receive the support they need or a chance at redemption. Like lost causes, many will fall through the cracks, forever imprisoned by the consequences of their choices: drugs, violence, incarceration, or death.

Dualities are inevitably linked to the struggles that lie ahead. It is only by dealing with the choices and consequences of their lives that those formerly immersed can progress in their attempts to build new ones. Despite the highs and the illusory glamour of it all, in the end it was all the same. Illusion no more; the time had arrived to find a new path, learn how to live without drugs, and face all they had done. It would be something that would require looking ahead while never forgetting what lay behind. Such a change involves dealing with the issues that lie within, as one attempts to forge new relations with the world around.

REMEMBERING AND LEARNING TO FORGET

This new reality requires that people remember certain things while letting others go. There is a need to learn to accept those things that can never be changed while changing those that can. It is something that is crucial but difficult. The process requires self-reflection, forgiveness, and the making of reparations to the extent that it can be done. At the end of the day, those who had lived the meth lifestyle were not the only ones affected. They were sons and daughters, brothers and sisters, mothers and fathers. They betrayed and crossed those they loved, carrying them along for the ride. Now it was time to simultaneously remember and forget—or at least to try—for themselves and those around them. The truth is that all they were capable of doing in the darkest moments of their lives will haunt them for years to come, if not forever. The transition is among the most testing aspects of postmethamphetamine life. It is part of the duality that exists as a result of the need to remember and the need to forget.

For these adults and others similarly situated, there will always be a need to focus on the things that keep them grounded in conventional life, while releasing those with the potential to lure them back. From this point forward, their focus must be directed at looking ahead. They will always struggle, because *they know*: they are forever cognizant of the highs of the drug, the lifestyle, and everything it gave them. It is something many still loved.

Reminders serve an important function in life after meth. They exist as anchors that tie people to the lives they live now in much stronger ways than to the ones they gave up. For Matthew, mental reminders were reinforced by physical ones, which he carried with him as he walked through life now. These were artifacts that provided solid proof, documentation of the person he once was and the negative consequences of his past. It was an important part of his recovery that he shared his experiences. It the midst of the interview he jumped up from the table and ran outside, reentering with a folder and book he retrieved from his car. He explained what the items were and their significance.

Matthew: I've got a folder I keep a lot of things like this in. I've got a book I keep all these in. I'll tell you why I carry these. I carry this almost everywhere I go, because when, I feel once you get sober, your body is sober, [but] *you're not sober.* I still have addictive personalities and thoughts. I still have them thoughts, they don't go away; the thoughts will go away in time, over time, my thoughts get better. I don't think about doing illegal activities as much anymore. I used to. When I first got somewhere . . . and times was tough, how easy it is to go make $200,000. I could do it [in] *one day,* I could make $200,000. No problem. And I go back to this, and I go back to that. And I carry these, I have in my truck [picture of him on meth] or I have it hanging in my house where I can see where I came from. And I never want to look like that again. I never want to be that man again.

The paperwork documented a lifetime of charges—numerous pages were stapled together. He held up a small black-and-white photo of himself at the time of his arrest. There were few similarities between the face in the picture and man now holding it. They appeared to be completely different people. In many ways they were not the same. He referenced the man in the picture while talking about his time on meth.

Matthew: I didn't worry. I wasn't scared to die. I wasn't scared to go to jail. I wasn't scared to kill someone. I wasn't scared of nothin'. I mean, does that look like somebody that is scared of much? I would walk into anywhere looking like that. It didn't matter and . . . That's me. That guy ain't here no more. I hope he stays gone.

Like a child at show-and-tell, he flipped through pages in his book on recovery. It helped him stay focused and grounded. These were more than just items; they were concrete reminders of everything he needed to remember and all that he needed to forget. No longer dealing or manufacturing, and clean for nearly six months, his life was changing. But it was challenging. He now had to relearn how to handle the ongoing stresses without methamphetamine and the money it could bring. For him, these were tests of faith.

Matthew: But right now, I'm going through a lot of tests. God is testing me. He took my house. He hasn't took my wife. My wife is hanging in there, strongly. We're movin' to a camper trailer. I bought a truck for $500, it blew up. So I'm rebuilding the engine. But God blessed me with a job. That's who I'm buying that truck from. It's all gonna work out. I don't care what God takes from me, I just got to walk through that hallway, now that hallway might be full of junk and I have to fight my way through that hallway, but when I get to the other side, it's gonna be glorious. I'm tellin' you, it's going to be glorious. You just can't give up. It's gonna get hard. You're gonna have bad days. People's gonna die. Bad things are gonna happen. That's earth. That's human. That's life.

At thirty-three, he had survived one stroke and two heart attacks. In addition to his difficulty remembering things, there were pressing physical reminders like high blood pressure and loose, broken, and missing teeth. Some reminders would eventually go away while others never would. He spoke about the significance of remembering and forgetting as he responded to a question about whether he thought he had quit using permanently this time.

Matthew: I've quit, I can't *honestly* say I've quit *permanently.* I can say I'm not high today. I am sober today. You can only worry about today. Don't look at tomorrow, because you're gonna overwhelm yourself. I'll tell you why you can't look any further than twenty-four hours. Okay. To explain it the best way I know how to explain it. At the first of the month, when you get all your bills in, you got this much money, this many bills. Your heart gets to racing, you're trying to figure out what to do. You just don't know. You just overwhelm yourself. Well, what do you do when you start overwhelming yourself? Some people eat. Some people drink. Some people get high. So I just worry about these twenty-four hours, just worry about today, 'cause actually all I have to worry about is twelve hours, because eight hours of the day I'm gonna sleep. And then, the next morning will be the end of today. So only worry about the day, *that day* and the time that you're awake. Because when you're sleepin', if you pray before you go to sleep, you don't have nothin' to worry about. Pray when you wake up, and just ask God to give you [today], ask God, "God, I'm not asking for two days, I'm not asking for a week. *Keep me sober today.* Keep me sober today and put good things in front of me and keep the evil away from me." Just worry about that, and worry about the moment you're in.

Relationships were critical for his sobriety. He had a supportive family but knew he would have to leave his fiancée if she relapsed.[1] Having to give up everything they had known was a common theme. The "successes" that accompany life in the world of methamphetamine are meaningless in the one that exists outside of it. Learning to live again meant starting over—without the money, power, and sex that had come with the drug.

Matthew had attributed much of his success to his belief in God. He wanted to share his story to help others, and had a desire to one day have the resources to start a sober living facility for fathers and their children. Despite the painful and sometimes self-deprecating information he shared about his former self, there was a purpose to his willingness to participate in the interview.

Matthew: Well, I hope, I pray, that it gets out there, and I hope one day that I'll get the funds and I'll be able to push on like you all are. That's why it's important for me to be here today. 'Cause you all are trying to do a lot of what I wanna do. Now, you all want to help, you all want to help people, and I, God, I want to help people so bad. I just, I want 'em to see life where I see it from. And it's not peaches and cream, but it ain't gotta be all bad, neither.

In the midst of her own struggles to regain normalcy, Lucy reminisced about the sense of safety that came with familiar things—and what she was familiar with was manufacturing meth.

Lucy: It's a lot more comfortable for somebody to go back doing what they know. I know how to go cook dope, I know how to get away with it, I know how to make good dope. That's a thousand times easier than it is here, facing the unknown, what I don't know, I don't know what to do. I don't want that, and it is easier for me to face the unknown and do something that I'm not familiar with. Not easier, it's not easier, that's easy, this is hard, but beneficial, and I know this is more beneficial to me and I know it's what I need to do. And not for me. For me, yes, but I mean my kids, I don't want my kids to go through it.

Her fragility was evident as she described her ongoing struggle to remember and forget. According to her own self-assessment, only a week earlier she might not have been strong enough to tell her story. Even speaking about manufacturing was a trigger.

Lucy: Girl, listen, I promise you, you don't think I've lived it? Day in and day out. But it's a good thing, because when you push it out of your mind you act like it's not there, and it is there. This is something I need to deal with, it's something that I need to understand, I've gotta beat these feelings, and I can't do it unless I visit them, I can't. Take your time, I'm alright, I'm okay, I have got an awesome support team on my side. Now if you would've contacted me a week ago, I would've done it, I don't know how I would've been afterwards but I know right here I'm protected. I've got people that care about me and love me unconditional[ly] in a way that the world can't, because they don't understand, they haven't been there, but these women have. I've been given page after page after page of people who, "You need something, call me, you have a problem, call me." You think I was released from prison with a piece of paper: you need anything, call me? Hell, no! They don't even give you a check, if you're from a different county than you're released in, they'll give you a bus ticket to get you back to the county that you were charged in, but that's it. You have to be resourceful. I'm a statistic, because I'm four years out of prison. I've relapsed once, but it's because of my will that I have it. I'm already beating odds. I guess probably it's because something was born in me strong, thank God. Thank God I'm not one of the weak ones, because you fall right back in the same crap, you do.

She knew she was a statistic. Though she had managed to stay clean for years following her release from prison, she had used meth during a three-week stint only seven months prior to her interview.

The nature of conventional life makes transitioning difficult. Regular existence is nothing like the one they described as they reflected on what they once loved about meth. In fact real life, in many ways, is everything that life on methamphetamine is not. For many, it is as Felix describes at the beginning of the chapter. Most people don't carry hundreds of dollars of disposable cash and have the energy to party for days. In the real world, everyday life is not a party. There are chores and work. There is hardship and struggle. It is part of the reason people become enthralled and seduced in the first place. It is part of the reason such problems continue today.

In the real world, people struggle in their attempts to cope with challenges, difficulties, and stresses. This makes transitioning back more problematic for those formerly involved with meth. Living high is the antithesis of what life is like afterward. This was something Emme spoke about as she reflected on the difference between the life she once lived and one the she lived now. She described the fragile adjustment she was trying to make.

Emme: It's fun. It's a high of its own. It's fun to do things on edge. Its fun not getting caught. I've always had to have been with the bad boys. I've always ran with bad crowd. It's just, it's *edgy.* It's, fun ... It's more exciting. You got to have some excitement. Even now, I still have to have a little bit of excitement. I don't do anything illegal or anything like that, but you know, sittin' at home with two kids kinda gets kinda boring after what I've done. So it's kinda like, so I would start bounty hunting or find other sources that are not illegal or bad.

The adjustment demands a complete change. The lowest days she experienced now were once fixable by meth.

Emme: There's days I have *horrible days.* That's just the way it is, and a lot of it's probably because of what I've done. I'm sure I'm gonna have effects from it. That's a lot. I'm sure things are going to happen to me when I get older. But I got out and I don't take it back, because I learned a lot from it. I've learned so much from it. I always wanted to know what that lifestyle was. It's almost like I found ... it. And I did. And I don't regret it. I know what I want to know, even though I don't practice it. I am not a very judgmental person. I don't judge anybody. I don't even judge the bum down the street, because *I know how it can be.* Maybe that's one of the best things that I got out of the situation.

Confronting the father of her child, who was currently serving time in prison, was something she would have to eventually face upon his release; he had been the one who introduced her to meth.

There were other reminders too. Felix had a physical response to meth, though he no longer desired to use.

Felix: Seeing it makes my heart rate pick up, I can feel myself, my body will respond to it, but I have no desire to do it . . . Physically I will respond to it . . . and if I'm around it long enough I'll start, my jaw will start working, my heart rate will pick up, but I have no desire to do it whatsoever.

It is a real part of life after meth. Ian was not even aware of the physical tics he still experienced from time to time.

Ian: I'm six years sober, ladies, and I still have a tongue deal and I don't even know I do it, it's just like breathing. Clients I work with kinda poke at me all the time. They just, I'm clean and sober, and I don't even know I do it. It's what's funny about it.

Though his exit from meth had been successful, the fragility of his foothold on conventional living remained. Even now, six years later, the ground that he stood on was shaky and unstable.

Ian: Well . . . I mean, you know . . . *I'm one bad decision away from death.* I realize that, and I'm never gonna be cured of this deal, and it's not just about not drinkin' or not druggin', it's about being, for me, it's about being reasonably happy most days. Everyday ain't gonna be an [Ian] day . . .

When asked whether he had quit permanently, he responded:

Ian: *My goal is to make it to midnight tonight.* There is nothin' that, I want you guys to know this, that I have a beautiful wife that I met in the rooms of Alcoholics Anonymous, and sometimes I look at her and I think, "What is she doing with me?" I have a real good life. I have a lot of friends, just a good life. But I put my recovery first, 'cause like I told you, if not, I'll trade my wife and my family and my good life. I will trade it for drugs and alcohol and, ah, so the way I'm sponsored is, I just try to make an amendment, I don't know what's gonna happen tomorrow. Tomorrow is not even promised, sober or not sober.

Q: [Being sober] for six years is great. You should be very proud.

Ian: I'm grateful. Pride will get me dead.

Lucas elaborated on the challenges he still faced, even today.

Lucas: I still have trouble every day. I wake up in the morning and I smell it. I walk outside and I can smell it . . . I smell it because there's a little thing in the back of your head that keeps you smelling that. It's something my drug counselor was telling me, that it'll let off so much of the endorphins that you remember, and possibly later on it will burn out, but sooner or later it'll go away where I don't smell it anymore. But I'm begging. Please let it go away soon, because there's days I go out to work and I have to stop in my tracks and sit down, because I'm sweating and shaking so bad. And it's just the smell.

Smelling it was only part of his ongoing struggle.

Lucas: It's still a struggle, every day it's a struggle. There's some days that are great, and I can walk out and bebop right to the truck and get in the van and go to work. But there's mornings when I get up, I can't even hardly walk. And my teeth hurt so bad. I get a headache because my teeth are falling out.

He continued to describe the realities he lived with.

Lucas: The aftereffects is what I dislike about methamphetamine . . . My bones hurtin', my teeth fallin' out. In fact, I'm gettin' fat without it. I don't have the energy that I used to have. My sex life is going to hell. I just don't have no enthusiasm for anything other than, you know.

Physical reminders are real and can be ever-present. They included things that were visible and those that were not. They were remnants of lives once lived; consequences that made life now more challenging. Bryant elaborated on what he disliked about meth now.

Bryant: Coming down, and I didn't do that very often. It's easier to stay high than come down and face [the] reality of life. It's like I tell people now, I can walk up to a . . . guy who is coming down . . . and I tell 'em it's easier to get high than deal with this. Life is hard now, I work hundred-hour weeks, I have to pay my bills, my credit sucks, it's hard to overcome the obstacles here now. But when I was high, hell it was easy just to blow 'em off.

Though not an option anymore, "blowing them off" seemed easier. Coming to terms with paths taken is an important aspect of adjusting to life after meth.

Physical reminders extend to the loss of the heightened sexuality that accompanied meth use. Once one of the key attractions, it became one of the things that needed to be forgotten. Adjusting to sex without meth can be problematic. It was one of the aftereffects many would have to deal with from this point forward. Bryant, too, was forced to adjust to the loss of the heightened sexual experiences he once enjoyed, as he describes in chapter 6. Though the night he tried meth had changed the course of his life, he had no regrets.

Bryant: I watched a lot of things go by that I probably could've changed differently had I not been in that room . . . That one night. Do I regret that night? Absolutely not.

He explained why.

Bryant: Because it's made me who I am today. I tell people all the time, I'm not ashamed of my past. I'm not happy with it, but I'm not ashamed of it, because had I not went down them roads, had I not traveled the avenues I've traveled, I wouldn't be sitting here today. I wouldn't be able to walk beside this young man and say, "Hey, let's find you a path." I'd be another sitting across the table here, talking to somebody like me. I enjoy where I'm sitting, I really do, and I'm proud of that.

Successfully transitioning required that he reframe his past experiences and find a new purpose. He was now dating a nonuser and had become certified as a peer recovery support specialist. He carried the certificate and photos of his family with him to the interview. He was proud of what he had become. He was making it. While still employed as a truck driver to support his ongoing transition, his aspirations were changing. His goal now was to help others like himself.

For Conner, the realization that he was about to lose everything served as the main facilitator for his exit. In a moment of clarity, the illusion that methamphetamine gave him everything vanished almost instantaneously. This realization changed the course of his life.

Conner: The main reason for stopping is 'cause I had caught a case, and I was scared to go to the penitentiary and lose my whole life, basically, they were offering me thirty-five years in the penitentiary, and I didn't wanna spend the rest of my life in the penitentiary, 'cause I have a family.

In the end, the lows he would go to for methamphetamine reminded him that what he truly desired, including the opportunity for a second chance, could only be obtained in a life without meth.

Conner: I made a decision basically that I had to be done with it, because it was gonna take me away from everything I ever wanted, which is my freedom, but yeah, I made a decision to quit . . . I'm the one that got myself busted from dealing methamphetamine. I'm the one that got myself into court procedures, so the courts didn't say, "You have to quit," you know, or "you're gonna go to prison." They're just saying, "You're gonna go to prison, for meth, because you this is what you did." And I said, well, I have to turn my life around, or I'm going to end up spending the rest of my life in prison and, and people don't realize, but you can turn your life around, and the courts will recognize it, but you have to be sincere about it.

Yet navigating the life he now so desperately desired proved to be more difficult than he anticipated.

Conner: This is the bad thing about meth. Once you use meth, and you quit using meth, you feel like your life is boring. That's the . . . hardest problem I had when I quit using, I just felt like I was just so bored, boring, my life was boring.

Q: Because you have this artificial high all the time?

Conner: Yeah. Plus you'd get out there and do stuff, and then after you use meth, you just wanna watch TV, or just bein' a normal person you feel like your life is boring. That's the hardest part about it.

Life after meth can be particularly problematic for those required to take medications after becoming clean. Some former users refused to take any drugs as part of their new lives. Ava, who needed medications to manage her health problems, developed a medication control strategy. It was a plan devised to minimize opportunities for abuse and relapse.

Ava: What I do, because I know I'm an addict, and once you're an addict, you're an addict, you always are, I have my mom fill my script, and she lives in [town], so she just mails me a certain amount every week, because I know me, and the best way for me to stay clean and to not mess up, if you know what your slip-ups are, it's best, I have to have something because I really had surgeries . . . If you have to take 'em, things happen, and so I just have my mom mail me a certain amount every week. Because that way I don't go overboard, I take it for what it's for, instead of taking it for pleasure.

She remained cognizant of her risk of relapse. Given the steady foothold she was gaining, it was a chance she didn't want to take. Despite having been clean for years, inevitable negative consequences continued to be part of her reality even now.

Ava: I've had a lot of friends die. I had one friend die two weeks ago. He accidentally overdosed on Oxycontins and alcohol and he suffocated in his own vomit and he was only twenty-four. I went to his funeral last Friday. Yeah, I've had a lot of friends die.

Like others, problems with her teeth continued to plague her.

Ava: But the worst thing that got me was my teeth. I had really, really pretty teeth when I was younger, and I've had braces twice, when I was younger, and [now] I don't have any teeth in the back at all.

Ava considered herself fortunate, since her front teeth were still intact. Eating hurt. She had sixteen teeth. She was only thirty years old. Though she had the support and resources to get them fixed before her later transition to the workplace, others were not so lucky. Olivia discussed her teeth problems.

Olivia: Yeah, these are all fake . . . I had to get 'em all pulled. Severe case of a meth mouth. It was bad.

She was only thirty-one. Though not everyone had teeth problems to deal with afterward, many did.

Forgetting is not as easy as it may sound. It is often hard to forget things you like and even harder to forget those you love. Even knowledge of how to manufacture, or the amounts of money once readily available, can become dangerous parts of the transition equation. These would be things that they would have to let go of, if not try to forget. Giving up the benefits of the meth-amphetamine lifestyle—the high, the rush, the sex, the money, the power, the confidence, and the control—was a requisite part of the transition. Accepting the loss of all that they had once liked was an essential part of their new lives.

Briana considered herself lucky, because she got in trouble with the law before ever learning how to make meth. At the time, she had been on a path that was leading her straight to manufacturing.

Briana: I would have, yes. If I hadn't gotten clean, that was the next step, absolutely. Nobody ever, ever offered. If they would have offered, if that cook in [city] would've offered to take me on [as] a cook I would've been there so fast.

Her lack of knowledge was a good thing now.

Part of the lifelong struggle for those who have come to love methamphet-amine is that they now know. Artificial, addiction, and all, they know. They know what it felt like to use a drug that seemed to offer everything one could want in the world—illusion or not. Those who crossed the Rubicon of loving methamphetamine could never go back. Though they may arrive at a point of recognizing that it was more bad than good, they can never unlearn their experiences. It is yet another part of what made escaping the world of meth-amphetamine and reentering conventional society difficult.

Knowing how to manufacture and understanding the high that accompa-nies the lifestyle are dangerous in life after meth. The pains were alluded to by Evan as he described the powerful experience of injecting meth:

Evan: I wish I didn't know. I wish I didn't know what that's like, because that is com-pletely different than . . . it's very . . . if you don't know what it's like, then don't ever find out. Because if you did find out, then you'd know, and you'd wish you didn't know.

His expressions and the intensity with which he spoke the words so carefully chosen in the moment were unmistakable; it was proof of the strong hold of methamphetamine. The seriousness was not by accident. He had learned, undeniably, in the most difficult way possible, of the undisputable danger of the journey he had taken, and now he had to live with this knowledge forever.

It is easier to have never known than it is to forget. Evan was one of many haunted by his memories of the person he had become. It defined all that he disliked now about methamphetamine and the associated lifestyle. It was a reality he had to face.

Evan: I like having possessions, and money, and a place to live, and a family, and people who care about me. I like having other people's trust. I like it when I say something, someone takes it for that's the truth, instead of looking at me like, "What are you trying to get out of me." I don't like looking at one of my friends' purse, sitting there, and wondering if she's got any money in it, if she'd notice if I took it out of there. I don't like calling my mother from [college], and telling her, "Hey, I'm not going to be able to pay my electric, I need $135," having her send me a check, and me go get dope with it. I don't like that. I like people trusting me. I'm not a piece of garbage. And I am when I use it. It's more important than anything, when I'm using it.

Still struggling five years after quitting, the words he spoke right after responding affirmatively to a question about whether he thought he had stopped using permanently said it all.

Evan: But still, even though I've quit permanently, I think about it all the time. I think about using it and then immediately I think, "No way. I'm not gonna do that." But still the thought's there. It's always there. I can't ever get it out of my head, because I know what it's like.

Challenges remained.

Evan: They tell you to try to get a hobby, or something to take your mind off, read something, go play basketball, do something else, do something else, they say to stay outside of yourself. Because when you get inside yourself, that's a big place to be, and it's easy to get down on yourself, and they want to know what the triggers are for you, to cause you [to] use it, and stay away from them.

Successfully navigating this exit continued to be the hardest thing he would ever do, and he was not alone.

The truth is that there is no way to completely forget or "not know." Life is not like that. It just isn't. Having lived in the world of methamphetamine, they would always know. They would always remember the highs and the lows. The things they loved and those they hated would always be part of their consciousness, as would the things they did and those they did not. They would forever be part of who they were and of who they had been. There are no do-overs or take-backs. Rather, such things will forever be part of the challenge inherent in transitioning—the challenge of simultaneously remembering and forgetting.

Things would be difficult enough if they stopped there. But they do not. Just as the harms and negative consequences of methamphetamine and manufacturing are expansive, so are the challenges of transitioning. The road that leads away from methamphetamine is long and arduous.

REESTABLISHING SOCIAL TIES AND REBUILDING LEGITIMATE LIVES

The dualities inherent in transitioning extend to people's social networks and relationships. Successful transitions require that people simultaneously repair and reestablish certain relationships and ties while severing and cutting others. For a multitude of reasons, those immersed in methamphetamine primarily interact with others similarly situated. To avoid detection, and in part due to the accompanying risks and dangers, they disassociate from nonusers, including family members and friends. The process of simultaneously severing ties in one aspect of life while trying to rebuild them in another can be difficult for anyone. Yet it is another critical aspect of what is required for those who escape methamphetamine. As with other facets of this transition, there are some who will succeed and others who will not.

Rebuilding conventional ties is essential. Once severed or broken, links to nonusing peers and family members now serve as anchors. In the same vein, links to others still engaged serve as threads that potentially lead back to meth. When conventional anchors are nonexistent or weak, the struggle to regain standing becomes more difficult. Sam described the conflict he faced in terms of returning to his former relationship; relationships mattered, serving as triggers or supports to help him stay clean.

Sam: Oh yeah, yeah, 'cause see, the ex-wife that I'm away from right now, she wants me, I could come back home right now, I could call her right now and tell her I'm ready to come home and she would take me in. I could be driving that [new] Camaro she's got right now, I could be back in my other truck that I have, I could be back with my two little kids, I still see them and all that, but she's a trigger for me and I can't go back to that trigger.

Sobriety was a new experience; it was one he would learn to enjoy.

Sam: What I'm learning now is I like being sober, I like my relationships, I like having my relationships back with my kids, I trashed everything. My finances, my house, my marriages, and it was all because that line of stuff right there.

When it came to social relationships, there were variations among the experiences of these adults. Some people maintained, reestablished, or entered new relationships with nonusing significant others and loved ones; others were not so fortunate. Some maintained ties with their children while others did not. Relationships with children are an important aspect of life after meth, given that the majority had children.

In general, the three outcomes for parent-child relationships were exemplified by Patrick, Lucy, and Katie. Though Patrick was in part responsible for getting his children involved with meth, at the time of his interview he and his children were off the drug. He was among the more fortunate, because he had managed to repair his relationships with his children, holding on to the family he once neglected. It was not possible for him to talk about the impact of methamphetamine in his experience without discussing his children.

Patrick: When I quit doing drugs, my entire family quit doing drugs ... All my kids quit. Best thing I ever done ... Best thing I ever done for my kids ... Me quitting, I had five kids. My four and my wife's ... all were messing with drugs when I quit. We're all clean now ... Greatest thing I ever done.

Though he did not elaborate on the extent of their use or how they stopped, it was clear that his own use and eventual desistance was linked to theirs. It was a victory that followed a path of absenteeism, loss, and heartache. His realization of what this had done to his and others' lives would be part of the reason he was willing to come and share his story. It would be to serve as a warning to others.

Patrick: You got to warn them about what's gonna happen. They got to see, where it leads 'em. I don't care how much fun it was, it still ... it still ruined my life.

The sad reality was that he was not alone. In the rural town he had grown up in, drugs had taken their toll. He recognized the limitations of his ability to share his story himself.

Patrick: You know ... I have ideas, what we should do, from an addict, from a manufacturer's point of view, but gettin' somebody to listen to a damned old truck driver out here in Oklahoma that, sure he's clean and sober three years, and he's been through these paths, but to get somebody that's got a three-piece suit up there in legislation to listen to me is a whole different deal.

At the time of her interview, Lucy was divorced, unemployed, and residing in a sober-living facility. She had given birth to seven children during the course of her addiction; her children now ranged in age from six to seventeen years old. She was unable to care for any of her children and was in limited contact with her eldest daughter—a pregnant runaway at risk for heading down a path similar to her own. Of her remaining children, one lived out of state, two lived with her ex-husband, and three had been given up for adoption.

Katie's circumstances represented another extreme. At the time of her interview, neither of her sons had anything to do with her. Despite the fact that she was sober and rebuilding her life, her children were not on speaking terms with her. It was the natural consequence of surviving a childhood where they had been placed second to drugs; all bonds were severed. Any remaining opportunities to repair these relationships were out of her control. It was one of her biggest regrets and one of the most significant challenges she now faced.

Becoming self-sufficient, with the ability to achieve general life stability, is almost a prerequisite for rebuilding broken relationships and mending ties with loved ones, especially children. This was particularly true for those who had placed their children in dangerous situations and at risk, living high and some-times even engaging in manufacturing while their children were in their custody. But achieving stability requires more than just desire. It requires becoming legitimately and gainfully employed. This represents yet another challenging aspect of the transition from methamphetamine to conventional life.

Gone were the days of fast money and large sums of cash. The money that it takes to build and support a new life—one outside of the manufacturing and dealing of drugs—comes much more slowly and with greater effort. In conventional life, legitimate money comes from legitimate work. Most had little if anything to show for all the money they had earned. Access to quick, disposal cash had to be given up. There were no more stacks of hundred-dollar bills. The reality is that the amounts of income generated postmeth will never match the amounts that were earned dealing and making the drug.

People varied in employability in life after meth. Those who were able to continue to work in careers they had been previously employed in, and those who were going back to school or finding new types of employment (e.g., drug counseling), were more likely to be successful in making the transition. But obtaining employment is only part of the challenge. Reminders sometimes remained even for those who had managed to find conventional employment. As a heat-and-air service worker, Ray sometimes smelled odors related to meth production in the houses he visited.

Ray: Oh, yeah, I have, because I can smell it, yeah, I could smell it in the house. I just go about my business. Most of the time, it's a house being rented. It's not the owner of the house. I'm just there to do my work and I leave.

Finding avenues that lead to legitimate employment and financial stability are difficult, and may end up being impossible for some. Many factors influence employability including skill sets (or the lack of), ongoing struggles with sobriety, and criminal records. It is yet another aspect of the difficulties inherent in adjusting to life after meth. Wes spoke about his decision to stop manufacturing.

Wes: Yes, yeah, and every day I make that decision, because I know the money that can come from it.

The fact was that most of these adults had the knowledge, experience, and skill to make methamphetamine. With the means to acquire necessary chemicals and supplies, reverting back to making money by manufacturing was always going to be an option, even when it really wasn't. In their more desperate moments of struggle, they would always remember the vast amounts of money that could be earned in the world of meth. It was a struggle that Lucy described as she talked about the challenges she was experiencing even now.

Lucy: And I can go get this [materials to cook meth] at the grocery store right now and I mean that's what's insane about the whole thing, you know what I'm saying. It has to be a will and it has to be a choice within yourself. Because it's so simple, when you have no job, you know the police are hounding you to the point you can't keep a job when you do get one, you can't find a place to stay. I have manufacturing charges, nobody wants to let me live in their house, why would they, I've cooked dope.

It was a dangerous cycle.

Lucy: But do you see the cycle? Do you see the cycle? It puts you in a predicament, to where anybody is gonna do what they have to do in order to survive. Whether it's selling your ass, or prostituting your kids, all kinds of stuff that people have done in order to survive. But when I know that I could go cook me dope and not harm anybody, I would never go put a gun to someone's head and rob them, I couldn't do that. It's more in my nature to go isolate my[self] somewhere, bust off a batch of dope and be $2,200 in the positive. That $2,200 is gonna go a long way if I'm not using dope.

For those lacking the experience, employment history, education, and social skills, the probabilities of making a smooth transition from a life supported by illegal money to one that is not are small at best.

LABELS THAT STICK: THE CHALLENGES OF ADDICTIONS AND CONVICTIONS

The problems of transitioning are compounded significantly by prior addictions and convictions. In addition to learning to live without drugs, there were arrests, convictions, and periods of incarceration to be overcome. As the adults shared their stories it became evident that addictions and convictions were labels that stick. It is one thing to have problems or get in trouble, and something else when past transgressions include labels containing words like "methamphetamine," and "manufacturing."

Many struggled with various types of addictions. These were not just the physiological, biological, and neurological effects of the drug and subsequent avoidance of withdrawal. Rather, their addictions related to the things— specifically the aspects of the life—they enjoyed and received pleasure from. While there are neurological and biological components to pleasure-seeking behaviors, it can also be about much more.

The labels that attached to them extended beyond those related to addictions. There were also the ones that came from formal criminal justice system involvement. Criminal justice labels create some of the most significant challenges to transitioning and barriers to reintegration. Labels forever become tied to identities. The descriptive labels of their past criminal activities are the ones most directly linked to the stigma that endures. They are the labels that are applied to those convicted of methamphetamine-related crimes, especially manufacturing-related offenses.

Thirty-one (93 percent) of these adults had prior interactions with the criminal justice system. Most had served time in jail or prison and had criminal records tied to their past. In a sense, they were fortunate that they were not now incarcerated or serving life sentences. While some faced lengthy periods of incarceration in the future if they failed in their attempts to remain sober and reintegrate, they were serving out their sentences in the community at the time of their interviews.

Among those who had gotten caught, the most fortunate were the ones given a second chance in lieu of being incarcerated. Katie's criminal record was extensive. Arrested more than thirty times, she had been convicted of twenty-six felonies and incarcerated three times. The vast array of property crimes she committed funded her drug habit. She would only ever be convicted of one drug charge. The charge got reduced to simple possession of a controlled dangerous substance (CDS). Her last arrest resulted in her getting the help she desperately needed to regain sobriety and stability.

Katie: I broke the law. I got seven felonies in one time ... I got possession of a stolen vehicle, possession of stolen property, breaking in, burglary 2, two counts of falsifying information to a pawnbroker, I forgot what all else, they just stacked it up on me, but

. . . my attorney came in and I told 'em, I said, "I don't understand," I said, "Y'all are always wanting to put me in prison," and I said, "I'm a drug addict." I said. "*I need help.* Y'all throwin' me in prison, as you look at my rap sheet, throwin' me in prison is not helping," I said. "You got all these programs out here for different people, women in recovery, drug court." He said, "What are you saying?" I said, "I need help. I don't want to go back [to] prison," 'cause I was looking at twenty-five years . . . He said, "Well, let me see what I can do." Well, I had to plea before drug court and they turned me down, because they said I had too many white-collar crimes . . . They told me even though I committed the white-collar crimes to get drugs, I didn't have any drug charges.

Not a drug offender on paper, it would be the diagnosis she received after placement in a state hospital years earlier that made her eligible to enter a mental health program for drug offenders. She had been diagnosed as bipolar paranoid schizophrenic.

Katie: I told this to my attorney, and next thing I know I had a woman coming in from the mental health court system, and they evaluated me. I don't know how, all I can tell you is it had to be the grace of God that allowed me to get in there, because I had too many crimes to be placed into the mental health court system, but God allowed me to go in there, and that's where I'm at today, and it's actually changed my life tremendously.

Clean for two years, she was scheduled to graduate from the program in forthcoming months. She had been given a second chance that she almost didn't receive. It was an opportunity that would make all the difference.

Aside from a few alcohol-related arrests as a juvenile and despite decades of involvement, Vanessa had no encounters with the legal system until an arrest and conviction for endeavoring to manufacture. The charge carried an automatic sentence of seven years to life. After serving over a month in a county correctional facility, she was offered a ten-year prison sentence in exchange for a plea. She elaborated on the situation at the time.

Vanessa: Everyone that had an endeavoring charge, that's what they were offering. *You could take it or not.* If you took it you took the chance of getting more. So my offer was ten years, I could have counteroffered, I could have went to jury trial, or could take a blind plea. So my public defender, who came and seen me one time before my court date, I was like "I'm going to take a blind plea." So that meant that I put myself at the mercy of the judge only. So that he would make the decision, which means, ultimately, if he wanted to he could have put me away for life, even though state minimum is seven years. We spent eight hours in the court going back and forth over why I felt I should not go to prison for this charge and he, so wonderfully, amazingly allowed me, in the process, to mostly speak for myself. The district attorney would have their say and then he would give me my opportunity. It wasn't my lawyer speaking for me, it was me speaking for myself, and he was very, very, clear in the fact that he was addressing me, and all the questions were addressed to me, and he wanted to hear my answers. And my plea to the court was that I have lived in addiction and I just didn't know where to get help. I don't think that prison's the answer. I actually had my children in the courtroom with me. There was a new program that existed, brand new to the state of Oklahoma, the only one of its kind, actually, in the nation, and they came up and interviewed me and accepted me based on their criteria, and even though the state continued to object to the last breath, I was given the opportunity to go into the program.

It was an offer that would change the course of her life. When asked if she had made a voluntary decision to quit, she responded:

Vanessa: No, I did not, I went to jail. I wouldn't have, I wouldn't have stopped. I was so lost at that time, that I wanted to, to die, *I mean I just wanted to use until I died.*

Serving a seven-year suspended sentence in the community, she was among the first female offenders to be convicted for such a crime and not be imprisoned. She was now clean and employed full time.

The significance of second chances should not be understated. Methamphetamine and manufacturing are highly stigmatized and criminalized. Negative public and societal perceptions are exacerbated by the reality that those who engage in methamphetamine-related crimes place innocent parties and others at risk of harm when making the drug in dangerous and volatile ways. During her interview, Lucy pleaded for societal support for a second chance. Her situation was not unique. She carried the never-ending weight of a methamphetamine-related felony conviction forever tied to her identity.

Lucy: We're here begging the community to give us a chance, we are decent people, yeah, we've messed up but I'm still who I am, and just because you have a conviction and they've got my number, they've got my number forever. I will be attached to that DOC [corrections] number, and if they think, you go get a job and you have a clean record . . . you can go look and see if anybody's been arrested, what they've been charged for, it's a requirement. But what saddens me is that you can go look up my DOC number and you can see those things, but those things aren't me. Those aren't me, but it's forever tied.

Q: It almost follows you?

Lucy: No, baby, it does, forever, forever, that will be and that's it! And that's what people don't understand, you get this, you're charged with that, you're condemned for life . . . I mean it is sad, it's very sad, especially when you got mothers of kids, I mean it's stuck, it's sick, it's sick, there's nothing right about it at all.

For her and the others so labeled, convictions equated to a life sentence; only this is one served both in prison and out. In addition to having no money and no job, her transition was complicated by challenges that came with the labels tied to her name and the knowledge that everything she needed to make the drug was within reach. The clashing realities ensured a precarious transition. The $2,200 she used to earn for an ounce of meth would solve a lot of the problems she faced now. The problem was that it would simultaneously create many more. Though she had escaped her former life, her journey towards normalcy had only just begun.

Jackson's and Troy's situations and circumstances were characteristic of those living on the shakiest of grounds; each for different reasons. At the time of their interviews, both were serving community sentences, living in a halfway house, and facing additional time in prison if they failed to maintain their sobriety or violated the conditions of their probation.

A divorced father of three, Jackson had an extensive history using, dealing, and manufacturing. Though arrested more than ten times, he had only one felony conviction for endeavoring to manufacture. He had served seven months in prison on a two-year sentence and was now being supervised by an electronic monitoring device attached to his ankle. Having already been at the halfway house for six months, Jackson was about to reenter the community. He had a twenty-five-year suspended sentence on top of the two years served in prison. During his height, he was using and manufacturing meth daily, earning upwards of $600-$700 a day. He had lived immersed in the meth lifestyle for eighteen years of his adult life, and he was only thirty-eight years old. Despite the fact that Jackson had been fortunate in that he had not received a life sentence for his crimes, the difficulties that lay ahead seemed insurmountable. He had no license and no job. He needed to pay $1,000 to get his license back. Though he had completed a year and a half of college, he had no marketable skills and a felony conviction. He faced an uphill battle in the days, weeks, months, and years ahead. Having received some drug treatment during his stay at the halfway house, he had been clean and separated from the lifestyle for more than two years. He commented on the challenges he encountered as he spoke about the difficulties making reparations.

Jackson: I know they want you to pay it. I'm thirty-eight years old, well I'll be thirty-eight in December, and I've probably had my driver's license ten years out of my life, rest of 'em was suspended.

Q: I had no idea they did that, wow.

Jackson: Yeah, they make it hard on 'em, they really do. For me to get my driver's license right now it'd cost me $1,000, without any way to get back and forth to work it's hard to come up with $1,000. And then being a convicted felon on top of that it's, it's ... they say that people don't discriminate against convicted felons *but they do.*

If he ever got in trouble again or failed a drug test, he would be sent back to prison for twenty-three more years. He had not lived without methamphetamine for even one day of his adult life while on his own. He would now have to figure out a way to make it successfully into his sixties to avoid returning to prison. It would be a challenge, given that he would be returning to the same small rural town in which he had used, dealt, and made methamphetamine.

Troy was a thirty-four-year-old male with a twelfth-grade education. Heavily immersed in the lifestyle for years, he had four convictions, the last two for second degree arson and endeavoring to manufacture. He had tried to burn down his house to evade detection for his manufacturing activities. He had served four years on a ten-year sentence and was out in the community serving the last three years of a five-year probationary sentence. Though he knew he could receive a life sentence if he was ever sent back to prison, he had started using meth again only a year after being released. In the months preceding his interview, he had failed multiple UAs (i.e., urine analyses), testing positive for methamphetamine. He explained what followed.

Troy: So they said I needed [to] come, he was gonna *revoke my probation* and send me back to prison and I said, "Okay," and then he called me back a week later and he said, "Well, I'm gonna give you another chance if you'll try treatment." I said, "I've never had no treatment before," I said, "I'll do it." And I'm right here and I've been clean for almost a whole month.

Troy had no control over his addiction. His eventual relapse and inability to stay sober were related to the fact that he was still around users and the drug. Though he had not resumed manufacturing, he started using again.

Troy: When I got out for like a year, I didn't mess with it, and I could be around people and watch them do it, and then one day me and my wife, I guess, almost talked each other into it, and it just took that one time and that's why I'm here.

He had been using "up to five times a day" before his failed drug test. As one of the ones with the shortest periods of sobriety, he was on the shakiest of grounds. The five-month sentence in the halfway house that lay ahead of him would help ensure his sobriety, at least for that amount of time. The real challenges would begin upon his release back to his old life and the small rural town he too had come from. Though not currently using, he still desperately craved the drug.

Troy: Anything could trigger it, I couldn't be around people doing it, because I'm going to be right back in that situation if I'm around that.

Currently living in a halfway house, he was away from his regular life and his wife. He had no idea whether or not she too was getting clean or was still using meth. It would be something he would learn and have to face upon his release back into the community. In all likelihood, like many others he would have to completely disassociate from the people, places, and things that served as triggers. But doing so is easier said than done, especially in small rural towns.

Natalie put herself into drug treatment to get the help she needed to support her transition out of meth. Her desire to seek help occurred after the son she had given birth to was taken away because she tested positive for meth. She explained what it took to get to this point.

Natalie: I didn't find my way out of it ... It sounds funny. I know it does to most people. I surrender to God every day to help me. I could go back to my way of thinking really easy. I pray every day and every night. The only thing that save me was my breaking point. When I had lost my mind completely, and I was praying so hard to die, just take me.

Q: Was this before or after he was born?

Natalie: After he was born. When they took him, I lost it. Well, I'd lost it way before that, but I really was just way into my addiction then, and I wanted to die. When I went to treatment, because [child protective services] said outpatient treatment. Little do they know about drug addicts, especially one that was ... in it for twenty-seven years. Outpatient treatment was not going to do it for me, for any addict, I don't think. I was dirty the first time I went to test and I couldn't stay clean. And I knew that [would happen] unless I locked myself up and my actual breaking point was just getting so bad that I had nowhere else to go.

While her transition was less stable at first, she had successfully completed treatment and was now surrounded by the support she needed to stay on stable ground. She had to pay for the treatment she needed to exit her former life. It was something she was still paying for now. She talked about the cost and need for more treatment beds.

Natalie: My treatment was $1,700 for 120 days. I was going to stay for thirty but I got there, and they figured out I had a lot more issues to deal with ... But there is state funding. There's over nine thousand people right now waiting to get into treatment and they're building more prisons.

Q: Instead of treatment facilities?

Natalie: Right.

Aside from the two-and-a-half years she served in jail, she had lived in the world of methamphetamine for twenty-two years. This was not something she could navigate on her own.

The power of criminal justice system labels can best be demonstrated by the paths available to those who were once heavily immersed in the drug lifestyle but who, for different reasons, had managed to escape without the application of any formal labels that would stick. Ava's, Max's, and Felix's circumstances serve as examples.

Despite five to ten prior arrests, seven previous convictions, and a stint in prison serving multiple concurrent sentences, Ava escaped without any meth-related charges or convictions. The opportunity for her second chance came after she was released from prison on medical parole. Her only drug charge was one she received the last time she got in trouble, back in 2007. Rather than being convicted for her crime, she was given a deferred sentence with five years' probation and the opportunity to enter a drug rehabilitation program. Attending college at the time of her interview, she was working toward having her record expunged. She was planning to apply for a pardon upon completion of her probation. Access to resources and a good lawyer were crucial.

Ava: I've been in a lot of trouble and I have a really good lawyer, she is a friend of my mom's. My mom has her own business that takes care of mentally retarded people. And my lawyer's daughter is handicapped and so that's how my mom met my lawyer. Anyhow in [year] I'm eligible for a pardon, because all my crimes are nonviolent and I will be eligible for a pardon and then after that, she's gonna work on expungement. So that's why I'm working on two bachelors and I'm gonna go into the masters, because she told me to stay in school and she said by the time I graduate, all my legal matters should be taken care of and I should have a clean record. So I'm doing the best I can to keep my grades up.

Max similarly got in legal trouble due to methamphetamine and manufacturing. His three arrests occurred over a two-year period. He had been arrested for possession of a controlled dangerous substance, conspiracy to manufacture methamphetamine, and possession of chemical precursors, for stealing anhydrous ammonia. His last arrest resulted from an anhydrous ammonia theft sting operation. None of his arrests resulted in a conviction. Rather, with the assistance of his parents and the lawyer they hired, he was given the opportunity to complete a drug court program. Though he faced ten years in prison if he refused to attend, his record would be expunged upon completion. At the time of his interview he was attending college with no criminal record to document his former crimes. The chances he received would make all the difference in his ability to transition smoothly and unscathed from the world of methamphetamine.

Max: I had a really strong support system whenever I was in drug court, that's the only reason I think I made it, there's people that don't, and they don't make it. I still talk to my drug court coordinator and I play golf with the judge, so it's a pretty crazy deal but they're just like, well there was probably like six or seven of us that graduated within a three-month period, and now all of us are out, I guess they're having problems with the new people coming in, failing UAs and stuff like that . . . I really think it's all in your support, people that have families that do it and they're trying to, and staying clean is so hard, but my family they don't do anything.

The consequences of his greatest disappointment would be minimized by the final outcome.

Max: Well, my involvement in meth, the whole thing. I wish I wouldn't have, I could've graduated college a long time ago, at least two years ago, I'd already be working somewhere and I would've never had to go through all the stuff and pay all the money to be able to get everything off my record, but it's all fine now, because it's like it never happened anyway.

Felix also managed to make it to adulthood with no adult criminal record of his crimes. The more than thirty arrests and seven adjudications he received occurred while he was a juvenile, and those records are sealed. Restarting college for the second time, he was trying to find his way to a better life than any he had ever known. Somehow, he came to the realization that obtaining an education was his only escape from the world of drugs and crime. Clean for four years, he was now a regular college student making plans for the future.

Felix: A year and a half when I'm done with school, I can stand in front of a classroom as their teacher, like a valid profession, and I'm not gonna stop, by the time I'm thirty-seven I want to have a doctorate in education.

Though most people would never know about his past transgressions, he knew of the impact of his actions. The issue came up as he explained the motivations underlying his transition to his new life.

Felix: I didn't wanna go to jail . . . It's not what I want my legacy to be. I want my life to mean something more than, hey that guy was good at selling drugs . . . I don't want the way I'm remembered to be that. I've done some really torn-up stuff to people and one of the things that made me change it was . . . those people that I fucked over like that, it doesn't matter what I do, that's how they'll remember me. I can become the next president of the United States, and they will always see me as that crazy, violent . . . and that kills me. That can't be what I'm here to do. I refuse to allow that to be what I'm here to do.

He was among the luckiest of them all. His history with drugs and crime would forever remain invisible.

Despite his history of using, dealing, and manufacturing methamphetamine, Ray too had never been arrested for his activities and had only spent one night in jail, for driving without a license. No record of his past interactions with methamphetamine existed. This was something that would enhance the chances of successful reintegration. Though once heavily involved in the world of methamphetamine, the most fortunate ones managed to escape with no formal labels attached. You would never know them if you met them as there was no official documentation of their past offenses and transgressions. This outcome was not the norm.

Additionally, there are the challenges that go along with returning to the same environment—or any environment—where methamphetamine problems are still present. This is especially problematic for those who have only ever lived in rural areas and small towns. Moving from a small town to a bigger city is not an option for everyone, especially those without the necessary support and resources.

The most troubling cases were not those like Briana, who had managed to maintain sobriety for fourteen years and find secure, stable, and meaningful employment, or those like Bryant and Allie, who were on their way to stability and maintaining sobriety. Rather, the most haunting cases will be the ones who, at the time of their interviews, were on the shakiest of ground, still straddling the edge of life in two different and incompatible worlds.

Those with little stability and the most to lose in terms of long-term consequences for their transgressions will forever be the most worrisome. They include people like Lucy, Troy, and Evan; these were the ones without stable social networks, housing, skills, or education to obtain legitimate means of employment. With methamphetamine-related felony convictions and addictions that still called to them like sirens in the night, there was little doubt that they were highly at risk for relapse or reentry in the world of methamphetamine. Evan, despite being clean for years, was still haunted by the demons of his former life and had been unable to find anything comparable to methamphetamine in his current life. Even he knew, despite his love for the very thing that would destroy all that he was and take everything from him, that it never had really been all that it seemed. The stronghold methamphetamine continued to have on him was evident as he reminisced about why some people begin using methamphetamine and others don't.

Evan: Ooh, I've got a real good answer for you . . . I think it's almost a matter of hope. If you're living life and you don't have a lotta hope for things to get any better, or for things to change, or anything, you can do a little bit of crank and feel great about everything, all day long and all night long, and the only thing you gotta do to feel good again is just do a little bit more, and it's so cheap, and so effective, and it works so good, and it's a lie. It's a lie. It is a lie. When it lulls you into a false sense of "I'm gonna take care of everything. I'm here for you. I understand you." This is the drug talking now.

It had been a lie.

CONCLUSIONS

There is an exit door from the world of methamphetamine and there is hope for those who find it. However, the reality remains that only some will find it and even fewer will be able to open it. It is fortunate that the stories of these adults did not stop in the midst of the darkest moments. It is also fortunate that, unlike those who become irreversibly lost in the world of methamphetamine with no hope for escape, each of them had stopped using the drug and exited from life they once lived.

Though their reasons for desisting and periods of abstinence varied, at the time of their interviews they were out. Most were still in the process of transitioning. As anyone traveling this road knows or will learn, stopping use and disengaging from dealing and manufacturing the drug are only the beginning. There are many trials and tribulations that await them in weeks, months, and years that lie ahead. Understanding the challenges associated with reintegration into conventional society is necessary for comprehending the difficulties of overcoming methamphetamine and the associated lifestyle. They are critical components for appreciating why some people will succeed while others may be destined to fail.

The obstacles and barriers to be overcome during the transition from one life to the next include those that existed in the past, and those which will need to be faced in the future ahead of them. Dualities exist within such transitions. There is the challenge of coming to terms with all that they had done and the lives they had affected. These things must be remembered, while the once enjoyable and positive aspects of their former lives must now be forever forgotten. It is a reality made more difficult due to the fact many still talked about all they had once loved about methamphetamine and what it had brought into their lives. Their former lives, as destructive and unsustainable as they had been, were more exciting and pleasurable than the ones after meth. The incompatibilities between life as it once had been and life as it would be now had to be reconciled. Coming to terms with life as it is, without meth-amphetamine, can make successful transitioning more difficult.

Thus, an important aspect of life after methamphetamine is the require-ment that those who leave the life remember the negative aspects of their former lives while working to forget the positive ones. In rebuilding their lives they must learn how to live "normally," and handle the everyday stresses and challenges. They must live with the consequences of their former lives, be these physical reminders or mental ones. Above all else, they must learn to live again, find a sense of purpose and self-value, and learn to enjoy the highs of life, without meth.

While the transition to conventional life is one that must be walked alone, success is truly not possible without the support and assistance of others. It is another dimension of reintegration—the need to reestablish social ties and take the steps necessary to rebuild conventional lives. Personal and social relationships must be exchanged—those with persons in the drug lifestyle for those with persons who are not. There is a need to reconnect and reestablish relationships and ties with some people while severing all connections with others. The fact that many had cut all ties with prosocial others and had never obtained the skill set necessary to live conventionally makes the journey all the more treacherous. Skill sets and knowledge are needed to support both personal transformations and pragmatic, practical ones.

Stability can only be achieved on building blocks of life. People need pro-social relationships with family members, spouses or significant others, and nonusing peers. People need to develop the skill sets that will allow them to become gainfully employed. There is a need for stable housing and help over-coming mental, psychological, emotional, and physical reminders and traumas from the past.

Transitions become easier over time, as methamphetamine becomes a thing of the past. In their post-methamphetamine lives, some exist on more stable ground than others, with those living closest to the edge of both worlds being at greatest risk for relapse and reentrance into their former lives. The challenges of lacking necessary resources, supports, and a means of obtaining legal income can be compounded and overshadowed by the weight of criminal records comprised of felony convictions. For those so labeled, words such as "addiction," "methamphetamine," "manufacturing," and "felon" become tied to their identi-ties, sometimes forever. Past crime and transgressions transform into labels that will forever serve as reminders of the past and all they have done.

Transitions are simplified and smoother for those who managed to escape their former lifestyles without detection or the application of such labels; this includes those who never got caught and the others who were given a second chance. For some, the reality is that no one, beyond those that they themselves might choose to tell, would ever know the truths of what they did. Despite the fact that they had engaged in many of the same behaviors as the others, they would be insulated from the consequences that come with the application of stigmatizing labels. The potential impact of their former life on their new one would be reduced and minimized.

One should not minimize the challenges that lie ahead. The reality is that some of them were still in the midst of arduous and heavy uphill battles; these included those with the shortest periods of sobriety, those lacking life stability, those facing lengthy periods of incarceration upon failure to transition successfully, and those still carrying the mental and physical reminders of their pasts.

Their transitions are not worth less simply because methamphetamine was involved or because many poor choices were made along the way. All of life's transitions are challenging; even positive ones can be difficult and nerve-wracking. This is part of the reason it is often easier to stay on one path than it is to change to another. Transitions are, by their very nature, shaky and uncertain. They require shifts in how we think, what we do, and changes in how we do things. They require new ways of thinking and being. They necessitate moving from lifestyles that are known to those that are not. To the extent that the transitions in this case involve leaving the highs of a methamphetamine-fueled life, they are more complicated and subject to being compromised. There are many uncertainties in the pathways that lie ahead. And often these people, like anyone else, are more comfortable with the things they know than the ones they don't.

The unspoken truth of life after meth is that, despite access to support and the acquisition of stability, the realities of all they had known and all they had done were parts of their lives they would have to live with forever; past experiences and memories of previous encounters would be, for many, imprinted on them for the rest of their lives. They, like us all, would forever have to face the demons that haunted them. The reality is that many will continue in their struggles, forever straddling the two incompatible worlds they had experienced in their lives. This would be among the greatest feat of their lives.

Even those who eventually succeed will never be able to make up for lost time and undo all the harms that had been done. The truth is also that, in the end, only some will make it. However, it is not by chance that many of their stories would end with a message of hope; it would be the reason they had been willing to share such stories with a complete stranger. At the end of it all, they wanted their past mistakes to serve as a warning to others and to provide concrete evidence, by the very lives they were leading, that there is a way out. There is life after meth. It was something they had to learn the hard way. Roman summarized it best.

Roman: [Meth] ruined my life. I was about to lose my wife, she was gonna take my son. I about lost my job. The thing about this stuff, methamphetamine or whatever, the disease as we call it, it only wants the stuff that is most important in your life. It don't want the small stuff. It wants your family; it wants your money; it wants your house; it wants your car; it wants your life. That's what's weird. Until you get sober you don't realize that, but it don't want nothin', the only thing it wants is the most important things in your world.

He went on to say:

Roman: The way I look at it now, because I used to always live in the past, well, that's done. *There ain't nothin' I can do to change it.* What's important is right here in the now. I can't control anything that happens tomorrow. I live in the now. Man, for the first time in my life, Rashi, I'm content in my life.

He finally found what he had been looking for all along.

CHAPTER 10

The Journey Ends?

All I can think of is . . . If somebody was reading this or listening to this who was maybe at a crossroads where they were maybe thinking about doing some methamphetamine, trying it out, or maybe if they had tried it a few times or even if whatever, using it, all I can say is, just don't, don't do it, cause it's not, you're not going to make it out of it . . . Three ways out. You can quit, you can go to jail, or you can die. And that's it. There's no success stories with methamphetamine . . . It's a bad life. It's a bad life. You can't have good things, it's not wholesome. It's not good. You won't have anything. You might have a lot of flash and a lot of show, but that's all gonna go. And it's not worth it.

—Evan

ILLUSION AND DISILLUSIONMENT

In the end, the high life had only been an illusion. Eventually, they all would see things as they really were, even those still struggling with their love for meth. Moving forward, however, requires not only seeing things as they really are but envisioning how they could be. Only by seeing both contradictory and seemingly incompatible perspectives can the gap that separates the two begin to narrow. Eventually, delusions must be replaced by reality. It is an endeavor many resist for as long as possible.

While these adults never really knew what they were seeking, they believed they had found it in methamphetamine. In reality, what meth offered was no more than an illusion, presenting herself as a friend, lover, soother, and seductress. She offered them joy, excitement, pleasure, and a sense of self-worth. She made their bodies feel powerful and strong. She altered their perceptions of reality and enticed them into believing they could conquer the world, all while making them feel alive in a way many had never experienced before. However, in the end, none of it was real.

There is nothing that can make you happy all the time and no drug that can fix all the hardships, difficulties, and challenges of life. People were never meant to stay awake for days on end. Pain, suffering, and tragedy are inevitable parts of life. No drug can make them go away. Yet people continue to use and abuse various types of drugs as they have for thousands of years.

Even after coming to terms with the devastating, life-altering consequences of their former lives, some still referred to it as love. The illogical and perplexing nature of it all prompted me many times to stop mid-interview and directly ask them how they could still love something that had destroyed them, their loved ones, and their lives. It is a contradiction that can be seen from Lucy's explanation of the impact of her immersion:

Lucy: I mean I'm a mother, I've been a mother since I was fifteen years old. I'd live or die for my kids, they were everything to me. They're gone. I have [to] deal with that, I have to deal with the fact that I've messed their life up forever. I have to deal with the fact that I have [a criminal] record forever. I have to deal with the fact that this is me . . . and I have to be okay with that and coming to terms and understanding who I am and how to deal with me. I don't have proper coping skills. First thing I want to do, I'm a very emotional person, anything that affects me emotionally, first thing I want to do is shut 'em out and shut down . . . So it's a sick sad thing I tell you.

Her words seemed rational and logical, until in her next breath she went on say:

Lucy: I loved it, loved it! Hated what it did to me, hated what it did to my life, but that's the sickness in it . . . and that's why meth I think is so [fuckin'] serious.

It is an essential piece of the puzzle.

AN INEFFECTIVE APPROACH

The illusion of methamphetamine expands beyond these adults. We are in a state of denial when it comes to drug policy in the United States, and we have been for decades. Rather than accepting reality, we hold steadfast to the belief that we can make drug abuse go away through prohibition, criminalization, and punishment. For decades, we have increased penalties to stop drugs. We do this in spite of evidence that indicates nearly half of all Americans have used drugs at some point in their lives. It is only now, after decades of direct and indirect harms, tragedy, and death, that the tide is slowly beginning to turn.

The methamphetamine problem and life experiences described throughout this book emerged, flourished, and adapted under the umbrellas of prohibition and the war on drugs, which failed not only in the United States but in countries around the world.[1] Prohibition did not work for alcohol. It has not worked for cocaine, heroin, or methamphetamine. It is time to reevaluate current policies to assess whether they achieved their goals.

Drugs are accessible, and in some cases, cheaper and more potent, despite decades of ever-increasing numbers of arrests, convictions, and incarcerations for drug-related offenses. For the first time in history, some state legislatures are allocating more funds to criminal justice system expenditures than education.[2] Like other social problems, this one is not only extremely complex but it evolves and changes over time. The failures of our drug laws have been documented for years.[3]

The recognition that this approach would be futile was recognized decades ago. In a 1969 report Ploscowe foresaw challenges that lay ahead, stating:

> Since all confirmed addicts cannot be incarcerated, permanently, there will always be addicts at liberty to serve as customers for an illicit drug traffic. Even where drug addicts are sentenced to penal or correctional institutions, they eventually come out . . . Severe penalties and strict enforcement may deter or discourage some drug peddlers. But there will always be others attracted by the lure of the large profits to be made in the drug traffic. The very severity of law enforcement tends to increase the price of drugs on the illicit market and the profits to be made therefrom. The lure of profits and the risks of the traffic simply challenge the ingenuity of the underworld peddlers to find new channels of distribution and new customers, so that profits can be maintained despite the risks involved.[4]

Though the language may have changed, the broader points have not. It is evident there are no simple solutions for multidimensional and multifaceted problems.

Before substantial changes can begin, three facts must be acknowledged. First, legal classification is not a true representation of drug-related risks, dangers, and harms. Two of the most harmful and deadly drugs, alcohol and tobacco, are not only legal, but tolerated and advertised. Second, attempts to reduce supply in the drug market are doomed to fail; the profits of the black market and illicit drug trade are too high. Third, current policies fail to provide treatment and services to those with the greatest need, as heterogeneity is not taken into account. Few who violate the law and are criminally sanctioned for drugs ever receive the help they need.

We no longer have a right to continue on a broken path that contributes to the problems we face. This is our responsibility. This is a social problem and a public health problem. It is one with a very real potential to adversely affect generations to come. We ignore it at our own peril. The time is now.

ENVISIONING CHANGE: ESSENTIAL ELEMENTS

So where do we go from here? Programs and policies aimed at reducing America's demand for drugs and minimizing the harms related to them at all levels must be supported, developed, and refined as needed.

Initiating change will require a willingness to consider new responses and alternatives, collaboration at all levels and among diverse stakeholders, and monetary and nonmonetary investments in programs, solutions, and communities plagued by drugs. This is not something federal responses can address alone. Nor is it one that state and local communities can pursue in the absence of federal or private monetary support. A collaborative approach based on data, evidence, and input from diverse parties—including academics, practitioners from law enforcement and child welfare, medical professionals, local community members, and those formerly involved with drugs is needed. Drug policies and responses must include both those based on sound scientific data and new, innovative and possibly "untested" solutions that break new ground.

At the national level, there is a need for a presidential commission to study drugs and drug policy. The success of such a commission would depend on the polity having the political and ideological will to seriously consider recommendations and support needed changes. To the extent that the methamphetamine problem is one that proliferates in rural communities, where few opportunities for social and economic advancement exist, future responses need to include strategies aimed at revitalization and community investments. In places where few opportunities for social advancement and livable wages exist, drugs will always be one of the solutions for those seeking escape and a way to earn otherwise unattainable amounts of money.

The following three areas serve as a starting point. In many ways, each applies to the stories shared here.

DRUG PREVENTION, EDUCATION, AWARENESS, AND OPPORTUNITIES FOR OPEN DISCUSSION

Prevention and education are critical to prevent some from ever using drugs and giving those who experiment and use them with the information they need to stay safe. This could be achieved through the following:

- *Fact-Based Prevention and Drug Education Programs:* There is a need for programs that provide accurate information on the effects and side effects of drugs, including risks and benefits. Educational efforts should move beyond messages that induce fear, overstate risk, and proliferate propaganda.

- *Increasing Awareness of Potentially Harmful Activities and Trends:* Concentrated and directed information campaigns should be developed for specific target audiences, including adolescents, parents, and others. Such efforts should address not only illicit drug use but other risky behaviors as well.

- *Safe Havens for Open Discussions about Risky Behaviors:* While hotlines are currently available for rape, sexual assault, domestic violence, and suicide, no such avenues are available for drugs. As a result, these activities continue to take place underground and remain hidden from adults, caregivers, and medical professionals who may be able to help. This could be achieved through community programs and via 1–800 hotlines.

TREATMENT, REINTEGRATION, AND OPPORTUNITIES FOR REPARATIONS

Support is needed for those who abuse drugs and become immersed in drug lifestyles. The types of services to be developed and supported should be based on the input of local communities and discussions about local needs, and ideally should include persons familiar with the current systems available as well as critical gaps. Assistance is needed in multiple areas. These include:

- *More Effective Mental-Health Services and Treatment Programs:* Research is needed to better understand the utility and value of different types of programs, services, and approaches for those addicted to different types of drugs. Treatment programs must be designed to be more comprehensive in terms of treating more than just addiction to drugs. Mental health components and attractions to other dimensions of drug lifestyles must also be addressed.

- *More Comprehensive and Systematic Reintegration Programs:* Programs that support education, job-skill development, and other prosocial behaviors are needed to assist with reintegration efforts. In addition, means of reducing the stigma and shame of addictions and related behaviors are needed.

- *Opportunities for Reparations:* Those convicted, incarcerated, or otherwise labeled as criminals should be provided with opportunities to make amends for past wrongs.

ADDRESSING PUBLIC HEALTH

The responsibility for addressing public health requires collaboration, innovation, investment, and commitment by all levels of government, as well as those in the private sector and local communities. To the extent that public health risks extend beyond those directly engaged, the responsibilities for sharing in the development of solutions and responses do so as well. Recommendations include:

- *Better Responses, Services, and Follow-Up for At-Risk Youth:* Comprehensive and systematic responses for handling at-risk children must be developed within each state for implementation at all levels.
- *Syringe Exchange/Needle Access for IV Drug Users:* Syringe or needle exchange or provision programs and mechanisms for disposal need to be implemented in communities where intravenous drug use occurs.
- *Tracking and Remediation of Toxic Places:* More comprehensive and systematic responses need to be developed for the tracking and remediation of toxic places.
- *Alternatives Aimed at Reducing Drug Violence:* Innovative approaches aimed at reducing drug-related violence need to identified and implemented.

CHANGE IS ON THE HORIZON

Recent events and shifts in policies and responses to drugs leave us with a sense of optimism for the future. Changes are occurring at various levels of government and across state lines. On April 24, 2013, President Obama unveiled his plan to reform federal drug policy. Presented as the "twenty-first-century drug policy," one of the most noteworthy shifts was illustrated by the inclusion of the statement, "Drug policy is a public health issue, not just a criminal justice issue."[5] Four specific points serve as the foci of the new direction: preventing drug use through education, expanding access to drug treatment, reforming the criminal justice system, and supporting those in recovery while lifting the stigma that accompanies substance-use disorders.

Efforts to minimize drug-related harms are also occurring at federal and state levels. In 2013, New Jersey Governor Chris Christie signed into law a piece of legislation aimed directly at reducing drug overdose–related deaths. The "Good Samaritan" law provides immunity from prosecution for those who report drug overdoses. Similar laws are now in place in numerous states. In 2014, former Attorney General Eric Holder began urging law enforcement agencies to train and equip their officers with naloxone, a heroin overdose antidote.[6] Police officers and other first responders in cities across the country are now being provided with heroin overdose antidote kits. Without broader changes in attitudes and responses, such efforts are likely not to be utilized to their fullest potential, because the very real risks of detection, arrest, and prosecution remain high.

The severity of this issue and the urgency of the need for better responses took center stage when on January 8, 2014, Governor Shumlin of Vermont devoted his State of the State Address to the topic of drugs and abuse. His recommendation for reframing responses included addressing drugs as a health crisis, strengthening law enforcement, and retooling the criminal justice system. He continued, saying:

> But these actions represent basic, good government responses to an emergency. Just as you expected us to work across agencies and across state and local government to help us all recover from the devastation of a tropical storm, so too should you expect us to approach this crisis of drug addiction with coordination and effective action. All of us, together, will drive toward our goal of recovery by working with one another creatively, relentlessly, and without division.[7]

The implications of failing to respond in long-lasting and effective ways are significant. The financial costs of our failed efforts are high, including the costs of social services, the criminal justice system, and incarceration.

Change is not something that can be achieved by a few academics through a handful of studies. Rather, it will take a collective effort, with the greatest minds from diverse disciplines working in collaboration with experts from multiple areas of specialization for the purpose of identifying better solutions and responses. The potential stakes of failing even to attempt to do better are high.

AN ONGOING PROBLEM

Methamphetamine continues to be a problem in the United States, and increasingly abroad. It remains widely available and is becoming cheaper and purer than before.[8] While methamphetamine may not be the biggest or dead-liest drug problem worldwide, in the communities and lives of families plagued by it, the urgency and life-altering consequences are undeniable and real. It is easy to understand why this persists in small and isolated rural communities where the closest towns may be hours away. With limited economic oppor-tunities and few avenues for social advancement, drugs fill a void. Dealing and manufacturing provide otherwise unachievable avenues of success. The true extent of the problem is unknown, because much of what goes on remains hidden and undocumented.

People use drugs because of their biological, neurological, psychological, and social effects. They use them as a way to alter perceptual and physical experiences, and their underlying motivations at least at first, and at least for some, are similar to the reasons people use alcohol. While drug use is often framed as abnormal, deviant, or criminal, the enjoyment of altered states has been around for centuries. Whether we are comfortable admitting it or not, rebellion and curiosity are part of the normal transition to adulthood. The problem is that sometimes things get out of control.

Though some might argue that the adults in this study made a series of poor decisions over time, less-than-rational decision-making is not restricted to those who use illicit drugs. People of great stature place their families, careers, and entire life's work in jeopardy for something they desire. The fact that people are sometimes willing to risk all for sex, money, or power may seem completely irrational and nonsensical, but it is a reality that is not too far out of the bounds of what goes on in the world of methamphetamine.

The cost-benefit assessments that underlie decisions about methamphet-amine were evident throughout the interviews. Explanations for continued involvement alluded to something more than physical addiction. Benefits, which were weighed against costs and risks, evolved and changed over time. Though decisions are not typically "rational" in the economic sense of the word, they do fit within the notion of "satisficing." That is, decisions were good enough at achieving specific and purposive outcomes. Even in the midst of their addiction, as behaviors spiraled out of control, some knew what they were doing. They were making choices and decisions, albeit constrained, about what they were going to do and how they were going to do it.

The inconsistency of responding to drug abuse simultaneously as a disease and as a crime lies at the heart of the problem. In *Addiction: A Disorder of Choice*, Heyman raises the point:

That current policies have nineteenth-century precedents does not mean that legal prohibitions should continue to be maintained or that the view that addiction is a disease is correct. History does not reveal the best drug policy or explain why people continue to inject themselves with heroin despite the realization that heroin is undermining much of what they hold valuable.[9]

He ends the book discussing the complexity of human behaviors using an array of examples of how social proscriptions and rationality combine to influence drug use; "The population trends and lever-pressing rates tell the same story: choice tends to produce less than optimal outcomes. Addiction is a disorder of choice."[10]

There is little question that, for the adults in this study, it was about more than just the drug. There was an attraction to the lifestyle that accompanied immersion. Though the seductive manner in which some of them described their former experiences was unexpected, in retrospect it should not have been. Crime and other behaviors hold an attractive and seductive element, as shown by Katz in *The Seductions of Crime*:

> Something important happened when it became obscenely sensational or damnably insensitive to track the lived experience of criminality in favor of imputing factors to the background of crime that are invisible in its situational manifestation.[11]

Scientists are still in the process of trying to understand the complexities of human behavior. The concept of "addiction" is not as clear as it once seemed. The adults in this study didn't just talk about their addiction to the drug; there were those who became addicted to other aspects of the lifestyle, including money, power, and the sheer ability to manufacture meth. There is growing evidence that some people become addicted to nondrug activities including gambling, sex, food, and video games. While there are likely neurological and physiological components at play, perhaps these behaviors stem from something more. It is time to think outside of the box and develop creative and innovative responses to drugs.

IN CONCLUSION

This story ends where it began—with the truth of the tragedy that is methamphetamine. It is the illusion of methamphetamine, that it gives you everything you ever wanted, while the truth is that it takes everything you have.

This story is, at its very core, a story of delusions, mistruths, and misperceptions. Methamphetamine devastated peoples' lives. Stories of loss and destruction were repeated over and over. These adults sacrificed everything, including relationships with the most important people in their lives—parents, spouses, and children. Wes summarized how methamphetamine impacted his life.

Wes: Gosh, in every way, physically, emotionally, spiritually, environmentally. Everything. All of 'em negative. I became somebody I wasn't.

The truth of the tragedy is the hard-core, in-your-face reality that results when one comes to terms with life as it is, not as it appears to be. It is a life that at times, especially in our most difficult of moments, seems to lack purpose and presents itself as unbearable. It is in our weakest moments that we are most vulnerable. In many ways the journeys of these adults parallel our own. Each person in this world is on their own journey through life. Each makes decisions. Each makes mistakes. Each will struggle within themselves and the world around them to find purpose, value, and meaning in life. Each is forced to find the ways he or she will cope with the realities of life. Each will fight to maintain a stronghold on the dreams and hopes they once carried as a young child.

Each dimension was interrelated, and yet they were also distinct. Not everyone progressed from using to dealing to manufacturing the drug. Levels and patterns changed and shifted over time. Involvement with methamphetamine, like other aspects of life, is dynamic and subject to change. There were differences between people, and variations in individuals' experiences over time. While each of the individuals in this study eventually arrived at a point of needing to stop using and get out, some had used for years and even decades before their drug use and lifestyle spiraled out of control. As the data show, people do stop using and leave the lifestyle. They stop using, dealing, and manufacturing. While it may not always be because they want to, and not always be on their own, they stop. The methamphetamine lifestyle ultimately proves unsustainable.

Over time, they became increasingly engaged in the diverse dimensions of the drug lifestyle and intertwined in social networks with others who were similarly involved. During progression into the methamphetamine life, focus is maintained on the benefits of the drug and accompanying lifestyle. Dealing and manufacturing are a means to an end. They are ways to support an increasingly expensive habit and the life that goes with it. In addition, they provide other attractions that bind people to the seductive aspects of the life including money, power, sex, and the ability to create the very thing that they and those around them desire. So why did they do it? They did it because they wanted to. They did it because they were in a social context and physical environment where such activities were not only possible, but ongoing. They did it because they could.

Life in the world of methamphetamine is the antithesis of normal life. This is part of the reason they use the drug. It becomes a very real part of why getting out becomes difficult. In the end, however, for those most heavily immersed, the intoxicated life is unsustainable. Inevitably their journeys ended with suffering, pain, loss, and heartbreak. For them, there was no other outcome. In addition to losing everything they had, they lost themselves. It would be the main reason they were willing to come and tell their stories. The tales they told illuminated the dark world of methamphetamine and served as a testament to the fact that people can and do get out. There was an urgency to show the world of methamphetamine for what it is, and to warn those who might be tempted to visit and downplay the tragedies that exist within it. The life experiences and tragedies described here serve as a warning and call for action. The true purpose for allowing documentation of their lives was clear— to help others.

Over time, the highs of methamphetamine and the accompanying lifestyle transform. The highs of intoxication turn into experiences characterized by paranoia, diverse types of hallucinations, and for some, psychosis. Drug-fueled hallucinations become indistinguishable from reality. Interactions shift from ones primarily engaged with peers and friends to ones with those on the periphery of life. Methamphetamine and money become inextricably linked with risk and danger. The life evolves from one that is intoxicating to one that is risky, and finally into one that is dark. Things did not appear as they actually were, at least in the beginning. Rather, the lifestyle transformed and changed as entanglement increased. In each new dimension, experiences became riskier and more dangerous. Eventually, what started out as fun ends up deadly. In the end, things become dark and all lines of ethics and morality are crossed. It is only then that the original illusion begins to dissipate and the world of methamphetamine reveals itself for what it really is.

Getting out of the lifestyle and desisting from use were only the beginning. There are many struggles to be overcome in life after meth, including physical, mental, emotional, and legal ones. Rebuilding lives included finding new, legal activities and connecting or reconnecting with relationships that had been abandoned or broken along the way. Those who escaped the life and evaded the label of methamphetamine offender, or worse yet, manufacturer, faced fewer struggles than those for whom such labels were attached.

The burning question remains—*where are they now?* Did they succeed in their transitions to conventional life, or did they get pulled back into the lives they once lived? The truth is that we will never know. We are left with snapshots of where they were at time of their interviews. They had emerged from the world of methamphetamine to share their stories, tragedies, and experiences. To some degree, all of the adults in this study were still in transition; some were more stable and securely settled into their new and primarily conventional lives than others. In reality, the risk will always exist that they could relapse or reenter their former lifestyle. Even after years of sobriety and conventional living, reentry to meth is possible. The stories presented here don't end with these adults and whether or not they succeed. An overwhelming majority of them had children. Thus, a bigger and somewhat more concerning question is, what happens to them? It is a question that must be asked and one for which there is no answer.

The issues today are drugs, crime, incarceration, public health, and our future. They collide with striking force when it comes to understanding the world of methamphetamine as it exists in the underground of the world around it. There should be little doubt at this point that the methamphetamine problem is real. It is dangerous. It is destructive. It is deadly. It is hard core. It is the most dangerous drug for those who become immersed, and for those affected by them.

If it were just about the high, it wouldn't be as bad as it actually is. But as the discussion about ancillary public health concerns demonstrated, it's more than that. If the intensifying violence in Mexico is any indicator, many large-scale traffickers and manufacturers are themselves "addicted" to the money and power that accompanies involvement in the life. Authorities have confiscated record seizures in recent years in countries around the world. Yet, these only represent the ones detected and caught. Unknown quantities of methamphetamine remain available on the streets today.

Our failure stems from not learning the lessons of history and hoping the problem will someday just go away. Reductions in local manufacturing in the United States, following the implementation of precursor controls, were hailed by some as a victory in the fight against meth. Within years of harsher laws and controls, offenders adapted.[12] Local manufacturers started making smaller batches via the shake-and-bake method, and traffickers offset reductions in local supply by trafficking more into the United States to meet and create local demand. As a whole, manufacturing is not solely attractive to those addicted to the drug. It is attractive to those who want money.

It is no longer okay to say that what we are doing will work. Methamphetamine is out of the bag. Recipes on how to make it are easily accessible. It's too late to start over or hit the reset button. There is no reset button for this issue. We need more creative approaches to drug policy. The time has arrived to start thinking outside the box. The challenge is to see through the illusions and help think of more effective responses to the problems that plague society. The challenge is to no longer support a political discourse that holds steadfast to the mantra that what we are doing is working, works good enough, or is better than any alternatives.

The stakes of not responding in more effective, innovative, and creative ways are high. The methamphetamine problem is expansive, and the harms and dangers it promulgates have the potential to reach far beyond those directly engaged in using, dealing, or manufacturing the drug.

The time for better responses is now. We sit here, four decades into the clandestine methamphetamine manufacturing problem. We must accept the reality that our failed responses have contributed to the dangerous presence of purer methamphetamine that is cheaper and more widely available on the streets of the United States. It is critical that we continue in our attempts to prevent methamphetamine use and accelerate efforts aimed at helping those who have passed this point and become problematically immersed.

We must be courageous enough to have the social and political will to change direction and open our minds to new and innovative responses. We must be willing to take risks in our approaches to drugs in general and methamphetamine specifically. This may require entering unchartered territory, where the outcomes and risks are unknown. This may require accepting the realities as they exist and making every attempt to minimize the harms done along the way.

The words of political philosopher Hannah Arendt ring true for this book and are reflective of the truths and realities of our times just as they were when first published back in 1950s. Though focused on a topic completely unrelated to drugs (i.e., totalitarianism), the words are haunting in their application to this problem in our time today:

Comprehension does not mean denying the outrageous, deducing the unprecedented from precedents, or explaining phenomena by such analogies and generalities that the impact of reality and the shock of experience are no longer felt. It means, rather, examining and bearing consciously the burden which our century has placed on us—neither denying its existence nor submitting meekly to its weight. Comprehension, in short, means the unpremeditated, attentive facing up to, and resisting of, reality—whatever it may be.[13]

Those captivated by the television series *Breaking Bad* may be interested in how the stories presented here fit with the fictional methamphetamine cook Walter White. Despite parallels between the story portrayed on TV and the one told here, differences exist. Unlike these adults, Walter White never consumed the drug he was manufacturing. His initial motivation for manufacturing never had anything to do with his own personal desire or need for meth. In the beginning, he cooked for one reason—the money. As a result of the unsurpassed quality of methamphetamine he was able to produce, he eventually rises to become a preeminent cook, giving his alter ego the name Heisenberg.

Yet even Walter eventually becomes seduced by the world and all it offers. Over time, he too is drawn into the lifestyle associated with the production of the drug. There is danger. There is risk. There is power. There is control. And there is money—lots of money! As Walter becomes immersed, he begins to value the things that come with the lifestyle more than he does himself or his loved ones. Even Walter crosses a Rubicon in his journey into the drug world, and he arrives at a point of willingness to sacrifice anything; to sacrifice it all. As he too eventually finds out, there would be no happy ending. Though his motivations and patterns of production varied, in the end lives were destroyed and people were hurt. And yet, in the end even Walter finally admits, "I did it for me. I liked it. I was good at it. And, I was, really . . . I was alive."[14]

Season after season, viewers came to appreciate the danger, risk, and seduction of the world of methamphetamine. The show was not palatable for everyone, because of the darkness portrayed. Yet the darkness is real. It is parallel to the darkness that exists in reality, on the streets where meth is bought, used, made, traded, and sold.

The time to learn from those who have lived in the world of methamphetamine and escaped is now. For people do escape the world of methamphetamine. This book and these stories are evidence of that. But for all who get out, there are many who never will. The paths into and out of the world of methamphetamine are littered with dangers, risks, destruction, and death. This is not just another drug scare, and is not just a fad that will somehow eventually go away by itself.

While not representative or generalizable, the findings presented here are insightful, informative, and likely to apply to others in similar situations. They shared their experiences to educate and inform others. For those who have never used methamphetamine, the message is to be forewarned. For those who have become immersed, the message is that there is a way out. For those who make policy, the message is one of desperation—something needs to be done.

These accounts shed light on the motivations underlying involvement with methamphetamine. People used, dealt, and manufactured for specific and purposeful reasons. However, heterogeneity existed within each dimension. Variations characterized what are otherwise commonly conceptualized as singular types of behaviors. Users expressed preferences about the types of methamphetamine they favored, methods of use, and social contexts within which they used. Dealers operated at different levels of the distribution chain, serving as the critical link between users and producers of the drug. People learned how to make methamphetamine from others in their social networks; some seized opportunities to learn, while others sought them out or purposefully created them. Cooks differed in the methods of production they utilized and the patterns of manufacturing. Risk was part of the game. They took whatever risks necessary to evade detection, often placing themselves and others directly in harm's way.

In the end their tragedies were not for naught. The ability to contribute to the discourse about the drug problem, methamphetamine, and drug policy brings meaning to the darkness they survived. No one says it is easy, but it is possible. At the end of the day they wanted people to know that if they could make it, so could others. Their strength and conviction were unexpected. These aren't just "faces of meth"—disturbing, scarred, beat-down, and out-of-control people. They served to remind us that at the end of the day even those immersed in drug lifestyles are not demons or monsters, but people, too. They are mothers and fathers, sons and daughters, brothers and sisters. None set out to live the life they led. Not one had grown up with the goal of becoming a user, dealer, or manufacturer. Yet they all became involved, and then, eventually, they all got out.

These adults had a story to tell. They shared what they had learned and lived through so that we might find better solutions and responses to the problems that had plagued them and the ones continuing to plague people and their communities. They risked revealing and reliving some of the darkest and most destructive things they had ever done in their entire lives, entrusting a complete stranger with stories they hoped would someday, somehow, make a difference. They had successfully exited the world of methamphetamine. At least for now. At least for today.

People do escape the world of methamphetamine. They do get out. Even those most heavily immersed in using, dealing, and manufacturing can get out. Maybe not all will. Maybe not many do. But there are some who will and some who do. I know. I met them. This is their story. It ends as one of hope. The line between illusion and reality is illustrated from a line from a fictional show: "Never give up hope. No matter how dark things seem."[15]

This book is the culmination of years of studies aimed directly at understanding why people were willing to be involved with methamphetamine, a drug that destroyed not only their lives but their bodies, health, and the lives of their loved ones. The questions from the very beginning were "What is going on?" and "Why?" After years of research, I am beginning to understand. It is my hope that now you are beginning to as well. The message shared is a powerful one—there is beauty in that there are lessons to be learned even in the darkest of things.

APPENDIX A

- Unusual, strong chemical orders (e.g., cat urine, ether, ammonia, acetone)
- Indicator items located in unusual places in a residence (e.g., chemical cans in the kitchen or bedroom rather than the garage)
- Numerous unusual items in/near a residence (e.g., damaged/dismantled lithium camera batteries, matchbooks, match heads, striker plates; these items are often found under homes or in burn piles further from the home on rural properties)
- Chemical stains on carpet, wood flooring, walls, sinks, tubs, or in yard
- Corroded plumbing pipes from acid meth-waste materials
- Booby traps located on a property (e.g., nails in the yard, pipe-bomb materials or devices stored/hidden on the property)
- Homeowners who are nervous about visitors to the neighborhood or their residence
- Cash payments for rent or large purchases
- High traffic at a residence, property, or location during unusual hours; different vehicles arriving for short periods of time
- Excessive amounts of trash (e.g., antifreeze containers, lantern fuel cans, red chemically stained coffee filters, drain cleaner containers, duct tape)

- Unusually high number of glass containers in a residence
- Darkened/blacked-out windows at a residence (covered with aluminum foil, plywood, sheets, blankets)
- Increased security surrounding a residence (e.g., video cameras, alarm systems, guard dogs, reinforced doors, electrified fencing) and overcompensation of security measures (e.g., multiple "Private Property" or "Beware of Dog" signs, or multiple looks on doors on certain rooms within a residence)
- Individuals exiting a residence to smoke cigarettes and/or cigars, especially during the winter
- Signs of negligence (e.g., little or no mail, visible trash, lack of newspaper delivery)

*Adapted from the Oklahoma Bureau of Narcotics and Dangerous Drugs

NOTES

1. AN INTRODUCTION TO DARKNESS

1. Dates have been changed to protect the identities of participants.
2. NIDA 2006; NIDA 2012; NIDA 2013; NIDA 2014
3. The administration of drugs rectally is referred to as "plugging."
4. See NIDA 2006; NIDA 2012; NIDA 2013; NIDA 2014.
5. See NIDA 2006; NIDA 2012; NIDA 2013; NIDA 2014.
6. "Tweakers" is a slang term used to describe methamphetamine addicts.
7. Garriott 2011.
8. Winter 2014.
9. Bland 2012.
10. Givens 2013.
11. Lambert 2013.
12. Christie 2013.
13. "Bloomfield Man Found" 2013.
14. South 2012.
15. WHSV News Staff 2013.
16. Cave 2012.
17. Mullen 2013.
18. Weisheit and White 2009; Shukla et al. 2012.
19. Ransley et al. 2011; Meade et al. 2012; UNODC 2011; UNODC 2014.
20. Scott and Dedel 2006.
21. NDIC 2008; NDIC 2011.
22. NDIC 2008; NDIC 2011; Shukla et al. 2012.
23. Scott and Dedel 2006.; NDIC 2008.
24. DEA 2000.
25. CDC 2005.

26. DEA n.d.a.

27. DEA 1996.

28. By 2011, funding for the Community Oriented Policing Services (COPS) methamphetamine grants dried up and the Drug Enforcement Agency (DEA) stopped assisting states with clandestine laboratory cleanup.

29. "Oklahoma Worries about Cost of Meth Lab Cleanup" 2011; Ban 2011.

30. These include the 1988 Chemical Diversion and Trafficking Act (CDTA), the 1993 Domestic Chemical Diversion Control Act (DCDCA), the 1996 Comprehensive Methamphetamine Control Act (CMCA), the Methamphetamine Anti-Proliferation Act of 2000, and the Combat Methamphetamine Epidemic Act (CMEA) of 2005. See Shukla et al. 2012.

31. International controls are beyond the scope of this discussion.

32. DEA n.d.a; Shukla et al. 2012.

33. O'Connor et al. 2009.

34. In 2006 Oregon became the only state to reclassify and require a prescription for products containing pseudoephedrine; Stomberg and Sharma 2012.

35. Cunningham and Liu 2005; Dobkin and Nicosia 2009; U.S. Government Accountability Office 2013; Stomberg and Sharma 2012.

36. Scott and Dedel 2006.

37. Edlin 2002; CDC 2002.

38. Molitor et al. 1998.

39. Jansen et al. 2006.

40. ONDCP n.d.

41. Grund et al. 2013.

42. Storrs 2015.

43. CDC 2009.

44. CDC 2013.

45. CDC 2014.

46. Beittel 2009.

47. Rochkind 2012: para. 2.

48. Marijuana continues to be the most commonly used illicit drug.

49. UNODC 2011; UNODC 2014.

50. Committee on Oversight and Government Reform 2012; Shukla et al. 2012.

51. NDIC 2011.

52. This information is based on recent interviews and discussions between the author and law enforcement officials in Oklahoma; Woodward 2014.

53. DEA n.d.b.

54. DEA 1996:vii.

55. The terms *knowns, known unknowns,* and *unknown unknowns* come from a speech given at a NATO press conference by former Secretary of Defense Donald Rumsfeld on June 6, 2002. In the speech, Rumsfeld states, "There are no 'knowns.' There are thing[s] we know that we know. There are known unknowns. That is to say

there are things that we now know we don't know. But there are also unknown unknowns. There are things we don't know we don't know. So when we do the best we can and we pull all this information together, and we then say well that's basically what we see as the situation, that is really only the known knowns and the known unknowns. And each year, we discover a few more of those unknown unknowns. It sounds like a riddle. It isn't a riddle. It is a very serious, important matter." Rumsfeld 2002: para 17–18.

56. Grateful acknowledgment to Dr. Marcus Felson for this point.

57. Sommers and Baskin 2006; Sommers and Baskin 2004; Lende et al. 2007; Boeri et al. 2009.

58. Haight et al. 2009; Boeri 2013.

59. O'Brien et al. 2008; Parsons et al. 2007; Sheridan et al. 2009; Carbone-Lopez et al. 2012.

60. Sommers and Baskin 2004.

61. Baskin-Sommers and Sommers 2006; Martin et al. 2009; Sexton et al. 2009; Sommers and Baskin 2004; Somers and Baskin 2006; Tyner and Fremouw 2008; Weisheit 2008.

62. Senjo 2005.

63. Pennell et al. 1999; Jenkot 2008; Weisheit 2008; Weisheit and White 2009.; Chiu et al. 2011; Sexton et al. 2006.

64. U.S. House of Representatives 2005: para. 1.

65. The term "most dangerous drug" has historically been used to refer to other drugs as well.

66. This study was approved by the University of Central Oklahoma Institutional Review Board.

67. Based on the distance from Thackerville, Oklahoma, which is located on the Oklahoma-Texas border, and Nuevo Laredo, Mexico, one of several towns near the U.S.-Mexico border.

68. United States Census Bureau 2014.

69. Christie 2013.

70. United States Census Bureau 2014.

71. This includes one who self-identified as being in a common-law marriage.

72. All names and dates have been changed.

73. Brownstein et al. 2012:31.

2. PATHWAYS TO METHAMPHETAMINE

1. Leshner n.d.

2. Counts are based on general drug categories.

3. Not including the individual who stole prescription tablets from his father the first time.

4. Variations in type and form of methamphetamine were discussed.

3. LOVING METH

1. *Merriam-Webster Online*, s.v. "Rubicon," http://www.merriam-webster.com /dictionary/rubicon
2. *Frontline* 2011.
3. Tolerance is also an issue.
4. *Merriam-Webster Online*, s.v. "heterogeneous," http://www.merriam-webster .com/dictionary/heterogeneous
5. Merriam-Webster Online, s.v. "Rubicon," http://www.merriam-webster.com /dictionary/rubicon
6. Langton 2007:28.

5. MANUFACTURING METH

1. Two had no participation with manufacturing.
2. Details of manufacturing processes are not discussed.

6. AN INTOXICATING LIFE

1. Katz 1988:3

9. LIFE AFTER METH

1. Matthew discusses his wife and fiancée during the interview.

10. THE JOURNEY ENDS?

1. Gray 2011; Pryce 2012; O'Mahoney 2008.
2. NAACP 2011.
3. Gray 2011.
4. Joint Committee of the American Bar Association and the American Medical Association on Narcotic Drugs 1961:20–21.
5. Kerlikowske 2013.
6. "Attorney General Holder, Calling Rise in Heroin Overdoses 'Urgent Public Health Crisis'" 2014; "Attorney General Holder Announces Plans" 2014.
7. Shumlin 2014: para. 46.
8. Shukla et al. 2012.
9. Heyman 2009:11.
10. Ibid.:173.
11. Katz 1988:311.
12. Shukla et al. 2012.
13. Arendt 1966:xxx.
14. *Breaking Bad* 2013.
15. *Star Wars: The Clone Wars* 2013.

REFERENCES

Arendt, H. 1966. *The Origins of Totalitarianism* (new ed.). New York: Harcourt, Brace & World.

"Attorney General Holder Announces Plans for Federal Law Enforcement Personnel to Begin Carrying Naloxone." July 31, 2014. *Justice News.* Retrieved from http://www.justice.gov/opa/pr/attorney-general-holder-announces-plans-federal-law-enforcement-personnel-begin-carrying

"Attorney General Holder, Calling Rise in Heroin Overdoses 'Urgent Public Health Crisis,' Vows Mix of Enforcement, Treatment." March 10, 2014. *Justice News.* Retrieved from http://www.justice.gov/opa/pr/attorney-general-holder-calling-rise-heroin-overdoses-urgent-public-health-crisis-vows-mix

Ban, C. July 18, 2011. "DEA Meth Cleanup Funding Hits Counties Hard." *National Association of Counties (NACO) County News* 43 (14). Retrieved from http://www.naco.org/newsroom/countynews/Current%20Issue/7–18–11/Pages/DEAmethcleanupfundingcuthitscountieshard.aspx

Baskin-Sommers, A., and I. Sommers. 2006. "Methamphetamine Use and Violence Among Young Adults." *Journal of Criminal Justice* 34: 661–74.

Beittel, J. S. May 27, 2009. *Mexico's Drug-Related Violence.* Washington, DC: Congressional Research Service (Report No. R40582). Retrieved from http://fas.org/sgp/crs/row/R40582.pdf

Bland, A. October 25, 2012. "Boy Riding on Father's Bicycle Handlebars Burned When 'Shake-and-Bake' Meth Lab Explodes." *Tulsa World.* Retrieved from http://www.tulsaworld.com/news/crimewatch/boy-riding-on-father-s-bicycle-handlebars-burned-when-shake/image_391613ae-6b65–55ef-b213-e30caea01f43.html?TNNoMobile

"Bloomfield Man Found with Needle Stuck in His Arm." May 5, 2013. *WBIW.* Retrieved from http://www.wbiw.com/

Boeri, M. 2013. *Women on Ice: Methamphetamine Use among Suburban Women*. New Brunswick, NJ: Rutgers University Press.

Boeri, M. W., L. Harbry, and D. Gibson. 2009. "A Qualitative Exploration of Trajectories among Suburban Users of Methamphetamine." *Journal of Ethnographic and Qualitative Research* 3:139–51.

Breaking Bad. September 29, 2013; season 5, episode 16. "Felina." Retrieved from http://www.imdb.com/title/tt2301455/quotes

Brownstein, H. H., T. M. Mulcahy, B. G. Taylor, J. Fernandes-Huessy, and C. Hafford. 2012. "Home Cooking: Marketing Meth." *Contexts* 11 (1):30–35.

Carbone-Lopez, K., J. G. Owens, and J. Miller. 2012. "Women's 'Storylines' of Methamphetamine Initiation in the Midwest." *Journal of Drug Issues* 42 (3):226–46.

Cave, D. February 9, 2012. "Mexico Seizes Record Amount of Methamphetamine." *The New York Times*. Retrieved from http://www.nytimes.com/2012/02/10/world/americas/mexico-seizes-15-tons-of-methamphetamine.html?_r = 0

Centers for Disease Control and Prevention (CDC). September 2002. *Viral Hepatitis and Injection Drug Users*. Retrieved from http://www.cdc.gov/idu/hepatitis/viral_hep_drug_use.pdf

Centers for Disease Control and Prevention (CDC). April 2005. "Anhydrous Ammonia Thefts and Releases Associated with Illicit Methamphetamine Production—16 States, January 2000–June 2004." *Morbidity and Mortality Weekly Report* 54 (14):359–61. Retrieved from http://www.cdc.gov/mmwr/preview/mmwrhtml/mm5414a4.htm

Centers for Disease Control and Prevention (CDC). January 19, 2009. *Research Update: The Choking Game: CDC's Findings on a Risky Youth Behavior*. Retrieved from http://www.cdc.gov/homeandrecreationalsafety/Choking/choking_game.html

Centers for Disease Control and Prevention (CDC). July 2013. *Policy Impact: Prescription Painkiller Overdoses*. Retrieved from http://www.cdc.gov/homeandrecreational safety/rxbrief/

Centers for Disease Control and Prevention (CDC). October 2014. *Prescription Drug Overdose*. Retrieved from http://www.cdc.gov/homeandrecreationalsafety/overdose/

Chiu, Y., B. Leclerc, and M. Townsley. 2011. "Crime Script Analysis of Drug Manufacturing in Clandestine Laboratories." *British Journal of Criminology* 51:355–74.

Christie, L. February 12, 2013. "My Home Was A Former Meth Lab." *CNN Money*. Retrieved from http://money.cnn.com/2013/02/12/real_estate/home-meth-lab/index.html

Committee on Oversight and Government Reform. July 24, 2012. *Meth Revisited: Review of State and Federal Efforts to Solve the Domestic Methamphetamine Production Resurgence*. Retrieved from http://oversight.house.gov/hearing/meth-revisited-review-of-state-and-federal-efforts-to-solve-the-domestic-methamphetamine-production-resurgence/

Cunningham, J. K., and L. Liu. 2005. "Impacts of Federal Precursor Chemical Regulations on Methamphetamine Arrests." *Addiction* 100:479–88.

Dobkin, C., and N. Nicosia. 2009. "The War on Drugs: Methamphetamine, Public Health, and Crime. *American Economic Review* 99 (1):324–49.

Drug Enforcement Administration (DEA). N.d.a. *Training Required to Sell Drug Products Containing Ephedrine Pseudoephedrine and Phenylpropanolamine by Mobile Retail Vendors.* DEA Office of Diversion Control. Retrieved from http://www.deadiversion.usdoj.gov/meth/trg_mobile_081106.pdf#xml=http://search.deadiversion.usdoj.gov/texis/search/pdfhi.txt?query=Training+requirements+to+sell+drug+products+containing+ephedrine+pseudoephedrine+and+phenylpop anone+by+mobile+retail+vendors&pr=Prod-static-walk&prox=page&rorder=500&rprox=500&rdfreq=500&rwfreq=500&rlead=500&rdepth=0&sufs=2&order=r&cq= &id=4fba96e02a

Drug Enforcement Administration (DEA). N.d.b. *Methamphetamine Lab Incidents, 2004–2012.* Retrieved from http://www.justice.gov/dea/resource-center/meth-lab-maps.shtml

Drug Enforcement Administration (DEA). March 1996. *Methamphetamine Situation in the United States: Drug Intelligence Report.* Washington, DC: U.S. Department of Justice. Retrieved from http://druglibrary.net/schaffer/dea/pubs/meth/toc.htm

Drug Enforcement Administration (DEA). 2000. *Chemical Control Actions—2000:* U.S. Department of Justice, Drug Enforcement Administration. Retrieved from http://www.gpo.gov/fdsys/pkg/FR-2000-09-25/pdf/00-24553.pdf

Edlin, B. R. 2002. "Prevention and Treatment of Hepatitis C in Injection Drug Users." *Hepatology* 36 (5 Suppl. 1):s210–19. doi:10.1053/jhep.2002.36809

Frontline. May 17, 2011. *How Meth Destroys the Body.* Retrieved from http://www.pbs.org/wgbh/pages/frontline/meth/body/

Garriott, W. 2011. *Policing Methamphetamine: Narco Politics in Rural America.* New York: NYU Press.

Givens, L. February 12, 2013. "Porta-Potty Meth Lab Found on Golf Course." *KFOR-TV News Channel 4.* Retrieved from http://kfor.com/2013/02/12/porta-potty-meth-lab-found-on-golf-course/

Gray, J. P. 2011. *Why Our Drug Laws Have Failed and What We Can Do about It: A Judicial Indictment on the War on Drugs* (2nd ed.). Philadelphia: Temple University Press.

Grund, J. C., A. Latypov, and M. Harris. 2013. "Breaking Worse: The Emergence of Krokodil and Excessive Injuries among People Who Inject Drugs in Eurasia." *International Journal of Drug Policy* 24 (4):265–74. doi:10.1016/j.drugpo.2013.04.007

Haight, W. L., J. D. Carter-Black, and K. Sheridan. 2009. "Mothers' Experience of Methamphetamine Addiction: A Case-Based Analysis of Rural, Midwestern Women." *Children and Youth Services Review* 31:71–77.

Heyman, G. M. 2009. *Addiction: A Disorder of Choice.* Cambridge, MA: Harvard University Press.

Jansen, K. L. R., D. Phil, and L. Theron. 2006. "Ecstasy (MDMA), Methamphetamine, and Date Rape (Drug-Facilitated Sexual Assault): A Consideration of the Issues." *Journal of Psychoactive Drugs* 38 (1):1–12. doi:10.1080/02791072.2006.10399822

Jenkot, R. 2008. "'Cooks Are Like Gods': Hierarchies in Methamphetamine-Producing Groups." *Deviant Behavior* 29 (8):667–89.

Joint Committee of the American Bar Association and the American Medical Association on Narcotic Drugs. 1961. *Drug Addiction: Crime or Disease?* Bloomington, IN: Indiana University Press.

Katz, J. 1988. *Seductions of Crime: Moral and Sensual Attractions in Doing Evil.* New York: Basic Books.

Kerlikowske, R. G. April 24, 2013. Drug Policy Reform in Action: A 21st-Century Approach. *Office of National Drug Control Policy.* Retrieved from http://www.whitehouse.gov

Lambert, J. January 30, 2013. "Meth Lab Found under Toddler's Mattress." *Local Memphis.* Retrieved from http://www.localmemphis.com/news/local/story/Meth-Lab-Found-Under-Toddlers-Mattress/d/story/biafhaUEfoKHnoSIV9GhOw

Langton, J. 2007. *Iced: Crystal Meth: The Biography of North America's Deadliest New Plague* (1st ed.). Toronto: Key Porter Books Limited.

Lende, D. H., T. Leonard, C. E. Sterk, and K. Elifson. 2007. "Functional Methamphetamine Use: The Insider's Perspective." *Addiction Research & Theory* 15 (5): 465–77.

Leshner, A. I. N.d. "Oops: How Casual Drug se Leads to Addiction." *NIDA.* Retrieved from http://archives.drugabuse.gov/Published_Articles/Oops.html

Martin, I., A. Palepu, E. Wood, K. Li, J. Montaner, and T. Kerr. 2009. "Violence among Street-Involved Youth: The Role of Methamphetamine." *European Addiction Research* 15 (1):32–38.

Meade, C. S., M. H. Watt, K. J. Sikkema, L. X. Deng, K. W. Ranby, D. Skinner, D. Pieterse, and S. C. Kalichmann. 2012. "Methamphetamine Use Is Associated with Childhood Sexual Abuse and HIV Sexual Risk Behaviors among Patrons of Alcohol-Serving Venues in Cape Town, South Africa." *Drug and Alcohol Dependence* 126:232–39.

Molitor, F., S. R. Truax, J. D. Ruiz, and R. K. Sun. 1998. "Association of Methamphetamine Use During Sex with Risky Behaviors and HIV Infection among Non-Injection Drug Users." *Western Journal of Medicine* 168 (2):93–97.

Mullen, J. February 28, 2013. "Australian Police Make Record Meth Seizure." *CNN.* Retrieved from http://www.cnn.com/2013/02/28/world/asia/australia-drugs-seizure

National Association for the Advancement of Colored People (NAACP). April 2011. *Misplaced Priorities: Over Incarcerate, Under Educate.* Retrieved from http://naacp.3cdn.net/01d6f368edbe135234_bq0m68x5h.pdf

National Drug Intelligence Center (NDIC). December 2008. *National Methamphetamine Threat Assessment 2009* (Product No. 2008-Q0317–006). Retrieved from https://www.hsdl.org/?view&did = 34482

National Drug Intelligence Center (NDIC). August 2011. *National Drug Threat Assessment 2011* (Product No. 2011-Q0317–001). Retrieved from http://www.justice.gov/archive/ndic/pubs44/44849/44849p.pdf

National Institute on Drug Abuse (NIDA). 2006. *Methamphetamine: Abuse and Addiction.* Retrieved from http://www.drugabuse.gov/publications/research-reports/methamphetamine-abuse-addiction

National Institute on Drug Abuse (NIDA). December 2012. *Methamphetamine.* Retrieved from http://www.drugabuse.gov/drugs-abuse/methamphetamine

National Institute on Drug Abuse (NIDA). September 2013. *Methamphetamine.* Retrieved from https://www.drugabuse.gov/publications/research-reports /methamphetamine/letter-director

National Institute on Drug Abuse (NIDA). January 2014. *DrugFacts: Methamphetamine.* Retrieved from http://drugabuse.gov/publications/drugfacts/methamphetamine

O'Brien, A.M., M. Brecht, and C. Casey. 2008. "Narratives of Methamphetamine Abuse: A Qualitative Exploration of Social, Psychological, and Emotional Experiences. *Journal of Social Work Practice in the Addictions* 8 (3):343–66.

O'Connor, J., J. Chriqui, D. McBride, S. S. Eidson, C. Baker, Y. Terry-McElrath, and C. VanderWaal. 2007. *From Policy to Practice: State Methamphetamine Precursor Control Policies.* Washington, DC: U.S. Department of Justice.

Office of National Drug Control Policy (ONDCP). N.d. *Synthetic Drugs (a.k.a. K2, Spice, Bath Salts, Etc.).* Retrieved from http://www.whitehouse.gov/ondcp/ondcp-fact-sheets/synthetic-drugs-k2-spice-bath-salts

"Oklahoma Worries about Cost of Meth Lab Cleanup after DEA Cuts Off Funding." March 7, 2011. *Fox News.* Retrieved from http://www.foxnews.com

O'Mahoney, P. 2008. *The Irish War on Drugs: The Seductive Folly of Prohibition.* Manchester, UK: Manchester University Press.

Parsons, J. T., B. C. Kelly, and J. D. Weiser. 2007. "Initiation into Methamphetamine Use for Young Gay and Bisexual Men." *Drug and Alcohol Dependence* 90:135–44.

Pennell, S., J. Ellett, C. Reinick, and J. Grimes. 1999. *Meth Matters: Report on Methamphetamine Users in Five Western Cities* (NCJ Report No. 176331). Washington, DC: U.S. Department of Justice, Office of Justice Programs.

Poe, E. A. 1960. *The Narrative of Arthur Gordon Pym of Nantucket.* New York: Hill and Wang.

Pryce, S. 2012. *Fixing Drugs: The Politics of Drug Prohibition.* New York: Palgrave MacMillan.

Ransley, J., L. Mazerolle, M. Manning, I. McGuffog, J. M. Drew, and J. Webster. 2011. *Reducing the Methamphetamine Problem in Australia: Evaluating Innovative Partnerships between Police, Pharmacies and Other Third Parties.* Monograph Series No. 39. Canberra, Australian Capital Territory: National Drug Law Enforcement Research Fund.

Rochkind, D. 2012. *Heavy Hand, Sunken Spirit: Mexico at War.* Stockport, England: Dewi Lewis Publishing.

Rumsfeld, D. June 6, 2002. *NATO Press Conference.* Retrieved from www.nato.int /docu/speech/2002/s020606g.htm

Scott, M. S., and K. Dedel. 2006. *Clandestine Methamphetamine Labs* (2nd ed.). Washington, DC: U.S. Department of Justice, Office of Community Oriented Policing Services.

Senjo, S. 2005. "Trafficking in Meth: An Analysis of the Differences between Male and Female Dealers." *Journal of Drug Education* 35 (1):59–77.

Sexton, R. L., R. G. Carlson, C. G. Leukefeld and B. M. Booth. 2009. "An Ethnographic Exploration of Self-Reported Violence among Rural Methamphetamine Users." *Journal of Ethnicity in Substance Abuse* 8 (1):35–53.

Sexton, R. L., R. G. Carlson, C. G. Leukefeld, and B. M. Booth. 2006. "Patterns of Illicit Methamphetamine Production ('Cooking') and Associated Risks in the Rural South: An Ethnographic Exploration." *Journal of Drug Issues* 36 (4):853–76.

Sheridan, J., R. Butler, and A. Wheeler. 2009. "Initiation into Methamphetamine Use: Qualitative Findings from an Exploration of First Time Use among a Group of New Zealand Users." *Journal of Psychoactive Drugs* 4 (1):11–17.

Shukla, R. K., J. L. Crump, and E. S. Chrisco. 2012. "An Evolving Problem: Methamphetamine Production and Trafficking in the United States." *International Journal of Drug Policy* 23:426–35.

Shumlin, P. January 8, 2014. *Gov. Shumlin's 2014 State of the State Address.* Retrieved from http://governor.vermont.gov/newsroom-state-of-state-speech-2013

Sommers, I., and D. Baskin. 2004. "The Social Consequences of Methamphetamine Use." *Interdisciplinary Studies in Alcohol & Drug Use and Abuse* (vol. 8). Lewiston, NY: Edwin Mellen Press.

Sommers, I., and D. Baskin. 2006. "Methamphetamine Use and Violence." *Journal of Drug Issues* 36 (1):77–96.

South, T. June 23, 2012. "13-Person Meth Case Ends with Sentencing." *Chattanooga Times Free Press.* Retrieved from http://www.timesfreepress.com/news/2012/jun/23/tennessee-person-meth-case-ends-with-sentencing/?print

Star Wars: The Clone Wars. March 1, 2013; season 5, episode 20. "The Wrong Jedi." Retrieved from http://www.starwars.com/tv-shows/clone-wars/the-wrong-jedi

Stomberg, C., and A. Sharma. 2012. *Making Cold Medicine Rx Only Did Not Reduce Meth Use: Analyzing the Impact on Oregon's Prescription-Only Pseudoephedrine Requirement.* Portland, OR: Cascade Policy Institute. Retrieved from http://cascadepolicy.org/pdf/pub/Oregon_Meth_Law.pdf

Storrs, C. May 26, 2015. "What Is Flakka (Aka Gravel) and Why Is It More Dangerous than Cocaine?" *CNN.* http://www.cnn.com/2015/05/26/health/flakka-gravel-illegal-drugs/

Tyner, E. A., and W. J. Fremouw. 2008. "The Relation of Methamphetamine Use and Violence: A Critical Review." *Aggression and Violent Behavior* 13:285–97.

United Nations Office on Drugs & Crime (UNODC). 2011. *World Drug Report 2011.* Vienna: United Nations. Retrieved from http://www.unodc.org/documents/data-and-analysis/WDR2011/World_Drug_Report_2011_ebook.pdf

United Nations Office on Drugs & Crime (UNODC). June 2014. *World Drug Report 2014.* Vienna: United Nations. Retrieved from https://www.unodc.org/documents/wdr2014/World_Drug_Report_2014_web.pdf

United States Census Bureau. 2014. "Oklahoma." Retrieved from http://quickfacts.census.gov/qfd/states/40000.html

U.S. Government Accountability Office. January 2013. *Drug Control: State Approaches Taken to Control Access to Key Methamphetamine Ingredient Show Varied Impact on Domestic Drug Labs* (Report No. GAO-13–204). Washington DC: Government Accountability Office. Retrieved from http://www.gao.gov/assets/660/651709.pdf

U.S. House of Representatives. December 2005. *The Methamphetamine Epidemic: International Roots of the Problem, and Recommended Solutions.* (Report No. 109–352). Washington DC: U.S. Government Printing Office.

Weisheit, R. A. 2008. "Making Methamphetamine." *Southern Rural Sociology* 23 (2):78–107.

Weisheit, R. A., and W. L. White. 2009. *Methamphetamine: Its History, Pharmacology, and Treatment.* Center City, MN: Hazelden Publishing.

WHSV News Staff. March 21, 2013. "Two Charged for Making Meth in Front of a Child." *WHSV.* Retrieved from http://www.whsv.com/news/headlines/two-charged-for-making-meth-in-front-of-a-child-199413211.html

Winter, M. July 8, 2014. "Police: Meth Addiction Led Utah Mom to Kill 6 Newborns." *USA Today.* Retrieved from http://www.usatoday.com/story/news/nation/2014/07/08/utah-mother-dead-babies-meth-addiction/12387475/?utm_source = dlvr.it&utm_medium = twitter&dlvrit = 206567

Woodward, P. October 31, 2014. "Pharmacists Stand Strong against Smurfing, Meth Use." *Tulsa World.* Retrieved from http://www.tulsaworld.com/opinion/readersforum/phil-woodward-pharmacists-stand-strong-against-smurfing-meth-use/article_1071faf4-da08–586d-a296–6c69f47efc36.html

INDEX

CPSIA information can be obtained
at www.ICGtesting.com
Printed in the USA
LVOW12s1826230517

535559LV00006B/1272/P